T5-AFM-138

THE STOCK EXCHANGE FROM WITHIN

Used by permission of F. Hopkinson Smith.
From Charcoals of New and Old New York. Copyright, 1912, by Doubleday, Page & Co.

BROAD STREET, LOOKING SOUTH FROM WALL STREET

The Stock Exchange is shown on the right.

THE STOCK EXCHANGE FROM WITHIN

BY

W. C. VAN ANTWERP

Illustrated from Photographs

GARDEN CITY NEW YORK
DOUBLEDAY, PAGE & COMPANY
1913

DREW THEOLOGICAL
FEB 7 - 1913
SEMINARY LIBRARY

PREFACE

In so far as these pages reflect the thoughts of a busy stockbroker, distracted by many duties and lacking in literary skill, they have but little merit and the writer entertains no illusions regarding them. But in the many quotations from the writings of the world's foremost economists that are here presented, and in the various legal and historical precedents cited, perhaps it is not too much to hope that this book possesses some slight value as a contribution to the vexed and vexing discussion of the Stock Exchange, and that it may serve in some degree both to dull the sharp edge of uninformed criticism and to strengthen the hands and hearts of loyal friends of a greatly misunderstood institution. The public is asked to disregard the utterances of demagogues and self-seekers and to consider facts. That done, the American spirit of fair play may be confidently relied upon.

The Stock Exchange authorities have had no hand in the preparation of the work, nor does it bear their endorsement. I say this lest it be thought an official *apologia*. Had it been such, the work would have been much more skillfully done, and its value greatly enhanced.

THE AUTHOR.

CONTENTS

ILLUSTRATIONS

CHAPTER I

THE FUNCTIONS OF THE STOCK EXCHANGE

CHAPTER I

THE FUNCTIONS OF THE STOCK EXCHANGE

EVERY now and then some one who has not given much thought to the matter asks the questions, "Of what real use is the Stock Exchange?" "What does it accomplish?" "Is it a necessary and useful part of our economic life, or is it merely a means of promoting speculation and gambling?" These are fair questions, and they are asked in good faith. To be sure they have been answered many times by writers on economic subjects, but the trouble is that in our hurried American life we do not read the economists, preferring to get our impressions from the hasty utterances of some one who knows no more about it than we do.

The study of any form of economic development, like the study of sciences and philosophies, requires infinite patience. But the "man in the street" is bored to death by such methods; he wants to take a short cut to his conclusions; merely tasting the Pierian spring he hurries on to judgments that are superficial, haphazard, and often crude and blundering. And yet at bottom this man, a good citizen with an open mind, invariably wants the truth. He may be too busy to dig it up himself, but he knows it when he sees it, and once he has grasped it he has no patience with those who seek to turn him from it. To this average man, who holds in his hands the balance of power in America, I venture to say something about markets.

The first thing a man asks when he wishes to buy is "the price." Every minute of the day, all over the world, that question is on men's lips. As it is a necessary prelude to all forms of trade, it follows that everything that enters into the making of prices becomes at once of primary importance. The more scientific the price, and the nicer and more accurate the making of it, the better the bargain for both buyer and seller and for trade generally, bearing in mind the distinction between prices, which are temporary and move rapidly — and values, which are intrinsic and move slowly. The price of a thing is what you can get for it; the value is its real worth to you, and hence it cannot be defined or measured, since a thousand considerations may enter into it, such as caprice, sentiment or association. If *real* values could be determined, they would necessarily be identical with prices, but as they cannot be ascertained in ordinary commodities of trade, prices become the really essential considerations and values the subordinate ones. Let us see, then, how prices are made, for this is one of the reasons why exchanges exist.

If you want to buy, let us say, a piano, you go to the dealer and ask the price, and as he is the only person in the neighborhood who deals in pianos, you must either accept his offer or look elsewhere. But to look elsewhere takes time and labor; dealers in pianos are widely separated; moreover, there is no open competition among them such as you would like, and so finally when you have bought you feel perhaps you have not secured your money's worth. You would have secured a much better bargain, no doubt, had there been twenty dealers in the room competing with each other, and a still better bargain had their number been fifty, or a hundred, or two hundred, because that would mean competition, and the more competition there is, in close contact and governed by rigid business rules, the more certain the approach to a perfect price. Everywhere in the world fairs and other gatherings of merchants are held at periodic intervals because people demand them in their effort to secure proper prices by competitive bidding and offering. One of the first travelers to penetrate the heart of Africa found among the natives this phenomenon of trade, showing that it is instinctive; indeed, it may be traced to the earliest known period in the history of any people. If you arise before daybreak in London and go to Billingsgate and Covent Garden, or in Paris to the *Halles Centrales* — Zola's "Ventre de Paris" — you will find there the modern type of these markets in their utmost perfection.*

This is why Exchanges exist, not only Stock Exchanges, but market-places of all kinds: Buyers seek the largest market they can get in order to obtain the lowest prices; sellers, in order to obtain the highest prices; and so it was learned long ago that economy of time and labor, as well as a theoretically perfect market, could be best secured by an organization under one roof of as many dealers in a commodity as could be found.† Bear in mind that this result, moreover, is best accomplished when the organization is so controlled by rigid rules of business morality as to insure to every one who does business there, great and small, rich and poor, an absolutely square deal. In such a market every purchase is made with the most thorough acquaintance with the conditions involved. Each dealer, each broker, each speculator, strives to obtain the best knowl-

* Principles of the Economic Philosophy of Society, Government and Industry, by Van Buren Denslow, LL.D., New York, 1888, p. 99.

† *Ibid.*, p. 107.

edge of the supply and demand, and the earliest news that may affect it, and each buyer or seller has an equal and a fair opportunity to profit by the resultant effect on the market of all these various agencies. The larger the body of brokers and traders, then, the more accurate the standards of value thus created. It is a pity you could not have bought your piano under such conditions.*

Demagogues have set the agricultural classes against Wall Street and against Exchanges, but producers everywhere, in default of exchanges, are forming quasi-exchanges of their own. Every day we hear of combinations, Farmers' Alliances, rural co-operative movements, etc., each designed to regulate the market for eggs, butter, potatoes, and such things, and each having for its purpose the very functions which govern a Stock Exchange in its own field—namely, the establishment of a fair price under the nearest possible approach to ideal conditions. It is now proposed in Congress that the Department of Agriculture shall collect and transmit to the agricultural districts by telephone and telegraph all available information concerning price movements, markets, and centres of supply and demand, this again embodying

---

* *Ibid.*, p. 101. Consult also "Theory of Political Economy," by W. S. Jevons, p. 92, and "A History of Prices," by Thomas Tooke, Part II, p. 46.

the essential functions performed in its own field by a great exchange.

In practice, of course, there can be no exchange to deal in perishable products of the farm, and this is a pity, because if such an exchange were practicable we should hear less of our old friend the cost of living. Why? Because at present the market for these commodities is controlled by commission dealers and by middlemen. The producer and the consumer are alike at the mercy of these people; the price is fixed by them; the number of bona fide dealers actually bidding against each other is limited, in many instances there is no competition whatever; the producer and the commission dealer are, moreover, widely separated; the man who sells has few sources of information, and it is the business of the dealer who buys to see that he gets none; the small producer therefore has to submit to a great inequality in price, and often to downright cheating. There is no standard. There are no rules governing the dealer, and no high-minded board to enforce his honesty. Naturally this sort of thing contributes to the cost of living, since the commission dealer, on his part, regulates his profits just in proportion to the ignorance, cupidity or remoteness of the farmer, while the middlemen, of whom there are sometimes three or four, apply the same iniquitous processes to the ultimate purchaser — who happens to be you or me. Every thinking man knows that this is rank economic error.*

A friend of mine owns a thousand-acre farm in the Shenandoah Valley, where he raised this year 10,000 baskets of peaches. He decided to seek one buyer, and he found him in the person of a Baltimore canner, who went down to Virginia, inspected the crop, and contracted for the lot on a basis of $1 for firsts, 70 cents for seconds, and 40 cents for thirds, delivered at Baltimore. Shortly after, the market was flooded with peaches from Georgia, and the Baltimore man, seeing that the crop would be plentiful, promptly "welched" on his trade, basing his action on the absurd contention that "firsts" should be three inches in diameter, although as every one knows peaches of this size are almost never to be had. This action threw all the grower's peaches into third class, which delivered at Baltimore would have netted him about 10 cents a basket.

In desperation he looked elsewhere, West, North, and South, only to hear the same monotonous answer from commission men, "we won't buy, but we will handle your crop on a commission of 10 per cent." Meantime the crop was ripening. To make

*Consult Report of the New York State Food Investigating Commission, September, 1912.

matters worse the railroad levied a prohibitive price, and refrigerator cars were not to be had. Finally there was nothing left but to ship by express and trust to the commission men to treat him honestly. The final accounting showed that on his first shipment he netted 5½ cents a basket, and on his second, 15 cents, not counting the expense of picking, packing, and hauling. So much for the producer. The consumer fared no better, for he had to pay $1.25 per basket for this fruit; one of this producer's friends actually purchasing a portion of this very consignment at that rate. The difference therefore between 15 cents and $1.25 contributes some food for thought as to the cost of living.*

Now contrast this experience of a grower having no exchange facilities with that of the Western farmer who deals directly with a Grain Exchange. The farmer can sell his crop, even though it has not been planted. Whenever he sells, and under whatever conditions, he enjoys the authoritative establishment of a price, fixed as clearly as matters are fixed in law. Moreover, the price at which he elects to sell is the best price, the fairest price, and the most scientific price that human agencies can arrive at, because it is made

* A detailed account of this incident was published in *Country Life in America*, July 1, 1912, from the pen of Graham F. Blandy, the producer.

by world-wide competitive bidding at the hands of skilled men in Chicago, in New York, in Liverpool, in Berlin, in Odessa, and in the Argentine, all competing by cable and telegraph. Think of the confidence he enjoys, and the liberty of action; think, too, what it means to him to know that the Exchange through which he deals is a body of honorable men, governed by rules, bidding publicly under one roof.

But, you will say, this is all very well in its application to a grain or cotton exchange, but how does it apply to the Stock Exchange? You concede that scientific price-making for commodities like grain and cotton is highly necessary, but you do not see that the same necessity exists for stocks and bonds. You feel, no doubt, that the one has to do with food and raiment and is therefore indispensable, while the other merely serves to stimulate speculation and gambling, and hence is altogether unnecessary. Now, in order to explain the error in this point of view, let us first see how bits of paper, called securities, came into being.

Long after Europe had emerged from the dark centuries following the fall of the Roman Empire, the needs of states and governments impelled their rulers to resort to credit, and it was discovered that the simplest way to do it was to issue securities, that is to say, certificates of the debt. Next, it was found that in order to insure success for these operations, a market was required. Intermittent or temporary sources from which credit could be obtained was not enough; *constant* sources of credit were essential, and, as these constant sources lay in the savings of the people, public markets in which investors could tell the value of their investments from day to day followed as a natural course.*

As time went on — necessarily the evolution was gradual — it was learned that companies having to do with all forms of business enterprises might also be formed on the same basis. The development of the world's business outgrew its infancy days of private partnerships, and corporate organization of necessity took their place, now that the discovery of credit, through the use of securities, had pointed the way. This corporate organization, which combines the small

---

* Bourses or Exchanges, as we know them to-day, undoubtedly owe their origin to the Jews. M. Vidal's scholarly work explains that the persecutions which those untiring and courageous merchants experienced in Spain after the expulsion of the Moors caused them to emigrate to Holland, where the market-place was called *Change* (Exchange) and where in later years there was to be established, aa s result of their labors, the famous Bank of Amsterdam, which was for a century the foremost institution of its kind in the world. The modern use of the word Change or Exchange is thus plainly traced. The word Bourse originated at Bruges, where, according to one authority, merchants gathered at the house of one of their number known as van der Burse. Other historians state that the word originated from the three purses (bourses) carved on the gable of the house in which the meetings were held.

savings of thousands into large sums and gives to the masses an intelligent directing force at the hands of highly trained experts, depends for its existence on the sale of its securities.

In order to understand that there can be no industrial progress without the issue of securities let us consider the locomotive engine. When in the early 1800's it became apparent that this contrivance could be used to operate an entirely new method of transportation, people looked upon it, at first, as an interesting but quite useless contrivance, because to build railroads was an expensive undertaking and nobody had enough money to finance it. The inventor's genius was not sufficient; another power was necessary to take it out of purely scientific hands and give it practical impulse. That power was credit; the way it was obtained was through the issue of securities, and the way securities were made popular vehicles of investment lay in providing a daily market for buyers and sellers.

As a natural result, organization followed. Capital was consolidated, the rights of owners were established, a great impulse was given to various new forms of inventive genius and powerful commercial enterprises of all kinds sprang into being. With this development the market-places or Stock Exchanges without which capital could not have been enlisted kept pace. It was found that transactions in the securities which represented the people's money should be rendered easy, quick, and safe, and that the very essence of the Exchange's functions consisted in protecting the people who were the actual owners of the enterprises by rules that would insure this result.

If we look about us to-day we find in all the great centres of the world Stock Exchanges at work in this important field. We find that just in proportion to the confidence which a country feels in the strength and uprightness of such a market, so enterprise goes forward with vigor, and so the national wealth increases. The success of one enterprise in its appeal to public credit through the medium of the Stock Exchange invariably leads to another; thus commerce and industry develop. Securities in America alone, aggregate the enormous total of forty-three billion dollars.*

Now, as our country's entire physical properties are valued at one hundred and thirty billions, it is

---

* Charles A. Conant, "The World's Wealth in Negotiable Securities," *Atlantic Monthly*, January, 1908, estimated the total American securities as of 1905, at $34,514,351,382. Since that time there has been added to the securities listed on the New York Stock Exchange alone, a total averaging about one billion dollars per annum. The total given above is, therefore, a conservative one, since I have added to Mr. Conant's 1905 estimate only Stock Exchange additions, and have taken no account of the millions added by small corporations.

apparent (after making allowances for securities that are held by holding companies and hence are duplicated in the foregoing estimates) that the nation's securities represent more than a third of the nation's wealth. Again, almost two million people are owners of these securities. The *Journal of Commerce and Commercial Bulletin* published Dec. 26, 1912, official statistics for 247 of the large corporations. This tabulation revealed the fact that the stock of these 247 corporations alone was owned by more than a million stockholders, and it is therefore quite safe to infer that the number of shareholders in all American companies approaches, if it does not exceed, two million. I think it will not be disputed that where two million people own a third of the nation's wealth, they are entitled, just as the farmer is, to a perfectly constructed price-making machinery that will enable them to invest their savings, or sell their holdings. Having learned the difficult lesson of saving their money and the still more difficult one of increasing their surplus capital by judicious investments, are not these people entitled to the safeguards afforded by a Stock Exchange? "There is no other way in which true prices can be made," says Mr. Horace White. "If the quotations so made are not precisely the truth in every case, they are the nearest approach to it that mankind has yet discovered."*

Think a moment. Until the last century property and trade were so insecure that, if a man saved money, he had to hide it, or lend it through money-brokers at such usurious rates as would compensate him for what he lost in bad debts. When Dr. Samuel Johnson wrote his dictionary in 1776 no such word as "investor" was known to the English language in a financial sense. There were pirates by sea in the old days and brigands on land. "Sovereigns and nobles," says the editor of the *Economist*, "extorted loans only to repudiate them; governments supplied their needs by debasing the coinage, or by issuing worthless money."† To-day all this is changed by banks

* "The Stock Exchange and the Money Market," "Annals of the American Academy of Political and Social Science," Vol. XXXVI, No. 3, November, 1910, p. 567.

† If the discovery had then been made that bits of paper could be used as a medium of giving mobility to capital, there would have been a Stock Exchange at Rome eleven centuries before Christ. M. Edmond Guillard's study of the subject shows that the *argentarii* (bankers) were then doing business at the imperial city, and that in addition to their central offices they had established branch offices at the Forum, where they gathered daily at a specified hour, together with the merchants, manufacturers, and capitalists, carrying on a business of money-changing in a public market that was, in its essentials, similar to our public financial markets of to-day ("Les Banquiers Atheniens et Romains, trapézites et argentarii," Paris, 1875 Guillaumin). As the business was introduced into Rome by freed Greek slaves, it is perhaps safe to say that the practice of dealing in public money-markets is in reality of still earlier origin. Plautus alludes to the crowd of merchants and bankers in the public square, and many chroniclers record the fact that at the time of Appius Claudius and Publius Sevilius, that is to say, five centuries before Christ, there was a public market in Rome known as the Assembly of Merchants (Collegium mercatorum).

and Stock Exchanges. Yet, despite these great inventions, capital is and always will be timid, and the small investor particularly must be protected and safeguarded in every possible way.

These small investors, no less than the large ones, require great convenience and promptness for their operations; they live in such widely remote parts of the country as to necessitate the placing of full reliance on prices made by the Stock Exchange; they must have the most accurate information; they must know that their brokers are working to obtain the best knowledge of supply and demand; they want prices fixed by the most scientific competition and by the largest possible number of competitors—brokers, speculators, and investors alike; they require a market in which thay can sell and get their money at once; above all things they must know beyond peradventure that they are dealing with reputable men who uphold a fine standard of honor. These are added reasons why the Stock Exchange exists.*

*"A hundred years ago the use of the cheque was hardly known even in London, and an English country gentleman would have had infinitely more trouble in making a small investment than would nowadays a remote Australian squatter, or a wheat-grower in the wildest West of Canada. A letter posted to London from a distant village of Saskatchewan in 1910 would arrive with far more certainty, and perhaps not less speed than a letter posted in 1810 from a village in Sutherland or Argyllshire. A penny stamp with a cheque enclosed in a brief letter of instructions to the banker, and the thing is done. But the thrifty Scot of 1810 would have had the utmost difficulty, and great expense as well as risk, in converting a similar amount of cash savings into an interest-bearing security. In 1710 the thing

If it did not exist, there would be no standard market for a large part of the country's material wealth, indeed, as we have seen, a very great deal of this wealth could not have been created at all. At the risk of repetition let me say that the investor on the one hand, and the patent or the railway on the other hand, have nothing in common. Left to themselves, they would never meet· they would be useless, because resources and money must be brought together in order to create wealth. A primary function of the Stock Exchange is to bring them together, and by standardizing prices, create values. Similarly, the investor, without the Stock Exchange to guide him, would have nowhere to turn for a fair price secured by competitive bidding. He might turn to his local banker, or to individual and unorganized brokers, and trust to their honesty to invest his savings for him, but the local banker and the isolated broker would then be in the same position as the com-

would have been practically impossible. The Bank of England had only just been called into existence, and, in fact, there were no bankers, no brokers, and no Stock Exchange in the modern sense of the word. A man who wished to invest, without personally employing his capital, had practically no choice but to buy property and let it out at a rent, or lend his money on mortgage. Bank of England Stock or National Debt had just begun to be a political speculation for the moneyed Whigs in London. Merchant venturers might risk a large sum in a joint-stock voyage. Otherwise the average Englishman at the beginning of the eighteenth century A. D. was hardly better off for investment than the average Athenian in the age of Pericles, or the average Roman in the days of Cicero."— "The Stock Exchange," by Francis W. Hirst, editor of the *Economist*, Williams and Norgate, London.

mission dealer and the middleman who played such havoc with that peach crop. It is painful to conceive such a situation.

Worse than that, without a Stock Exchange to create standards and define the difference between good and bad investments, very many simple people would be at the mercy of an army of dishonest promoters and bucket-shops, for the modern invention of securities has brought with it dangers and pitfalls. The United States once swarmed with these bandits — they are now rapidly being driven to cover — but they still ply their trade in other countries, where they flourish as "banks" or "investment" companies. These chaps, to quote the editor of the *Economist* (London), "have bought a lot of rubbish, usually called 'bonds,' from shaky industrial concerns or from half bankrupt states and municipalities of South America. They have bought, let us say, the 6 per cent. bonds of the Yoko Silk Company in Japan at 60, which they sell you at 90, the 5 per cent. bonds of the Brazilian Province of ——— at 55, which they sell you at 75, and a few other similar bargains. They tell you that if you spread your risks scientifically over different countries you will be perfectly safe. You perhaps do not realize that none of these securities which you are advised to buy are quoted in the London Stock Exchange.

If they were the game would be impossible." Which is only another way of saying that if there were no Stock Exchanges to uphold worthy enterprises and discourage bad ones, there would be no limit to the frauds practised upon gullible investors. And if this is true of a tight little island like England, how doubly true it is in a great country like ours where investors are so widely scattered.

The foregoing pages will serve to show the inquirer that what is happening in commerce, is happening in the securities which represent that commerce. Because commerce goes on expanding, securities must necessarily keep pace and the Stock Exchange must perforce grow in importance. That much maligned individual, the speculator, now regards the whole world as his field and is eager to enter foreign markets wherever there are opportunities. In 1910 more than three billion dollars of British capital were invested in American railways alone, returning one hundred and twenty-five millions annually in interest and dividends, to say nothing of the English millions in our lands, mines, and industrial enterprises. We too are large holders of foreign securities, and the list of such holdings increases yearly. But it may be accepted as a fact that this enormous mass of corporate securities would not

seen, these quotations are not a one-man affair, but the combined judgment of thousands of experts, bulls and bears, bankers and brokers, speculators and investors, all over the world, bidding and offering against each other by cable and telegraph and recording the epitomized result of their bidding in the prices current on the Stock Exchange. Such a man knows, moreover, that the price thus established is not merely the opinion of all these minds as to values to-day, but that it represents a critical look into the future. He knows, indeed, that financiers everywhere have in mind prospective values rather than present values, and so he acquires a double advantage in regulating his own action by the light of the superior knowledge thus freely given him. The importance of this "advance information" cannot be overestimated, and furnishes us with another reason why Stock Exchanges exist.

In 1906, for example, business conditions in this country were the best ever known. Good crops, big earnings, and general optimism prevailed. But Stock Exchange securities did not advance in the last half of the year, because trained financiers began to foresee the first signs of trouble ahead. In the early months of 1907 this knowledge became more general, and a severe decline took place, notwithstanding the fact that the business of the country at large continued to be excellent. "What is the matter with Wall Street?" was the question in the press and on the lips of the uninformed, but Wall Street, or rather the Stock Exchange, was merely fulfilling its function as a barometer and foretelling the coming storm.

At the height of the autumn panic, on the other hand, when the press was filled with dire forebodings and the ignorant layman was frightened out of his wits, securities stopped declining and began to rise because the Stock Exchange mind saw that the worst was over. The brightest financial students in the world then began another process of discounting the future; the barometer plainly foretold the end of the disturbance. And all this information — a fundamental law of price movements which indicated clearly when the trouble was coming and when it had ended — was given gratis to the world in the daily published quotations of Stock Exchange securities.

In another chapter I shall describe the method by which the Stock Exchange protects its patrons, the public. As this is of particular importance in connection with the matters just cited, I call the reader's attention to the remarks of Prof. S. S. Huebner, Ph.D., of the University of Pennsylvania.

"Importance must be attached to the protection and safeguards which organized Stock Exchanges give the stock and bond holder, in regulating brokerage transactions and maintaining a standard of commercial honor among brokers. . . . In this connection it should be remembered that the constitution of nearly every Stock Exchange defines the object of the Exchange as follows: 'Its object shall be to furnish Exchanges, rooms and other facilities for the convenient transaction of business by its members, as brokers; to maintain high standards of commercial honor and integrity among its members, and to promote and inculcate just and equitable principles of trade and business.' No person can be elected to membership until he has signed the constitution of the Exchange, and by such signature he obligates himself to abide by the same, and by all subsequent amendments thereto. The value of this organization becomes apparent when we take account of the gigantic frauds perpetrated upon innocent investors through advertising campaigns by persons unaffiliated with any recognized Exchange, or by certain members of unorganized curb markets. . . .

All Stock Exchanges provide for the arbitration of disputes which may occur between members, and if both parties are willing, between members and their customers. They also prescribe rules governing the nature of contracts, the making of all offers and bids, the registry and transfer of securities on the transfer books of the corporations, and the conditions upon which securities may be listed upon the Exchange for trading purposes. Practically all stock Exchanges also require that all transactions must be real, and that no fictitious or unreal transactions shall be permitted; that discretionary orders cannot be accepted by brokers; and that every member of the Exchange must keep complete accounts, subject at all times to examination by the governing committee or any standing or special committee of the Exchange, and under penalty of suspension, no member may refuse or neglect to submit such accounts, or wilfully destroy the same. Nor may any member, under pain of suspension (a serious penalty, involving not merely the loss of the rights and privileges of membership, but also the stigma attaching to the member as a factor in the business community), be guilty of 'any conduct or proceeding inconsistent with just and equitable principles of trade.'"*

One of the most important functions of the Stock Exchange is, as we have seen, the almost automatic ease with which it directs reservoirs of capital into channels of usefulness in the world's industry and commerce. The layman may feel that this use of the Stock Exchange does not affect him as an individual, but it does, and vitally. Every merchant and every manufacturer, great and small, all over the world, is directly benefited by it. One may see, for example, securities of railway equipment companies quoted for weeks at a low level. This shows that the business of these companies is not profitable, and it serves to discourage owners of capital from undertaking new enterprises in that direction, because the securities of such companies cannot be sold. Moreover, it shows investors, as plainly as words can tell, that this is an unsafe and unprofitable form of investment.

---

* "Scope and Functions of the Stock Market."— "The Annals of the American Academy of Political and Social Science," Vol. XXXV, No. 3. May, 1910.

Reverse the situation, and lines of industry are revealed where high and advancing prices of securities indicate a rising tide of business, with an outlook for large profits in the future. Capital then takes hold cheerfully; there is a market for the new securities and a proper basis for fresh commercial development, because investors and speculators have learned from the published daily quotations of these Stock Exchange securities that there is good warrant for the flow of capital into such channels, and that a reasonably safe return will follow an investment in them. In commenting upon these functions of the Stock Exchange, Mr. Conant says: "Through the publicity of knowledge and prices, the bringing of a multitude of fallible judgments upon this common ground, to an average, there is afforded to capital throughout the world an almost unfailing index of the course in which new production should be directed." Through the mechanism of the Stock Exchange, therefore, the public determines the direction in which new capital shall be applied to new undertakings. In this way our great railways were built, our Western country opened to progress, and our vast industrial undertakings made possible.

"The stock market acts as a reservoir and distributor of capital, with something of the same efficiency with which a series of well-regulated locks and dams operates to equalize the irregular current of a river. The hand of man is being stretched out in the valley of the Nile to build great storage basins and locks, and the waters which flow down the great river may be husbanded until they are needed, when they are released in small but sufficient quantities to fertilize the country and tide over the periods of drought. Something of the same service is performed for accumulation of capital by the delicate series of reservoirs, sluice gates, and locks provided by the mechanism of the stock market. The rate of interest measures the rise and fall of the supply of capital, as the locks determine the ebb and flow of the life-giving water. The existence of negotiable securities is in the nature of a great reservoir, obviating the disastrous effects of demands which might drain away the supply of actual coin, and preventing the panic and disaster, which, without such a safeguard, would frequently occur in the market for capital."*

Some day, no doubt, the United States will become a great creditor nation, as England is, and then the field of these operations will be extended to other countries. When that time comes we shall take a hand, through the machinery of the Stock Exchange, in the development of new and immense fields of human endeavor just as London does to-day. To what extent could capital exports of such tremendous economic significance continue if so useful and so indispensable an institution as the Stock Exchange were abolished or interrupted? It was Burke who said that "great empires and little minds go ill together," and so

* Charles A. Conant, "The Uses of Speculation," *Forum* (August, 1901).

it is with great markets and little critics. There can be no worthier purpose in the commercial world than the upbuilding of a great centre of credit designed to finance material enterprise, enrich the world, and extend the benefits of civilization to new lands and new people, based upon the credit supplied by the banker, the money provided by the speculator and investor, and the safeguards afforded by the Stock Exchange. And yet, curiously, the greater the effort in these directions, the greater the criticism. Just in proportion to the perfection with which all these agencies equalize prices, economize time and effort, and protect the public, so they seem to attract attention, comment, and attack.*

In Wall Street, according to this viewpoint, everything is tainted, sinister, reprehensible, covetous and unscrupulous, just as it follows the onward march of invention, science, and progress.

---

*Suppose for a moment that the stock markets of the world were closed, that it was no longer possible to learn what railways were paying dividends, what their stocks were worth, how industrial enterprises were faring — whether they were loaded up with surplus goods or had orders ahead. Suppose that the information afforded by public quotations on the stock and produce exchanges were wiped from the slate of human knowledge. How would the average man, how even would a man with the intelligence and foresight of a Pierpont Morgan, determine how new capital should be invested? He would have no guides except the most isolated facts gathered here and there at great trouble and expense. A greater misdirection of capital and energy would result than has been possible since the organization of modern economic machinery. "Wall Street and the Country," by Charles A. Conant, pp. 92–93. — G. P. Putnam's Sons, New York, 1904.

This sort of criticism will not, of course, continue. The man in the street — the average layman to whom I have ventured to address this chapter will learn sooner or later — in point of fact he is learning now — that the questionable practices in Wall Street which started all this hubbub, and which were a natural and a human accompaniment of the slowly developed technique of this or any other business, have now been effectually stopped. It has been a very long time, for example, since Jay Gould ran his printing-press for Erie certificates, and that incident cannot possibly happen again. The Keene type of manipulator has gone, never to return. "Corners," too, have seen their last day on 'Change, and so also have other artificial impediments in the way of natural supply and demand. It has been years since the Cordage scandal, and the Hocking Coal incident marked the end of that form of manipulation. Yet there are persons who talk of these things as though they were daily occurrences, overlooking the fact that the New York Stock Exchange, by its own efforts put a stop to the evils complained of, and will never tolerate their return.

McMaster in his "History of the People of the United States" tells us that in the early days in New England public sentiment was so aroused against the legal profession that lawyers "were denounced as banditti, as blood-suckers, pick-pockets, windbags and smooth-tongued rogues." At that period in our history feeling ran so high against banks and bankers that Aaron Burr was only able to procure a charter for the Manhattan (Banking) Company by resorting to the subterfuge of naming it, in the Act, "a Company to furnish the City with water." No doubt all this rancor and hostility seemed a very serious matter to the lawyers and bankers of those days, just as the criticism of to-day strikes home to members and friends of the Stock Exchange.

The lawyers made many mistakes a century and a half ago when the code and its practice were imperfectly understood in this country; so it was with the early history of banking; and so in our time Wall Street and the Stock Exchange have made the mistakes which any gradually developing form of enterprise must make. But these mistakes are dead or dying, and, in their place, no doubt, there will come a better understanding all around. When that day dawns the thoughtful American will realize that the particular rôle which the Stock Exchange plays in promoting all forms of commercial endeavor is a boon such as no country in the history of earlier days ever enjoyed. He will contemplate his country's progress with pride; he will rejoice in its capacity to outstrip other countries; he will acclaim its advancement toward the proud position now held by England, the banker and the clearing-house of the world. And he will learn — this thoughtful citizen — that material achievements like these cannot be attained without a market for capital and a market for securities.*

* The student who wishes to go more thoroughly into the subject of Stock Exchange usefulness is referred to "The Annals of the American Academy of Political and Social Science," Vol. XXXV, No. 3, May, 1910, Philadelphia. "Some Thoughts on Speculation," by Frank Fayant, New York, 1909; "The Stock Exchange," by Francis W. Hirst, London, Williams & Norgate, 1911; "Wall Street and the Country," by Chas. A. Conant, New York, G. P. Putnam's Sons, 1904; "Story of the Stock Exchange," by Chas. Duguid, London, New York, E. P. Dutton & Co., 1902; "The Stock Exchange, London," Methuen & Co., 1904; "The New York Stock Exchange," by Francis L. Eames, New York, 1894; "Der Deutsche Kapitalmarkt," by Rudolph Eberstadt, Leipzig, Duncker & Humbolt, 1901; "The Stock Exchange," (London), by C. D. Ingall & G. Withers, Longmans, Green & Co., 1904; "A Simple Purchase and Sale Through a Stockbroker," by Eliot Norton, *Harvard Law Review,* Vol. VIII, No. 8; "Stock Exchange Investments; History, Practice, and Results," London, Simpkin, Marshall, Hamilton, Kent & Co., 1900.

CHAPTER II

THE USES AND ABUSES OF SPECULATION

CHAPTER II

THE USES AND ABUSES OF SPECULATION

SOMEWHERE in each one of us lurks Stevenson's spirit of "divine unrest," the parent of speculation. To-day, as in wise old Greece in the morning of the world, philosophers sit under every tree, speculating upon the phenomena of the universe, and upon the practical application of them to the needs of humanity. Thus Archimedes came to know of things that we now call Copernican, seventeen centuries before Copernicus was born; thus Columbus and his argosy sailed into the great unknown, speculating upon an irrational and even shocking exploit; thus Pasteur saved to France through the meditations of his speculative mind a sum greater than the cost of the Prussian war and the colossal indemnity that followed it.

And so the "divine unrest" goes on and on, impelling men to speculations and explorations of the physical world and of the world that lies beyond our primitive senses, with here and there a high achievement, and now and then a miserable failure, but always on and on. The hypothesis of the spectacled professor blossoms into a boon; the dream of the inventor becomes a benefaction; the forlorn hope of the explorer points the way to wealth. Things that were speculations yesterday become realities to-day. To-morrow? — nobody knows. In a free field, not bounded by formulæ nor restricted by law of God or man, with money to encourage it and enterprise to spur it on, what may come from the speculations of the future passes understanding.

Now speculation is an all-embracing word, overworked, threadbare, and worn to the bone. Originally it meant "to see"; then "to view," "watch," "spy out"; then "exploration" or "contemplation." When thrift came into the language and men ceased burying their gold, it began to take on a new meaning. The spirit of legitimate adventure, that entered men's minds when the Most Christian Kings abandoned brute force and repudiation, led men to buy things in the hope of selling them at a profit. It was risky business at first, and capital, then as now, was timid. The High Finance of the Middle Ages was not easily forgotten. But little by little channels through which enterprise might flow into wealth came into being, and confidence came with them. This was called speculation.

By the time Adam Smith wrote his "Wealth of Nations" (1776) the word was firmly fixed in the language. "The establishment of any new manufacture," he said, "or any new branch of commerce, or of any new practice in agriculture, is always a speculation from which the projector promises himself extraordinary profits." How the early channels of speculation broadened into great rivers, how confidence grew as the art of making money and increasing it developed, how credit became established, how speculation led to the opening of new countries and the extension of immense advantages, through civilization, to the people of those countries — all this is a fascinating story. And yet the speculation of to-day is no different in its elementals from that of the early Greeks; the same spirit of "divine unrest" that spurs on the philosopher in his study stimulates the explorer of strange lands, beckons on the engineer and the builder of railways, and attracts the capital of the adventurous investor. We cannot stop it if we would, because hope, ambition, and avarice are fundamentals of human nature. The police cannot arrest them; they are fixed and immutable.

If there is more speculation in material things to-day than there ever was before, it is because there are more things to speculate in, more money to speculate with, more people to speculate, and more machinery, like telephones and telegraphs, to facilitate speculation. Capital, credit, and new undertakings grow day by day and open new avenues of possible profit. The per capita wealth of nations, growing by what it feeds on, constantly seeks new fields for enterprise and adventure. The intelligence of the people increases by leaps and bounds, and goes peering curiously into all the little nooks and crannies of the world for opportunities of gain — the apotheosis of speculative enterprise.

All forms of human endeavor in material things are, or were at their beginning, speculations. Every ship that goes to sea carries with it a speculation, and leaves another one behind it at Lloyds. Every man who insures his life or his house buys a speculation, and every company that insures him sells one. The farmer speculates when he fertilizes his land, again when he plants his seed, and again when he sells his crop for future delivery, as he often does, before it is planted or before it has matured. The merchant contracts to fill his shelves long before spring arrives; he is speculating. The manufacturer sells to him, speculating on the hope or belief that he will be able to buy the necessary raw material, and again on the labor, the looms and the spindles necessary to make the delivery. In the South the grower of cotton and in Australia the grower of wool are likewise speculating on the probability of a crop and on the price at which they may sell to this manufacturer. It sounds like "this is the house that Jack built" in its endless chain of sequences; a chain, indeed, and one no stronger than its weakest link. Interfere with any part of it, and the whole commercial structure which it binds together falls apart. The grower, the manufacturer, and the merchant *must* speculate.

There was twofold speculation on the part of our great financial barons who built our trans-continental railways, for they had to reckon not only upon the probability of profit in their under-takings but likewise upon the willingness of other speculators — you and I — to assist them by buy-ing a part of the securities which represented the outlay. To be sure it so happened that many of these vast speculations at first proved unsound. Some of them were a little premature; others pushed too far; they brought disaster upon the speculators who had put money into them. And yet who shall say that our great railways have failed to enrich the world and spread the comforts of civilization? "But for a verdant and ever-green faith," says a recent writer, "salted with the love of risk and adventure for their own sakes, how could mountains be bored and waters bridged? If there were not superstition there could be no religion; if there were not bad speculation there could be no good investment; if there were no wild ventures there would be no brilliantly successful enterprises."

This is not hyperbole; it is fact. The world of business and enterprise must go on; it cannot stop. As it goes on capital must be enlisted, which is another way of saying that speculators must be attracted. The only way that has been devised to attract them is through the medium of certificates of ownership or evidences of debt, called securities. But the business does not end there, for, as we have seen in the previous chapter, the capital of speculators will not take hold unless a market is provided. They want to know where they stand; before they venture upon the troubled waters of new enterprises they must be assured of a public market, a harbor where they can get ashore quickly if storms are brewing.

The only plan that the ingenuity of man has thus far devised to meet this emergency is a Stock Exchange. One man, or two, or a hundred cannot make a market, because the immense volume and variety of these securities make it impossible for any unorganized handful of brokers and dealers to determine a fair market price.

What is required, and what the man whose capital is wanted insists upon, is an organized body of brokers, speculators, and investors competing keenly, seeking to buy cheap and sell dear, gathering and disseminating all the news, and so sharpening the judgment and stimulating the higgling of buyers and sellers as to bring prices to their legitimate level and give them stability. Ten thousand competitors in this business of bringing prices and values together are of course better than one thousand; a hundred thousand would be better still. The Stock Exchange supplies this want, and will continue to supply it until a better plan is devised.* Meantime, since it has grown to its present stature by forms of speculation necessary to the maintenance of enterprise, any serious interruption of the facilities it affords will bring enterprise to a standstill and cause the whole sensitive structure of credit to collapse in terror. Let Professor Seligman explain this matter:

"If a railway or other industry, in launching a new enterprise, had to depend on the chance investors at the time of

* The Stock Exchange is an organization of individuals formed for the purpose of listing securities and for facilitating the sale and delivery of stocks. . . . Through its agency corporations are enabled to sell their shares and get the money capital to conduct their business. The Stock Exchange has come into existence because of a demand for trade facilities that will adjust differences of opinion in reference to future values of corporation securities and give the purchaser some idea of values. ("Modern Industrialism," by Frank L. McVey, Professor of Political Economy in the University of Minnesota. N. Y., 1904.)

the issue of the securities, it would be seriously hampered. The mere knowledge that at any moment there will be a ready sale on the Exchange greatly increases the circle of purchasers, many of whom may not intend to be permanent investors. The Stock Exchange aids the investment of capital, as the Produce Exchange aids the production of finished commodities. Business orders and corporate needs are intermittent, because they depend on temporary exigencies; the risks at one end, at all events, are eliminated by the unintermittent, continuous market which regular speculation affords. The Cotton Exchange was the result of the disorganization of the cotton trade after the Civil War; speculation in all other staples has in the same way been the consequence of the efforts of the manufacturer to avert the risks of intermittent and spasmodic fluctuations in the raw material. The result of regular speculation is to steady prices. Speculation tends to equalize demand and supply, and by concentrating in the present the influences of the future it intensifies the normal factors and minimizes the market fluctuation. Speculation so far as it has become the regular occupation of a class, differentiated from other business men for this particular purpose, subserves a useful and in modern times an indispensable function."*

Here we have an authority who tells us that speculation in securities, no less than in raw materials, is "an indispensable function" if business is to go ahead. The last census shows that 32½ per cent. of the population of the United States is composed of laboring men, not counting agricultural workers. This large army of men is

* "Principles of Economics," by Edwin R. A. Seligman, Professor of Political Economy in Columbia University (N. Y., 1905).

by no means independent; on the contrary it is strictly dependent on the ability of others to give it employment. Shut down the factories, curtail the operations of railways, close the mines and quarries, stop building and new construction, and in greater or less degree suffering and privation among these large masses must ensue.

Now go a step further, and we find that the managers of these railways, mines, and factories, are in turn dependent — wholly dependent upon capital. They cannot go ahead with the extensions and improvements necessary to efficiency without borrowing money; and credit, in turn, will not come to their support unless a broad market is provided, through the Stock Exchange, for the securities which represent these obligations. Hence we see that just as every farmer in the West and every cotton-grower in the South must have a stable market for his products, so every laborer in our great industrial field is directly concerned with the maintenance of a stable market for the securities of the company that employs him. The interests of one are the interests of all, and speculation, in one form or another, underlies all industrial progress. "Complaint is made of the evils of speculation," said the greatest of French economists, "*but the evils that specu-*

lation prevents are much greater than those it causes."*

Now that we have reached a point in our discussion that brings us face to face with the so-called "evils" of speculation on the Stock Exchange, let us pause and consider the difference between speculation, which is held by many to be abhorrent, and investment, which is generally thought right and proper. The first thing we encounter is the shadowy and indistinct boundary line that separates the one from the other. Does any one know where the one begins and the other ends? France has more conservative investors than any other country, yet, as Mr. Hirst puts it, the most critical and hidebound buyer of French rentes is a speculator in the sense that he not only wishes his purchase to yield him interest, but also hopes and expects that sooner or later he will be able to sell out at a profit, all of which is legitimate, proper, and human. The first question every man asks when the time comes to invest is, "Is this a good time for investment?" "Am I buying cheap?" by which he means "Are these investments likely to enhance in value?"

He may have bought Spanish bonds at low prices during the war between Spain and the

* "Nouveau Dictionnaire d'Economie Politique," by Paul Leroy-Beaulieu, Paris, 1892.

United States — a somewhat speculative investment — and in his purchase he believed himself an investor in a strict sense. Yet, when those bonds recovered to a normal basis and he sold out at a profit, was it speculation, or investment, or a little of both, that defined the trade? British consols are low to-day, and there is of course no safer investment, but the investor who buys them is influenced by the fact that a long period of peace seems to lie ahead, with reduced expenditures for armament and hence with diminished borrowings by the Government leading to a substantial recovery in the price of these solid securities. Such a man is "speculating" on England's abstention from war, on its limitation of military and naval expenditures, and on the probable effects of these matters on the price of his consols.*

The truth seems to be that all investment is speculation, differing from it in degree but not in kind. This salient fact was recognized as long ago as 1825, when, despite the comparatively limited field for investment enterprise, McCulloch saw what was coming and grasped the true idea of the part speculation and its handmaiden, investment, were to play in the industrial renais-

* Consult "The (London) Stock Exchange," Francis W. Hirst, London, Chap. VI, p. 164, Williams & Norgate, 1911.

sance. Coming at a time when speculation was new, and subjected, as all innovations are, to widespread criticism and doubt, his words have prophetic significance.

"It is obvious that those who indiscriminately condemn all sorts of speculative engagements have never reflected on the circumstances incident to the prosecution of every undertaking. In truth and reality they are all speculations. Their undertakers must look forward to periods more or less distant, and their success depends entirely on the sagacity with which they have estimated the probability of certain events occurring, and the influence which they have ascribed to them. *Speculation is, therefore, really only another name for foresight;* and, though fortunes have sometimes been made by a lucky hit, the character of a successful speculator is, in the vast majority of instances, due to him also who has skilfully devised the means of effecting the end he had in view, and who has outstripped his competitors in the judgment with which he has looked into futurity, and appreciated the operation of causes producing distant effects."*

A quarter of a century later we find England's foremost thinker sounding the same clear note. John Stuart Mill was by no means a hermit phil-

* "Principles of Economics," by J. R. McCulloch, London, 1825.

osopher feeding on theories. Traveler, sportsman, business man, statesman, and author, he saw things broadly and wrote for practical men. "Speculators," he said — and he was speaking of the "greedy" ones who buy and sell for gain — "have a highly useful office in the economy of society. Among persons who have not much considered the subject there is a notion that the gains of speculators are often made by causing an artificial scarcity; that they create a high price by their own purchases and then profit by it. This may easily be shown to be fallacious." He then shows, what I have outlined elsewhere, that the market is larger than any speculator or group of speculators, and, if this was true in 1848, I think it will not be disputed that it is quite true to-day.

Continuing, Mill says: "The operations of speculative dealers are useful to the public whenever profitable to themselves. The interest of the speculators as a body coincide with the interests of the public; and as they can only fail to serve the public interest in proportion as they miss their own, *the best way to promote the one is to leave them to pursue the other in perfect freedom. Neither law nor opinion should prevent an operation, beneficial to the public, from being attended with as much private advantage as is compatible with full and free competition.*" Mill makes no distinction here between investors and speculators; they are one and the same. In any case it is conceded that speculation is what makes the markets to-day, since 90 per cent. of the transactions that take place daily on the world's Stock Exchanges are speculations pure and simple. And this is a good thing. Before we go on with our subject, let Professor Emery explain why, and bring the teachings of McCulloch and Mill down to our own day:

"Speculation has become an increasingly important factor in the economic world without receiving a corresponding place in economic science. In the field in which it acts, in the trade in grain and cotton and securities and the like, speculation is the predominant influence in determining price, and, as such, is one of the chief directive forces in trade and industry. But treatises in the English language on general economic theory and conditions have given very little space to this influence, which is fundamental in the world of economic fact. . . .

"It is true that forty years ago speculation was far less important than it is now, and there was, therefore, more justification for disregarding it. Professor Hadley has given due consideration to the new conditions which prevail in modern business. At the same time it should be remembered that McCulloch, already in his day, had grasped the true idea of the function of speculation, a fact shown by the incorporation of his treatment of the subject into his chapters on Value. Wide as is the influence of speculation, its force is felt primarily in the field of prices. By making prices it directs industry and trade, for men produce and exchange according to comparative prices. Speculation then is vitally connected with the theory of value.

"From the point of view of theory, therefore, it is incorrect to attach so little importance to the function of speculation; in practice it is impossible to deal intelligently with the evils of the speculative system without first recognizing its real relation to business. Both the writer and the reformer must reckon more than they have yet done with the fact that speculation in the last half century has developed as a natural economic institution in response to the new conditions of industry and commerce. It is the result of steam transportation and the telegraph on the one hand, and of vast industrial undertakings on the other. The attitude of those who would try to crush it out by legislation, without disturbing any other economic conditions, is entirely unreasonable."*

Now we come to the evils of the business. That there are evils, really serious ones, no one will deny. To be sure many of the phases of speculation that are called evils are not evils at all; the statements made concerning them have what Oscar Wilde termed "all the vitality of error, and all the tediousness of an old friend," and yet, although the prevalent criticism is often stupid and superficial, there are undeniably offensive forms of speculation that one would like to see suppressed. Speculation is a comparatively new phenomenon, and it has brought with it dangers and pitfalls. So also have automobiles, electricity, and steam

* "Speculation on the Stock and Produce Exchanges of the United States," by Henry Crosby Emery, Professor of Political Economy at Yale University. New York, 1896.

engines. But while the Stock Exchange has created the arena for the display of these abuses, it has not originated them "except," as a recent writer puts it, "in the sense in which one may say that private property has originated robbery."

The great evil of speculation consists in the buying of securities or real estate or anything else with borrowed money, by uninformed people who cannot afford to lose. Its commonest form in speculation in securities is what is known as "margin" trading, this name being derived from the fact that the buyer, instead of paying cash in full for his purchase, deposits only a fractional amount of its cost, which is intended to serve as a margin to protect the broker from loss, while the broker pays the remaining sum necessary to complete the actual purchase. Thus the speculator may deposit $1000 on securities costing $10,000, while the broker furnishes the additional $9000. It is a system in use everywhere; on the London Stock Exchange it is called "Cover," on the Paris Bourse, "La Couverture."

There is no fixed amount of margin called for by brokers, as circumstances differ widely with the character of the securities dealt in, the standing of the buyer, and the condition of the market; but in a broad way it may be said that members of the New York Stock Exchange exact a margin equivalent to ten points on middle-grade speculative issues, twenty points on high-priced and erratic securities, and five points on very low-priced shares that move slowly. There are, of course, certain securities on which no payment short of actual outright purchase in full would be accepted by reputable brokers, while on the other hand, in the case of securities that fluctuate but slightly, such as our government, state, or municipal bonds, a 5 per cent. margin would be ample. This is also the practice in London and Paris, generally speaking. In Paris the *Agents de Change* always insist upon a greater margin than the *Coulissiers*, or outside brokers, and here members of the New York Stock Exchange invariably pursue the same policy.

This affords an opportunity to say that the local evil of stock speculation arising from insufficient margins is one that may be laid at the door of outside Exchanges rather than the "Big" Exchange, as it is called, because, in the minor Exchanges, margins are notoriously small, and the smaller the margin the greater the number of "victims." Indeed, if it were not for this practice it would be difficult for members of smaller Exchanges to exist at all. In so far as speculation in securities may merit criticism, this tendency to attract poor people by the bait of slim margins is undeniably a very real evil, and one which can only be corrected by the brokers themselves. The Hughes Committee, after devoting much time and labor to this matter, put its conclusions in these words:

"We urge upon all brokers to discourage speculation upon small margins, and upon the Exchange to use its influence, and if necessary its power, to prevent members from soliciting and generally accepting business on a less margin than 20 per cent."*

Every one connected with the New York Stock Exchange knows that this suggestion, like all the others made by the Commission, was received with approval by all hands, and, if a hard

* In its effort to study all possible remedial methods affecting speculation on margins, the Hughes Commissioners in 1909 put this question to the Governors of the Stock Exchange:

"*Would taxation of loans made on margin transactions tend to discourage margin speculation? If so, would it be desirable to graduate the tax in accordance with the margin ratio?*"

To which the Governors replied:

"In our opinion the taxation of loans could not be made upon margin transactions, as the lender of the money would be absolutely ignorant as to whether the securities pledged with him were carried on margin or whether they were owned absolutely. Any species of taxation upon loans would work a great injury to the money prosperity of the banking institutions of the City of New York. Loans are made to individuals and institutions upon bona fide property; they are also made to borrowers of money upon stocks and bonds offered to the institution, which are marginal in their nature; further, they are made upon securities only in part marginal, and any effort to distinguish would be practically impossible and would retard the entire business of the community. The effect of taxation upon loans would be to drive capital instantly from the city, and would force a species of financial institution to arise in every State which would profit by our inquisitorial laws, should such be enacted, to their own advantage and to our serious detriment. Such a restriction upon the free lending of money is not only unsound, impossible of enforcement, but could not help resulting in a constant evasion of the law."

and fast rule could have been devised to meet not merely the spirit but the letter of the recommendation, the Governors of the Exchange would have put it into instant operation. But there are difficulties in the way, and one of the duties of the Governors is to consider very carefully all sides of each perplexing question that comes before them, not merely in the interests of the Stock Exchange, but with due regard to the common law and the interests of the public. Margin trading is a matter of contract, and "the right of one private person to extend credit to another," as the Chairman of the Hughes Commission himself points out, "is simply the right to make a contract, which, under the Federal Constitution, cannot be impaired by any State Legislature."*

Here is a very considerable difficulty in the way of restricting margin trading, and one that is not fully understood by the outsider. He is prone to speak of contracts thus made as "gambling transactions," missing altogether the essential point that there is a vast difference between a transaction with a contract behind it, enforceable at law, and one that has to do with bucket-shops and roulette, in which there is no contract, and is

* "The Hughes Investigation," by Horace White, *Journal of Political Economy*, October, 1909, p. 537.

expressly prohibited by law. No matter what his intent may have been when he bought, and no matter what margin the broker accepted — the buyer has the right to demand his securities at any time, and the broker must always be prepared to deliver them; conversely, the broker may compel the buyer to pay for and to receive the securities he has bought. Motives and methods have nothing whatever to do with the transaction.

The broker who buys for a client to-day does not know, and sometimes the client himself does not know, whether the securities are "bought to keep," or are to be sold to-morrow; similarly the broker has no means of knowing whether the client, who deposited a ten-point margin at the time of his purchase, will or will not deposit another ten points to-morrow, and continue such payments until his securities are wholly paid for. In the large majority of cases the intent of the speculative buyer is to sell as soon as he can get a satisfactory profit, but that does not make him a gambler by any means. Why? Because, if he bets $1000 on a horse race, one party to the transaction wins and the other loses; whereas, if he deposits $1000 as margin against a stock speculation and makes a profit of say $500, the broker loses nothing by paying him that profit when the account is closed. No property changes hands in the one case, while, in the other, actual property is purchased and held ready for delivery on demand. The law is clear in classifying the operations of bucket-shops with gambling transactions, because in a large majority of instances no actual purchase is made; the "buyer" merely bets in that case as to what subsequent quotations will be; the "trade" is between two principals, one of whom must lose if the other wins.

The Hughes Commission, as I have said, went very fully into all these matters. It was in session six months, and many witnesses were examined. After considering all the pros and cons of margin trading, the experience of England and Germany in dealing with speculation, the three-years' debate in Congress on the Hatch Anti-Option Bill, and the voluminous reports of the Industrial Commission, the conclusion was reached "to urge upon all brokers," as shown in the paragraph cited, a general agreement on margins of not less than 20 per cent. It must be borne in mind that this was not in the nature of a formal recommendation, but rather as the expression of a hope that some measure of reform might be accomplished if such concerted action by brokers were feasible.

That members of the New York Stock Exchange endorse this view goes without saying.

They realize more fully than is generally known by the public that indiscriminate and reckless speculation by uninformed people who are beguiled into it by the lure of small margins is an undoubted evil that should be checked, and they are doing what they can to check it by discouraging such operations. For example, it would be very difficult to-day for a woman to open a speculative account with any reputable firm of brokers on the major exchange unless she were well known, peculiarly qualified for such transactions, and abundantly able to support them. Accounts will not be accepted from clerks or employees of other brokerage houses or of banks and other corporations in the Wall Street district; indeed, such transactions are expressly forbidden by the rules of the Exchange. No accounts will be accepted from any one who is not personally known to one of the firm's partners — and the practice resorted to in earlier years of employing agents to solicit business under the nominal title of "office managers," "bond department managers," and all that sort of technical subterfuge, is likewise forbidden.

Members of the Exchange are not permitted to advertise in any way save that defined as of "a strictly legitimate business character," and the governors are the judges of what is legitimate. The layman has but to glance at the bare and colorless announcements made by Stock Exchange houses in the advertising columns of our newspapers to see how rigidly this rule is enforced; indeed 90 per cent. of the members do not advertise at all. Best of all, speculation on "shoe-string" margins is now almost eliminated from the major exchange. The houses that notoriously offended in this respect ten and fifteen years ago are to-day inconspicuous in the day's dealings. Their business is gone — in its very nature it could not last long — and if rumor be credited its demise carried with it a part of the capital of the firms involved. It was a lesson and a warning. All these instances serve to show that the Stock Exchange is doing what it can to remedy this evil, and, if circumstances arise in which more can be done, the governors and members will be found a unit in enforcing whatever restrictions are necessary.

At the moment it is difficult to see how an inflexible rule of 20 per cent. margins could be put in practice without seriously interfering with really sound business. A telegraphic order may be received from a customer of the utmost responsibility who may happen to be in Europe. Any stockbroker, and any business man in mercantile trade, would be glad to execute for such a person all the orders he chose to entrust, regardless of margins. In such a case no question of motive enters into the transaction; it may ultimately prove to be a speculation pure and simple, or the buyer may cable instructions to deliver the securities to his bank, in which case it would seem to be an investment; but, regardless of that, an insistence by the broker on a 20 per cent. margin would be silly, and would merely drive the business elsewhere or prevent it altogether.

Numerous instances of a similar sort might be cited to show how difficult it would be to enforce margin prohibitions in all these perfectly legal contracts. Germany tried it in the law of 1896, with disastrous consequences, which I have described elsewhere. It is a matter that will always be a fruitful topic of discussion, yet it differs in no essential respect from the practice of a speculator in real estate who pays down a small percentage of a purchase price and borrows the balance on mortgage. It is similar to what the merchant does when he fills his shelves with goods bought with a fractional payment in cash and the balance at some future date. In all these cases involving property let me repeat that the deposit of a specified sum by the principal and an agreement or contract with the broker is a perfectly valid transaction.*

That newspaper criticism and attacks by social mentors should go to extreme lengths in deprecating stock speculation by crude, greedy, and unsophisticated people is perhaps, after all, a perfectly useful function, and if such critics err in going to great extremes, that too may be set down as right and proper, for it is perhaps better to go too far than not to go far enough. The interests of the Stock Exchange are the interests of the whole country; its welfare depends upon an intelligent and thrifty people; its aims are public-spirited and patriotic. Whatever it may lose in

* The governors of the Stock Exchange, when asked by the Hughes Commission, "Would a change in the practice of dealing on margins be desirable?" replied as follows:

"The practice of dealing on margins is absolutely essential to the conduct of many transactions, whether in stocks or bonds. To prohibit it would be to deny to a man the right to invest his funds and to purchase property upon such terms as he pleases. As well might the purchase of real estate, where a portion of the consideration is left on mortgage, be prohibited. The responsibility of the individual enters so largely into these transactions that it will be impossible to define specific instances where the margin would be too small or unnecessarily great. It is to be left to the discretion of the bankers, as well as to the judgment of those who furnish the money upon which these transactions are based. There may be certain classes of securities, like city bonds or government bonds, where a very small margin is ample. There may be other transactions in stocks selling at very high prices where a very strong margin should be required. Like many other details of a banking and brokerage business, these matters are frequently subjects of arrangement, whereby the broker protects himself and a satisfactory protection is given to him by his client. It would be manifestly impossible for the enactment of rules or regulations suitable to every case, and, in conclusion, we would say that it is almost unknown for an institution, bank, or trust company, to lose money upon any loans made on margins to members of the Stock Exchange in good standing."

the way of business from ignorant and silly people who are driven out of blind speculative undertakings leading to losses which they can ill afford, it will gain tenfold in imparting sound information through candor and publicity. On the other hand, unless we are prepared to abolish property altogether, do away with the instruments of credit, and suppress all forms of trading designed to supply our future requirements, we may as well reconcile ourselves to the inevitable and take what comfort we may in the reflection that prudence, thrift, and foresight are not to be eliminated, merely because the proletariat below stairs sometimes indulges in speculation and suffers the consequences of its folly.

"Finally," writes Professor Emery, "the question must be faced of the effect of eliminating the public from the speculative market even if it could be accomplished. It is supposed sometimes that such a result would be all benefit and no injury. On the contrary, the real and important function of speculation in the field of business can only be performed by a broad and open market. Though no one would defend individual cases of recklessness or fail to lament the disaster and crime sometimes engendered, the fact remains that a 'purely professional market' is not the kind of market which best fulfils the services of speculation. *A broad market with the participation of an intelligent and responsible public is necessary. A narrow professional market is less serviceable to legitimate investment and trade and much more susceptible of manipulation.*"*

One of the difficulties with which men have to contend in a big country like this is the apparent inability of large masses of the people to understand other large masses. Distances are so great, occupations so diverse, and enterprise so confining, that one whole section of the country may not and often does not know what another section is doing. Men are too busy to learn by travel and reading that which, in the interest of the whole country, they should thoroughly understand. Thus it happens that a section of the country given over, let us say, to agricultural pursuits, having first acquired the notion that speculation in securities is only a form of legalized robbery, assumes that to New York City and the New York Stock Exchange is confined a greater part of the stock speculation of the world. We have seen the fallacy in the first of these hasty conclusions; the second may easily be explained away.

Yankee speculation in securities is not a marker to speculation in London, where the day to day

* "Ten Years' Regulation of the Stock Exchange in Germany." *Yale Review*, May 1908, *q. v.*, *post*.

trading vastly exceeds ours, and where the "Kaffir Circus" of 1894–5 and the "Rubber Boom" of 1909–10 exceeded any similar outburst ever known in America. France is the most prudent and thrifty of nations, yet the Panama mania which collapsed in 1894, although followed by a period of the utmost repentance and conservatism, found a parallel in the crazy French speculation in Russian industrials which crashed in 1912. There was an extraordinary speculation in Egyptian land and financial companies in Cairo in 1905–6, which, in proportion to the number of participants, greatly exceeded any boom in New York. China awakens slowly, but, once its political reforms are effected, a field of extraordinary speculation will open there without a parallel in history. The Chinaman is not only a shrewd and competent business man, but he is, Mr. Hirst tells us, "a confirmed and incurable" speculator. "From time to time," says this writer, "the Shanghai Stock Exchange becomes a scene of the wildest speculation, and it is safe to predict that, when a new China is evolved, Stock Exchanges will spring up in all the large towns. Of this, a foretaste was afforded in the spring and summer of 1910, when Shanghai caught the rubber infection from London. All classes and races took part, but the native Chinaman plunged deepest. When the break in prices came, one Chinese operator was so heavily involved that, on his failure, many of the native banks had to suspend payment, with the result that for months the trade and credit of this great shipping and business centre were disorganized.*

I mention these incidents to show that speculation is not confined to geographical limits. It is all a part of the "divine unrest" inherent in each of us, and it develops and grows intense just in proportion with the march of the civilization it serves to benefit. In new countries, as in China, it may often go too far; sometimes in old countries it oversteps the bounds of prudence, but any student of these phenomena knows that, as economic processes become understood by the masses, the intervals of time between the panics that result from over-speculation grow wider and wider.

Another mistake of those sections of the country that do not understand the Stock Exchange results from the indiscriminate blending of that institution with Wall Street. Let us hear from Mr. Horace White on this point. He was the chairman of the last committee that investigated the Stock Exchange; he is one of our foremost economists, and he may be assumed to understand his subject:

* "The Stock Exchange," by Francis W. Hirst, London, 1911, p. 101.

"There is a widespread belief that Wall Street and the Stock Exchange are one and the same thing, and that all the fluctuations on the Exchange are caused by Wall Street. This is an error as glaring as it would be to suppose that all the water in the Mississippi River comes from the adjacent banks, ignoring the innumerable streams and rills that contribute their quota from countless unseen sources. Wall Street and the Stock Exchange are two different things. The men on the floor of the Exchange are the agents of others, executing the orders which they receive both from Wall Street and from other parts of the habitable globe. Some of them speculate on their own account, but the speculating members of the Exchange are divided into bulls and bears. They do not all push in the same direction at any one time. They simply aim to anticipate, each for himself, the drift of financial public opinion in order to take advantage of it.

"This is what Wall Street outside of the Exchange does; and the only advantage which speculators in Wall Street have over those in other parts of the country is derived from larger capital, more direct and ample sources of information, and greater skill and promptness in the use of it. Wall Street speculators are likewise divided into bulls and bears pushing against each other; and all their advantages do not save them from making mistakes, which often result in losses proportioned to the magnitude of their operations. The 'rich men's panic' of 1903 was such an instance. The panic of 1907 was another. It is sometimes said that Wall Street can put prices on the Stock Exchange up or down at its own pleasure. This is a delusion."*

Members and friends of the New York Stock Exchange view with apprehension the periodic

* "The Hughes Investigation," by Horace White, *Journal of Political Economy*, October, 1909, pp. 532–3.

attacks upon their great institution made by those who, for reasons not to be discussed here, wish to attract popular attention. But there is no reason why these matters should excite alarm. The Exchange purified itself long ago of the old abuses, new ones as they occur meet with severe disciplinary measures, and it has a certificate of good character in the report made to the sovereign State of New York by the Hughes Commission. This commission has stated explicitly that margin trading is a matter of contract guaranteed by the Federal Constitution. It is not conceivable that any legislature can ignore such a report, by such a commission, nor is it possible that, in such event, any court could be found to uphold legislation directed at random against an institution that bears the endorsement of all students of economics.

One has but to read the decisions of the courts to see that the matter of non-interference with the great Exchanges, on technical grounds, has become a fixture in our jurisprudence. "The Exchanges," said Judge Grosscup of the United States Circuit Court, "balance like the governor of an engine the otherwise erratic course of prices. They focus intelligence from all lands, and the prospects for the whole year, by bringing together minds trained to weigh such intelligence and to forecast the prospects. They tend to steady the markets more nearly to their right level than if left to chance or unhindered manipulation."* In somewhat similar vein Justice Holmes of the United States Supreme Court, said: "Speculation . . . is the self-adjustment of society to the probable. Its value is well known as a means of avoiding or mitigating catastrophes, equalizing prices, and providing for periods of want. *It is true that the success of the strong induces imitation by the weak, and that incompetent persons bring themselves to ruin by undertaking to speculate in their turn. But legislatures and courts generally have recognized that the natural evolutions of a complex society are to be touched only with a very cautious hand, and that such coarse attempts at a remedy for the waste incident to every social function as a simple prohibition and laws to stop its being, are harmful and vain.*"†

With these opinions before them, so long as the governors of the Stock Exchange continue their policy of a wise and dignified administration in the interest of the public they serve, there is nothing to fear. Corrections, remedies, improvements, and reforms will be found to be necessary from time to time — some of them are necessary

* "Board of Trade Case," 88 Fed. 868.
† "Chicago Board of Trade Case," May 8, 1905.

at this moment, and the governors are hard at work on the task. To accuse them of indifference or neglect of duty is to deny them that form of intelligence which enables a man to protect his property. Their splendid institution has grown to its present importance and power through economic development that could not have been foreseen nor prevented. Speculation on a large scale has accompanied its growth, and contributed to it; and speculation, as we have seen, is a highly desirable and useful part of all business. This speculation numbers among its adherents people in all parts of the world who have a perfect right to speculate, and who do vastly more good than harm in their operations.

It has also attracted a great many people who have no business to speculate, and who would be prevented from doing so if it were possible. The ignorance and cupidity of these people is so great, and the pitfalls provided them by unscrupulous, methods outside the Exchange are so many and various that something has to be done to protect them. The Stock Exchange does not encourage them, but it recognizes that they have legal if not moral rights, and it stands ready to help them. It gives to such people the same information that it gives to the richest investor in the land. The securities in which it deals are known to be free from taint; all forms of crookedness are prohibited; every transaction within its walls is made openly, as a result of free competitive bidding, and published broadcast to the world. What more, and what less, can be done? Has there ever been a time in the world's history when property and trade were so secure, and when speculation, which makes property and trade, was so jealously safeguarded?

---

*Several authorities among those quoted in this chapter have been taken from Mr. Frank Fayant's pamphlet, "Some Thoughts on Speculation," N.Y., 1909. It would be difficult to compress in small space a more instructive array of data than that presented in Mr. Fayant's work.

CHAPTER III

THE BEAR AND SHORT SELLING

CHAPTER III

THE BEAR AND SHORT SELLING

THE operations of "bears" in the great speculative markets and the practice of "short selling" are riddles which the layman but dimly comprehends. Buying in the hope of selling at a profit, and if need be, "holding the baby" for a long time and "nursing" it until the profit appears, is simple enough; but an Oedipus is required to solve the enigma of selling what one does not possess, and of buying it at a profit after the price has cheapened. It is the most complicated of all ordinary commercial transactions. How the thing can be done at all is a mystery; how such a man can serve a really useful economic purpose by this process is unfathomable. The layman who tries to figure it out thinks there is an Ethiopian somewhere in the wood-pile; the thing is unreal and fictitious. The only way he can understand it is to turn bear himself and learn by experience.

Why there should be so many bulls and so few bears can only be explained on the ground that optimism is the basis of speculation, and hope the essence of it. Yet the market can only go two ways: it is quite as likely to go down as up. Since sentiment should have no place in speculation one would think there should be as many bears as bulls, more of them, in fact, because the market almost always goes down faster than it goes up, and because nine out of ten of the unforeseen things that occur result in lower prices.

Accidents like diplomatic entanglements, rumors of war, earthquakes, and drought are constantly occurring to upset the plans of bulls and bring fat profits to bears in a hurry, while matters that bring about higher markets are generally things long anticipated, in which the profits that accrue to the bulls come about slowly and laboriously, and always with the attendant risk that a disturbance in any corner of the globe may bring on a sudden smash that will undo the upbuilding of months. In theory, therefore, there should be at least as many bears as bulls in all active markets, but in practice the large majority are always bulls, to whose sanguine and credulous natures the bear is a thing apart — a gloomy and misanthropic person hovering about like a vulture awaiting the carrion of a misfortune in the hope of a profit. Naturally the layman cannot understand him, and would like to suppress him.

Despite the fact that the odds seem to favor

the bears, there is an old and true saying that no Ursa Major ever retired with a fortune. Wall Street has seen many of them, and with perhaps one exception the records agree that the chronic pessimists have not succeeded. Fortune seems to have smiled on them at intervals; in the country's early days of construction and development mistakes were made that brought about disaster, but in the long run such tremendous progress has resulted in America as to defeat the aspirations of any man or group of men who stood in its way. The big bears, as a rule, have "over-stayed the market." Imbued with the hope that worse things were in store, they have been swept away by the forces they sought to oppose. One of them, a power in his day, was so obsessed with the notion that all prices were inflated, that he has been known to sell stocks short "for investment." One night when a lady at his side remarked on the beauty of the moon, he is said to have replied with that absent-minded mechanical skepticim inherent in the bear, "yes, but it's too high; it must come down."

One would think the ideal temperament for a speculator would be absolute impartiality, with an open mind uninfluenced by sentiment, ever ready to take advantage of all fluctuations as they occur. The ups and downs of a stock market always show, on average long periods, a practically equivalent swing each way, so it would seem that the speculator most likely to profit by these fluctuations would be one without preconceived prejudices, ready at all times to turn bull or bear as the occasion required. As a matter of fact, this type is the rarest of all, being confined, generally speaking, to the professional "traders" on the large exchanges, necessarily a very small minority of the speculative group, yet withal perhaps the most uniformly successful. These men, it must be understood, are not speculators, but traders, a nice distinction involving "catching a turn," as opposed to the speculative habit of "taking a position."

In active times I have known one of them to operate simultaneously in the New York Stock market, in the cotton market, and in the wheat market, trading at the same time in London and Paris, "shifting his position," or "switching" from the bull to the bear side twice in a single day, and closing all his trades at three o'clock with a total net profit of less than a thousand dollars on a turnover of 30,000 shares, to say nothing of the transactions in cotton and grain. It goes without saying that to do all these things in one day requires a curiously mercurial temperament, and calls for nerve and celerity altogether foreign to the average speculator. Such a man, moreover, contributes but little to the making of prices and values, which is the function of large markets; his chief economic usefulness lies rather in the enormous revenues he pays to the State. The man whose operations I have just described contributed in a single year $75,000 to the State Government in stock-transfer taxes.

The scientific way to measure the value of speculators in wide markets is to consider the bull as one whose purchases in times of falling prices serve to minimize the decline, and the bear as one who serves a doubly useful purpose in minimizing the advance by his short sales and in checking the decline by covering those sales. All these operations serve useful economic purposes, since the more buyers and sellers there are, the greater the stability of prices and the nearer the approach of prices to values.

This, as I have said, is the scientific way to look at it, and the correct way, but the popular way is something quite different. From this point of view the man who sells property he does not immediately possess is thought to be a menace, who depresses prices artificially and works a disadvantage to the investor or, in the produce markets, to the producer. Nothing could be more fallacious than this, because of the fact that just as every routine sale of actual stock requires a buyer, so every short sale by a bear requires a purchase by him of equal magnitude. And it is precisely these repurchasing or "covering" operations of the bears that do the utmost good in the way of checking declines in times of panic or distress.

When there are no bears, or when their position is so slight as to be inconsequential, declines are apt to run to extreme lengths and play havoc with bulls. One often hears among acute and clever speculators the expression "the bears are the market's best friends," and, though this may seem incongruous, it is quite true. In the month in which these lines are written there has occurred, for example, a really severe break in prices on the Stock Exchanges at London, Paris, and Berlin, arising from the periodic Balkan crisis. This decline ran to disproportionate extremes, and, in fact, approached such demoralization that more than 300,000 shares of American securities held abroad were thrown on the New York market for what they would bring. The reason for the severity of this decline was easily explained. The outstanding speculative account at all European centres, while not actually unwieldy, was almost entirely in the nature of commitments for the rise. There was no bear account. Therefore all Stock Exchanges were supersensitive since they lacked the steadying influence which covering by the bears invariably brings about. The bears are then, in truth the market's best friends, and the more there are of them, the better for all concerned when trouble comes.

Throughout all the political agitation in Germany which culminated in that disastrous failure, the Bourse Law of 1896, there appears to have been very little opposition to the bear and the practice of short selling; nevertheless in that section of the law which prohibited dealings for future delivery the bears found their activities restricted. The law has now been amended, having proved a wretched fiasco, but in the decade which attended its enforcement it was curious to note the unanimous cry that went up in Germany for the restoration of the bear. His usefulness in the stock market no less than in the commodity market was recognized; his suppression was deplored. It was found that just as his activities were restricted so the tendency toward inflated advance and ultimate collapse was increased. The market became one-sided, and hence lop-sided; quotations thus established were unreal and fictitious. Moreover there was an incentive to dishonesty, for unscrupulous persons could open a short account in one office and a long account in another, and if the bear side lost they could refuse to settle on the ground customarily resorted to by welchers.

"The prices of all industrial securities have fallen," said the Deutsche Bank in 1900, "and this decline has been felt all the more because by reason of the ill-conceived Bourse Law, it struck the public with full force without being softened through covering purchases" — i. e., by the bears. Again, four years later, when the law was still in force, the same authority states "a serious political surprise would cause the worst panic, because there are no longer any dealers (shorts) to take up the securities which at such times are thrown on the market." The Dresdner Bank in 1899 reported that the dangers arising from this prohibition cannot be overestimated "if with a change of economic conditions the unavoidable selling force cannot be met by dealers willing and able to buy."

"Short sellers do not determine prices," says Professor Huebner. "By selling they simply express judgment as to what prices will be in the future. If their judgment is wrong they will suffer the penalty of being obliged to go into the market and buy the securities at higher prices. Nine tenths of the people are by nature 'bulls,' and the higher prices go, the more optimistic and elated they become. If it were not for a group of 'short sellers,' who resist an excessive inflation, it would be much easier than now to raise prices through the roof; and then, when the inflation became apparent to all, the descent would be abrupt and likely unchecked until the basement was reached. The operations of the 'bear,' however, make excessive inflation extremely expensive, and similarly tend to prevent a violent smash because the 'bear,' to realize his profits, must become a buyer. The writer has been told by several members of the New York Stock Exchange that they have seen days of panic when practically the only buyers, who were taking the vast volume of securities dumped on the exchange, were those who had sold 'short,' and who now turned buyers as the only way of closing their transactions. They were curious to know what would have happened in those panic days, when everybody wished to sell and few cared to invest, if the buying power had depended solely upon the real investment demand of the outside public.

"In reply also to the prevalent opinion that 'short selling' unduly depresses security values, it should be stated that 'short sellers' are frequently the most powerful support which the market possesses. It is an ordinary affair to read in the press that the market is sustained or 'put up' at the expense of the 'shorts' who, having contracted to deliver at a certain price can frequently easily be driven to 'cover.' Short selling is thus a beneficial factor in steadying prices and obviating extreme fluctuations. Largely through its action, the discounting of serious depressions does not take the form of a sudden shock or convulsion, but instead is spread out over a period of time, giving the actual holder of securities ample time to observe the situation and limit his loss before ruin results. In fact, there could be no organized market for securities worthy of the name, if there did not exist two sides, the 'bull' and the 'bear.' The constant contest between their judgments is sure to give a much saner and truer level of prices than could otherwise exist. 'No other means,' reports the Hughes Committee, 'of restraining unwarranted marking up and down of prices has been suggested to us.'"*

So much for the functions of the bear in markets that deal in invested capital. In the commodity markets he becomes of even greater value, indeed, he is well-nigh indispensable. The Hon. Horace White, who was the Chairman of the Hughes Investigating Committee, cites this instance: "A manufacturer of cotton goods, in order to keep his mill running all the year round, must

* "Scope and Functions of the Stock Market," by Prof. S. S. Huebner, Ph. D., University of Pennsylvania. "Annals of the American Academy of Political and Social Science," Vol. XXXV, No. 3, May, 1910.

make contracts ahead for his material, before the crop of any particular year is picked. The cotton must be of a particular grade. He wishes to be insured against fluctuations in both price and quality; for such insurance he can afford to pay. In fact he cannot afford to be without it. There are also men in the cotton trade, of large capital and experience, who keep themselves informed of all the facts touching the crops and the demand and supply of cotton in the world, and who find their profit in making contracts for its future delivery. They do not possess the article when they sell it. To them the contract is a matter of speculation and short selling, but it is a perfectly legitimate transaction.

"To the manufacturer it is virtually a policy of insurance. It enables him to keep his mills running and his hands employed, regardless of bad weather or insect pests or other uncertainties. The same principles apply to the miller who wants wheat, to the distiller, the cattle-feeder, and the starch-maker who wants corn, to the brewer who wants hops and barley, to the brass founder who wants copper, and so on indefinitely. Insurance is one of two redeeming features of such speculation; and the other, which is even more important, is the steadying effect which it has on market prices. If no speculative buying of produce ever took place, it would be impossible for a grower of wheat or cotton to realize a fair price at once on his crop. He would have to deal it out little by little to merchants who, in turn, would pass it on, in the same piecemeal way, to consumers. It is speculative buying which not only enables farmers to realize on their entire crops as soon as they are harvested, but enables them to do so with no disastrous sacrifice of price. When buyers who have future sales in view compete actively with each other, farmers get fair prices for their produce."*

And, it may be added, the same satisfactory result is attained when bears who have sold the farmer's crop short come to cover their short sales by buying in the open market; their buying steadies the market if there is a tendency to decline; if the market is strong, their buying helps make it stronger. In either case they are the farmer's best friends, because the farmer profits as prices advance.

Speaking of farmers, it is well known that much of the opposition to short selling and dealing in futures in the large markets finds its chief advocates among the Western and Southern politicians whose constitutents are the agricultural classes. These gentlemen fulminate strongly against the

* *Journal of Political Economy*, October, 1909, pp. 531–2.

New York Stock Exchange and the grain and cotton exchanges, and in currying favor with their bucolic supporters they do not hesitate to condemn margin trading, short selling and every other phase of speculative markets. Yet it does not occur to them, or, if it does, they dare not refer to it, that in forming pools and combinations to hold back their wheat and cotton their constituents are doing the very thing which they so strongly condemn in speculative centres. The farmer is, of course, richer than he ever was before, but nevertheless he grows his wheat to sell, and only a few can carry it for any length of time without borrowing from the banks. The farmer who goes into one of these pools with wheat valued at $10,000 and who borrows $8000 on it from his local bank, is nothing more nor less than a speculator in wheat on a 20 per cent. margin, and the same horrid appellation describes the cotton-planter who resorts to similar practices.*

Now, of course, there is no moral reason why a farmer should not speculate if he chooses, but what touches us on the raw is his Phariseeism in doing for himself what he professes to abhor and condemn in others. One is tempted to say unkind things to the farmer at such times, to remind him, for example, that he is to-day the most back-

* Consult the *Wall Street Journal*, February 18, 1909.

ward and unprogressive factor in American business life. Despite the fact that the Department of Agriculture has spent $100,000,000 on his education in the last twenty years, he has not yet begun to learn what the German, Dutch, and French farmers learned years ago in intensive farming, nor has he mastered the art of cattle-raising in anything like the degree it is understood in the Argentine. Nature has smiled on him; he waxes fat with her bounty, but he does not keep pace with the growth of the country. Although enhancing prices are paid him for his product, he is unable to raise a crop proportionate in any degree to the facilities put at his disposal in the way of fertilizers and machinery. One would like to "rub it in" on the farmer, but one doesn't, "because" as a recent writer puts it, "the farmer is a farmer, and therefore not a person to be lectured like a mere banker or broker in Wall Street."

To the farmer, the politician, and the layman generally, short sales of cotton or grain are understood, approved, in fact, if the grower happens to be the one who profits by them. But substitute stocks and shares for wheat and cotton, and talk of "operations for a fall," and the layman thinks he smells a rat. He sees the bale of cotton or the carload of wheat actually moving; it is a concrete thing; it appeals to his senses, it is comprehensible. But talk to him of bits of paper called stock certificates, and by a curious process he concludes that a short sale has no basis of reality and is therefore menacing and improper. He persuades himself that short selling ought to be prohibited by law, and, since Wall Street harbors the chief offenders, he finds in the nearest politician a handy ally to assist him. These gentlemen, who obstinately refuse every other medicament, could be cured of their ailment by a strong diet of economics. They become subjects of medical, rather than financial, interest. They should dip themselves into Conant and Leroy-Beaulieu; they should cool off in the pages of Bagehot and Emery; and, by the time they have got into the soothing columns of the Hughes Commission's report, they will be ready for new points of view.

As a preparatory lesson: suppose a speculator buys from a commission merchant a carload of coal of a specified grade. The coal is not in the possession of the commission merchant, but he knows where he can get it, and he knows that he can deliver it on the date agreed upon. Accordingly he sells it short, and enters into a binding contract which, happily, the courts construe to be perfectly legal. Now suppose the same purchaser wishes to buy 100 shares of Pennsylvania Railroad stock. All Pennsylvania stock is the same, that is to say any 100 shares of it is just as good as any other 100 shares of the same property — the number on the certificate is of no importance whatever.

The dealer to whom he applies does not happen to have 100 Pennsylvania on hand, but he knows where he can get it, and he knows that he can deliver it to the purchaser on the following day. So he sells it short, and all that remains to complete his part of the contract is the actual delivery. He is then a bear on Pennsylvania stock. He may, if he chooses, go into the open market and buy the stock at once, so that he will be able to deliver it in the easiest and most direct way. Or he may feel that by waiting he may be able to buy at a lower price than that at which he has sold it, hence, in order to make the delivery promptly, he borrows the hundred shares from one of his colleagues, to whom he pays the market price as security for the temporary loan of the certificate.* In a day or two the price of the

* "The borrower is also bound to pay the lender whatever interest by way of coupons or dividends or otherwise and all bonuses and accretions that would have been paid to the lender on the securities he has lent had he kept them. These are in practice treated as increases to the market price of the borrowed securities. The reason for this provision is that the lender is the actual owner of the securities and as such owner he is entitled to whatever they may earn by way of interest or in any other way. He has simply temporarily let another have the use of them, and, since the securities can be and are disposed of by the borrower, the lender would lose the interest,

stock may have declined, whereupon the bear goes into the market and buys the 100 shares of Pennsylvania at a price, say, 1 per cent. lower than that at which he sold it.

When this certificate is delivered to him next day, he delivers it in turn to the man from whom he borrowed the original 100 shares; his security money is then returned to him, and the transaction is closed. It is just as real a transaction as any other, and just as legal. Morever, since it is always possible to buy, but not always possible to sell, the active presence in the market of large numbers of bears who *must* buy, whether they want to or not, is the very best policy of insurance that a holder of securities could have.

Many years ago there was a law on the French Statute books, subsequently repealed, prohibiting short sales. M. Boscary de Villeplaine, a deputy chairman of the association of stockbrokers, was conversing with Napoleon regarding a pending discussion in the Council of State looking to the repeal of the law. "Your Majesty," said de

---

etc., which is paid on the borrowed securities between the date that they are borrowed and the date when they are returned and the loan cancelled, unless the borrower paid an equivalent amount to him. On the other hand, any assessment the lender would have had to pay on the borrowed securities during the continuance of the loan is a charge against him; for such an assessment is a burden adherent to ownership. In practice it is treated as a reduction of the market price."— Eliot Norton "On Short Sales of Securities through a Stockbroker." The John McBride Co., New York, 1907.

Villeplaine, "when my water carrier is at the door, would he be guilty of selling property he did not own if he sold me two casks of water instead of only one, which he has?" "Certainly not," replied Napoleon, "because he is always sure of finding in the river what he lacks." "Well, your Majesty, there is on the Bourse a river of Rentes."*

Napoleon felt, no doubt, that there was something inherently wrong in selling short; even as these lines are written, counsel for a Congressional committee is attempting to make witnesses admit that the practice is "immoral." But why, where, how is it immoral? It pervades all business; no question of morals or ethics enters into it at all. The man who sells you a motor-car has not got it; he accepts your money and enters into an agreement to deliver the car next spring because he knows or believes that he can make it and have it ready for delivery at that time. Meanwhile he has sold short. A gentleman of my acquaintance has sold thousands of storage-batteries on the same basis, although plans for them have not yet been designed to meet the specifications. At Cape Cod the cranberry-growers sell their crop before it has begun to mature; all over the land contractors and builders are "going

---

* (Memorial of the stockbrokers addressed to the Minister of Finance, 1843, p. 44, footnote. Quoted by Vidal, *q. v.*, p. 46.)

short" of the labor and materials which, at some time in the future, they hope to obtain to fulfil the terms of their agreements. Are all these worthy people "immoral"?

If it is immoral to *sell* for a purpose, it is equally immoral to *buy* for a purpose; in each case the purpose is the hope of a profit. Buying for a profit is approved by every one; why not selling? In both instances you have bought or sold for a difference in price; the *sequence* of the events in no way involves a question of morals, since there is no ethical difference and no economic difference between buying first and selling last, and selling first and buying last. Moreover, in selling short you do no injury, since you sell to a buyer, at his price, only what he wants and is willing to pay for.*

All suggestions of impropriety in short selling

* Some of those who admit the value of the stock market have subjected to severe criticism those who speculate for the fall of stocks. One reads constantly of the "bears" trying to accomplish such and such results by depressing securities. Napoleon had a long talk with Mollien, his Minister of Finance, in seeking to demonstrate that those who sold "short," in the belief that national securities would fall, were traitors to their country. He argued that if these men were selling national securities for future delivery at less than their present value they were guilty of treason to the State. But Mollien replied in substance: "These men are not the ones who determine the price; they are only expressing their judgment upon what it will be. If they are wrong, if the credit of our State is to be maintained in the future at its former high standard, in spite of your military preparations, these men will suffer the penalty by having to make delivery at the price for which they sold, for they must go into the market and buy at the price then prevailing. It is their judgment, not their wish, that they express." — "Wall Street and the Country," by Charles A. Conant, pp. 111–112, G. P. Putnam's Sons, New York, 1904.

are grotesque in their absurdity. But suppose, for purposes of argument, that economic errors of some sort were actually involved in this practice. How could it be regulated or controlled? As the governors of the Stock Exchange stated to the Hughes Commission in 1909, short selling is of different descriptions. There is the short sale where the security is held in another country and sold to arrive pending transportation. There is the short sale where an individual sells against securities which he expects to have later, but which are not in deliverable form; and in this connection I call your attention to the recent sale of $50,000,000 of Corporate Stock of the City of New York where deliveries were not made for a period of about three months, and which stock was dealt in enormously, long before it was issued.

"If a market had not been provided for it under those conditions," said the governors, "the loan could not have been placed. Then, again, there is the short selling of stock against which different and new securities are to be issued; the vendor knowing that he is to receive certain securities at a distant date, but desiring to realize upon them *at this time*. Beyond this, there is the regular selling of short stock, either by parties who do so to hedge a dangerous position upon the long side of the market, or the sale purely and simply with the intention of rebuying at a profit, should circumstances favor it."

Finally, there is the investor with stock in his strong-box actually paid for and owned outright. He may wish to sell in a strong market with the hope of repurchasing at lower prices, but for reasons of his own he may borrow the stock for delivery rather than deliver the securities bearing his own name. Technically he is short; he is a bear. But in his case, as in that of the others here cited, how can this perfectly proper method of doing business be "regulated" or interfered with in any way? I do not think it necessary to pursue so palpable an absurdity.

It has been said that the bears often resort to unfair methods to bring about declines in prices, circulating rumors designed to alarm timid owners of securities and thus frighten them into selling. That this is done every now and then is undeniable, but the opportunity of the bear in these matters is very limited, and may be easily and speedily investigated, whereas similar practices by the bulls in inflating values by all sorts of grotesque assertions and promises are by no means so easily run to earth, and do incalculably more harm.

The bear who drags a red-herring across the trail now and then interrupts the chase, but he cannot stop it; the genial optimist who has a doubtful concern on his hands, with a pack of enthusiastic buyers in full cry at his heels, is a much more serious matter. Good times and bull markets engender many questionable practices of this sort. "All people are most credulous when they are most happy," says Walter Bagehot; "and when much money has just been made, when some people are really making it, when most people think they are making it, there is a happy opportunity for ingenious mendacity. Almost everything will be believed for a little while, and long before discovery the worst and most adroit deceivers are geographically or legally beyond the reach of punishment. But the harm they have done diffuses harm, for it weakens credit still further.*

If this book were written for people instructed in economic matters there would be no occasion to dilate upon the usefulness of bears and the value of short selling, but since we are addressing laymen who do not understand how the bear can be a useful factor, we may venture to say once more that insurance is the chief advantage in his operations. Ex-Governor White's contribution to the subject, which I have quoted in this chapter, is strongly supported by Mr. Conant, who shows that valuable progress in opening new countries and developing new industries is often made pos-

* "Lombard Street," p. 158.

sible by "bearish" operations designed to "hedge" or insure the new undertaking against loss.

"The broker who has a new security which he desires to place from time to time in the future, making possible, for instance, the opening of a new country to railway traffic, protects himself against loss resulting from future changes in market conditions by selling other securities for future delivery at current prices. These securities will realize a profit when the date arrives for delivery if the market has in the meantime become unfavorable, and will offset the loss upon his new securities. They will have to be bought at a loss if the movement of prices has been upward, but the upward movement will afford a profit upon the new securities which he is seeking to place upon the market. Thus, to quote Georges-Levy, 'there is a genuine insurance, which the broker will have himself organized and on which he will willingly pay the premium for protection against any accident.' "*

An instance such as this serves to show the difference between gambling and speculating, terms that are often misapplied by critics of stock markets. A gambler seeks and makes risks which

* Charles A. Conant, "Principles of Money and Banking" (New York, 1905). The reader is invited to consult, in this connection, that portion of the Report of the Hughes Commission, (see Appendix) having to do with short selling.

it is not necessary to assume, and which, in their assumption, contribute nothing to the general uplift. But the speculator — in the instance just cited, a bear who sells short — volunteers to assume those risks of business which must inevitably fall somewhere, and without which the mine, or the factory, or the railroad could not be undertaken. His profession, and the daily risks he assumes, call for special knowledge and superior foresight, so that the probability of loss is less than it would be to others. If he did not do it — if there were no bear speculators — the same risks would have to be borne by others less fitted to assume them or the useful projects in question would not be undertaken at all.

So general is the employment of these hedging or insurance operations that in the case of cotton — to cite but one instance — the business is regarded by practically all cotton merchants as an absolute necessity under modern methods of conducting business. "An idea of the value of the hedging function may be obtained," says Herbert Knox Smith, Commissioner of Corporations, "when it is stated that in Great Britain banks very generally refuse to loan money on cotton that is not hedged. Moreover, it is almost universally conceded that, since the introduction of hedging, failures in the cotton trade, which had previously been frequent, have been materially reduced as a direct result of the greater stability with which transactions in spot cotton can be conducted."*

In conclusion it may be noted that as early as 1732 an attempt was made in England to prevent short sales by law, that the law was recognized a mistake and subsequently repealed. To-day there is no law on the English Statute books restricting speculation in any form. In America the New York State Legislature enacted a law in 1812 and the Federal Government in 1864, both designed to prevent short selling. These laws have also been repealed and they will not be revived. The bear has come to stay. As a spectre to frighten amateurs, he may continue for a time to stalk abroad o' nights; as a necessary and useful part of all business he is a substantial reality. And he is not "immoral."†

---

* Report of the Commissioner, Washington, 1908.

† Despite the effort to avoid technical terms in these pages, the value of the bear should be considered from still another angle. Smith, a bear, sells short to Jones, a bull. The economic usefulness of Jones then becomes problematical, since he may sell out at any moment. His permanence as a holder or owner is merely optional, and his usefulness in the economic scheme of things is impaired. As a market factor he may be ignored. But there is nothing optional about Smith's position, for he is now a *compulsory* buyer; his economic status is fixed; he has become a very real potential force.

CHAPTER IV

THE RELATIONSHIP BETWEEN THE BANKS AND THE STOCK EXCHANGE

From the rare George Holland print owned by the Stock Exchange Luncheon Club

BROAD STREET IN 1797

The street in the lower left hand is Exchange Place. The site of the Stock Exchange of to-day is indicated by the man standing on the sidewalk in the middle distance.

CHAPTER IV

THE RELATIONSHIP BETWEEN THE BANKS AND THE STOCK EXCHANGE

"A MILLION in the hands of a single banker is a great power," said Walter Bagehot; "he can at once lend it where he will, and borrowers can come to him because they know or believe that he has it. But the same sum scattered in tens and fifties through a whole nation is no power at all; no one knows where to find it or whom to ask for it." This explains the power of Wall Street. Money flows there for the same reason that water flows downhill. The great agricultural districts of the West, for example, will gather from their crops this year several hundred millions of dollars. They have no real economic use for all this money in the farming districts; the large commercial and industrial undertakings that help to make America rich and powerful are not in that neighborhood.

Particular trades settle in particular districts, and the money they require must be sent to them from other districts. "Commerce is curiously conservative in its homes;" the steel trade concentrates in and around Pittsburg, the grain trade at Chicago, wholesale merchants in special lines are always to be found huddled together in our big cities in neighborly intimacy; and once a trade has settled in one spot it remains there. The millions that go West to pay the farmer must therefore go elsewhere to pay others as fast as a demand for money arises, because the price that will be paid for it elsewhere is greater than the price it will bring in the farmer's pockets. This is doubly true because, as we have said, there are no imperious demands for money for commercial undertakings in the farmer's neighborhood, and, even if there were, home enterprises are seldom attractive; curiously enough there is a familiarity about them and their local promoters that breeds contempt. Besides, these millions are scattered in small sums all over the agricultural States; there is no cohesion, no concentration.

What then becomes of these vast sums? They are deposited in the local banks, and the local bankers, who are wisely permitted by law to deposit three fifths of their legal reserves in a city bank, promptly transfer the funds that are not required at home to the bank that will pay interest on them. In this way large capital accumulates, and when we say this is a wise provision of the law we mean that scattered reserves in local country banks are of no more avail in emergencies than the five-dollar bills in the people's pockets; but, gathered into one great central fund that will aggregate a sum large enough to provide every solvent bank and business house with ample support in times of distress, they accomplish a purpose worth talking about.

This is the way they do in Europe, but say "Central Bank" in America, and people are frightened out of their wits. They say politics would dominate it; "the interests" would control it. The bigness of things seems to paralyze them. But to attack a thing merely because it is big and powerful is no argument. In a country full of big things it does not ring true; it is un-American, and, as for the bogy of a centralized banking control, there is infinitely more of it in New York to-day, under the existing system, than there could possibly be under the plan proposed by the original Aldrich measure. However, the idea of a great Central Bank is not the subject under discussion.

When money flows into the New York banks the popular notion seems to be that it is used to facilitate speculation on the Stock Exchange. But this is only one of its many sources of employment. It will supply the payroll at Pittsburg, it will ship grain to Europe, it will discount the bills of merchants, it will return to the West and South when they call for it to move the next crop. If Canada or Europe wants it, and bids high enough for it, they will get a share of it. Wherever capital is most profitable, there it will turn; it will rapidly leave any country that cannot pay for it. It is the old simile of water finding its own level. The first step consists in gathering the idle hoards of individuals into banks; the next consists in centralizing these deposits where they will be available for other sections of the country that have use for them.

In order to attract these funds and so facilitate the business of the country smoothly and economically, the New York banks are accustomed to paying 2 per cent. interest on such deposits. Critics who seem to feel that there is something objectionable in the laws of gravitation, would prevent country banks from depositing in the cities by forbidding the payment of interest on deposits by national banks. But the laws that govern national banks, as Mr. Horace White suggests, are not the laws that govern State banks and trust companies, and, as these would gladly pay the 2 per cent. interest on deposits, they would be given an unfair advantage.* Critics also say

* "The Stock Exchange and the Money Market," by Horace White, "Annals of the American Society of Political and Social Science," Vol. XXXVI, No. 3, Nov., 1910, pp. 563-573.

that country banks should not be allowed to keep three fifths of their reserves in city banks, but then they would be at a disadvantage with the State banks in their neighborhood, since the prohibition would not apply to them. Moreover, if country banks were not thus permitted to deposit three fifths of their reserves, what would they do with their funds? For long periods the money would remain idle, and idle funds are as unhealthy for the community as they are for the banks.

There is no other way but for the country banker to take care of his customers first, and then send as much of his surplus as the law permits to the centre that will pay him the best return and the safest return. This is good business; it makes money; it is sound economics. And before the critic goes into a paroxysm over the fear that speculation in stocks will absorb all this wealth once it finds its way to New York, let me remind him, to cite but one instance, that short-time commercial paper, representing actual commodities moving to market, has the first call. The Minneapolis miller's ninety-day bill, accepted by a reliable merchant and based on an actual carload of flour, has in all normal times a preferred claim on the banker's funds.

This discounting of commercial paper is the

ideal function of banking, to quote Mr. White, and if there were always a sufficient supply of good bills to absorb all the bank's loanable credit, with an inflow of cash from maturing bills equal to the outgo of new ones, there would be no occasion for bankers to look elsewhere to keep their funds mobile — and the critic would be out of work.* But this does not often happen, because the bank's loanable funds normally exceed the amount of acceptable paper, and at such times the banker makes advances on goods or securities, and, if goods and securities are not pressing for loans, he will place his funds elsewhere, where a demand exists. But securities for which there is always a ready market are such thoroughly good collateral for loans that bankers are glad to get them.

The stockbroker is, in a way, a dealer in merchandise. Whether he buys for investment or for speculation — and remember that the boundary line between investment and speculation is often shadowy and indistinct — he pays cash for everything he buys. He then seeks advances of credit upon his wares just as the merchant does, supplementing his own capital and the deposits (margins) of his customers with call or time money from the banks. To deny him these facilities is exactly the same as to deny credit to a mer-

**Ibid.*, p. 564.

chant; both are doing a perfectly legal business, and both contribute to the economic welfare of the community.

The popular idea is that loanable funds thus borrowed by Stock Exchange houses constitute a diversion of money from the merchants who need it. Not so. Even if the banks were disposed to use all their loanable funds in mercantile loans and discounts they could not do so, because a part of these funds may be called for at any time, and it is not good banking to lend too large a proportion of call money on time. The merchant wants 30, 60, and 90 day money, and he wants it at a rate not to exceed 6 per cent.; the stockbroker is compelled by the nature of his business to borrow a large part of his money on call, and he pays whatever the banks choose to charge for it. Incidentally it may be said that no usury law is violated, even if 100 per cent. is charged, because the New York law legalizes any rate of interest on call loans of $5000 and upward, secured by collateral.*

* The Stock Exchange authorities were asked by the Hughes Commissioners in 1909 what effect would result if this law were repealed. An interesting historical summary is involved in the reply to this question.

"In our opinion the repeal of such a law would simply lead to constant evasions, which would cause the law to be practically a dead letter, and it is far better to leave it as it is, and to allow the supply and demand to regulate the rate for money.

"It is reasonable to assume that the repeal of this law would result in a recurrence of the conditions which existed prior to its enactment. Prior to 1882, when this Act was passed, such loans were subject to the drastic

As a matter of fact, far from being put at a disadvantage by the banking methods that provide call loans to Stock Exchange houses, the merchant or manufacturer enjoys banking facilities which the Stock Exchange may never hope to enjoy. The merchant is able to secure banking accommodations upon his personal credit, that is, by discounting his own promissory notes or single-name paper unsecured by pledge of collateral. But the stockbroker, however ample his resources and his credit, can only obtain loans upon collateral securities. Any attempt to resort to his personal credit or his personal paper would be construed as a confession of weakness, and his good name at the banks would suffer accordingly.

Persons who conjure nightmares over the prac-

---

provisions of the Usury Law, which imposes the forfeiture of the principal as a penalty for violation. The Usury Law, however, as to this class of loans, had for years been a dead letter, and whatever risks were incurred through its penalties were taken by lenders without hesitation. Demand loans were made at interest plus a commission, and in times of money stringency the interest rate represented by the so-called commission attained proportions which have been unknown since the passage of the Act of 1882. Extreme instances are to be found of a rate as high as 700 per cent. per annum.

"Such violent fluctuations in the rate have been unknown since the passage of the Act of 1882. Since that time all quotations of interest on call loans have been at so much per cent. per annum, not, as was formerly the case, at ⅛ or ¼ of 1 per cent. per day. Through the extreme stringency which existed in the autumn of 1907, the rate ran from 12 to 30 per cent., with the exception, perhaps, of one or two days when practically no money was procurable at any price, when the quotation ran up to 100 or 110 per cent. per annum. It would seem demonstrated by experience that the law of 1882 has been a most potent factor in reducing the interest rate in times of stringency and in rendering it at all times more stable and equable."

tice of the banks in loaning surplus funds to stock-brokers are deceiving themselves. Instead of losing by this system, every merchant and manufacturer in the land profits by it in greater or less degree. The stockbroker deals in the bonds and shares of great railway and industrial companies, which, in order to succeed, must be able to sell their certificates to the public and so raise the money necessary to provide the extensions and new construction that are constantly demanded by the public. If fresh capital could not be enlisted in this way, additions and improvements would cease. The merchant who requires the railroads to ship his goods, and the manufacturer whose demands for new side-tracks, cars, and other equipment are unceasing, are therefore directly interested in the maintenance of a broad and stable speculative market for securities at all times, because in that way only are funds to be raised for the requirements of trade and industry. There would have been no railroads in this country had there not been speculators to build them, nor could the money have been raised had there not been other speculators to buy the shares with the aid of the banks.

Prevent the banks from lending money to facilitate stock-market operations and business ceases; interfere with it or hamper it and confidence is impaired, and when these things happen the industrial system collapses in terror. Such has been the experience of modern times. Until a system is devised whereby large undertakings may enlist public support in other ways than by offering securities in our great Exchanges and by maintaining a market for them there, it is useless to talk of interfering with that necessary relationship which exists between the banks and the stock market. On the one hand we have the cobwebs and windy sophistries of politicians and doctrinaires; on the other hand the test of proved effectiveness in the conduct of business. And the country's business cannot stop; it must go ahead.

In the last six years more than a billion shares of stock have changed hands on the New York Stock Exchange, together with bonds of a market valuation exceeding five billions of dollars, and, under the rules, each purchase made was paid for in full by 2:15 P.M. of the day following the transaction. If all these purchases had been made for cash — i. e., if every customer of every brokerage house paid in full for his purchases, there would be no use for bank loans to brokers; there would be no speculation, and hence no progress. Securities purchased in the six-year period quoted were, in the majority of instances, bought on margin, that is, they were only partially paid for by the purchasers, the balance required being funished by the broker from his capital and by the banks from their loanable funds.

There is a popular fallacy as to the amount of actual cash required to finance these enormous Stock Exchange transactions; persons who are not well informed often entertain the impression that it is much larger than it really is. As a matter of fact considerably more than 90 per cent. of the business of the banks is done through the Clearing House, an institution designed, as every one knows, to minimize the transfer of actual cash and to simplify the payment of balances. If these clearings seem large — they are, in fact, twice as large in New York as in all the other cities of the Union added together — it is not alone because more speculation in securities takes place in New York, but because this happens to be the centre where many other cities balance their claims against each other.

Furthermore, when critics who do not understand the subject look askance at the volume of loans of the New York banks, they must remember that the lending power of such institutions is always four times greater than the supply of money in its vaults. The reserve of 25 per cent. which the banks are required to maintain means that every million dollars of actual cash added to their funds renders possible an expansion of four million in loans, and every withdrawal of funds involves a proportionate reduction of these loans. These matters are self-evident. The point to bear in mind is that through this expansion and contraction of loans stock-market operations are increased or diminished by almost automatic processes. "Money talks" is an old aphorism. In this case it is not money that talks, but credit, and the credit extended to stockbrokers by the banks is always wisely regulated to meet conditions as they arise.

The customer of a brokerage house buys, let us say, 1000 shares of St. Paul at 120, on which he deposits a partial payment or margin of $15,000. The bank will loan to the broker 80 per cent. of the market value of the stock, or $96,000, which, added to the $15,000 deposited by the customer, leaves $9000 which the broker supplies from his firm's capital. The broker gives to the bank, with the securities, a note on one of the bank's printed forms, which gives the bank absolute authority to sell the collateral whenever the margin shall have declined to less than 20 per cent. This note is so sweeping in its terms, and gives the bank such complete power, that a reproduction of it, in small type, would fill two pages of this book.

It empowers the bank to sell as it pleases — if the broker fails to pay the loan on demand, or to keep the margin at 20 per cent. — all the securities in the loan; it authorizes the bank to seize any deposit the broker may have in the institution; the bank may itself purchase all or any part of the securities thus sold, and all right of redemption by the broker is waived and released. This instrument would seem, *per se*, a pretty strong hold on the broker, but the bank's security does not end there. In making the loan the bank knows that the borrower is a member of the New York Stock Exchange, and that presupposes capital, with at least one Stock Exchange membership, worth to-day about $60,000. It knows, too, that a fundamental rule of all Stock Exchange brokers is to protect the bank at all hazards, not merely because the personal honor of the broker is involved, but because the business could not be conducted otherwise.

It is apparent from a consideration of all these elaborate precautions that the lending of funds to stockbrokers is a safe business, indeed in all the criticism directed against Wall Street methods I have not yet heard it questioned. The department of the bank entrusted with such matters watches the tape with vigilance to see that the

20 per cent. margin is not impaired; if it should happen to be impaired, the broker's messenger is almost always on hand anticipating with his additional collateral the call that the banker will make. So excellent is Stock Exchange collateral, thus secured and thus protected, that the losses resulting from this class of business are infinitesimal. I am not a banker, but I hazard the opinion that it constitutes, in fact, the minimum risk in all the departments of the bank's business.

In any case, when trouble comes and panic conditions prevail, it requires no stretch of the imagination to say that the stockbroker's loan is a better loan than that of, let us say, the silk merchant, for he, perhaps, cannot easily repay. He is under immense liabilities in various directions and he has many obligations; whereas the stockbroker feels every minute of the day that his first duty is to the bank; the customer who owns the securities in the loan must either deposit sufficient margin or the broker will sell him out, in which case the loan at the bank is paid off. Finally, it may be added that in the October panic of 1907, when merchants' failures were announced daily, and when certain banks and trust companies closed their doors, not a single failure was announced on the New York Stock Exchange.

Another objection often lodged by critics of present-day banking conditions, has to do with the practice of New York banks in the over-certification of brokers' checks. These over-certifications are held to be objectionable because the National Banks are forbidden by law to certify for a sum greater than the drawer has on deposit. In practice it works out this way: The broker's clearing-house sheet of to-day tells him what payments he has to make, so on the following morning he acquaints his bank with the fact that payments are to be made necessitating certifications beyond the amount of his deposit. He then sends to the bank the promissory note of his firm, payable on demand, and the bank credits his account with the proceeds. As the day advances the broker's checks come in and are credited to the account, which is always balanced and the note paid off before the close of the day's business. The risk is nominal.

Of course a few hours elapse between the certification and the receipt of the broker's checks, and in this brief interval it would be possible for a dishonest man to abuse the privilege extended him, but the fact that such a thing does not happen affords tenable ground for the belief that it will not happen. The bank does not deal with an individual, but with a firm, and it knows that the firm has a membership in the Stock Exchange, with a cash balance on deposit in the bank that extends the accommodation. Any banker will bear witness that the business is quite satisfactory and that it involves no loss. Moreover, this certification of stockbrokers' checks is essential to the maintenance of broad speculative markets, and, whether that portion of the public that criticises the practice likes it or not, speculation is a necessary part of our business life.

It may be pertinent to remark in this connection that the law prohibiting these certifications by National Banks is unnecessary and unwise, as is evidenced by the facility and safety with which it is honored in the breach. State Banks in New York are under no such restriction, nor has it occurred to our lawmakers that a necessity for the prohibition exists. The experience of these banks in the matter of certifications, like that of the National Banks, shows that the business is safe and sound. If the merchant discounts his paper for thirty, sixty, or ninety days, why prevent a similar accommodation to stockbrokers for an hour or two? Both are engaged in a strictly legitimate business upon which the welfare of the community in greater or less degree depends, and the fundamental purpose of a bank is to promote and encourage such business. That is what banks are for, and bank officers are supposed to know something about how, when, and where accommodations may be extended with safety to all concerned.

Mr. Horace White cites the year 1909 as an illustration of the employment of loanable bank funds by brokers which brings up another point. For long periods in that year, money loaned on call on the floor of the New York Stock Exchange at 1½ per cent., while our banks were paying 2 per cent. to the interior banks to which the money belonged. This does not necessarily mean that the banks were losing money; because the greater part of these funds was employed in time loans and in commercial discounts at 3 and 4 per cent., thus raising the average income rate. There is also to be considered the unearned increment which the bank gains by "holding" its depositor, even though no large profit accrues from the funds thus deposited.*

As the ratio of reserves to liabilities at that time was much above the legal requirement, it might be inferred from this and from the 1½ per cent. rate that money was easy; but it was not, as many persons in commercial pursuits learned when they tried to borrow it.

*Cf. Mr. White's article *supra*, p. 570.

There was a great deal of money that was not being used in daily business, and one of the reasons was that the period was one of distrust. Stockbrokers got funds at 1½ per cent. while many other borrowers were required to pay stiffer rates, because the banks that controlled the money market — i. e., the loanable funds — were unwilling to part with them except for short periods and on instantly marketable security, and this state of mind on the part of the New York bankers was shared by the bankers of Europe. It was good banking, because it was prudent and conservative. In other words, at a time when danger threatened, bankers in all important centres of the world regarded Stock Exchange collateral as ideal security, and, as we have seen, the aggregate of their loanable funds pressing on the market kept call rates down to 1½. If in times of doubt and distrust this form of collateral proves its safety, is it not a fair hypothesis that it is safe at *all* times?

If the critics are correct in their contention that pressure of easy money in the New York market holds out inducements for foolhardy speculation on the Stock Exchange, the year 1909, just cited, should have witnessed a great boom in securities. If speculators could borrow at 1½ per cent. on securities that netted 5 and 6 per cent., the theory of our adversaries is that this disproportion entices a large number of people into such speculative ventures that inflation takes place, followed by collapse. That nothing of the sort occurred shows that critics, like other less gifted persons, may err; it shows, too, what every thoughtful person knows, that booms are not created on the Stock Exchange, which merely reflects in its dealings external conditions of all sorts, among them psychological processes which neither brokers nor money markets may hope to control. As a matter of record, 1909 showed but little increase in the volume of business transacted on the Stock Exchange as compared with 1908, and the increase, such as it was, represented nothing more than a natural recovery from the paralysis following the débacle of 1907, plus an investment of funds at attractive levels. The same state of affairs prevailed in 1910. From June to December of that year call money rates almost never exceeded 3 per cent., and time money might be had at from 3½ to 5, yet far from stimulating speculation — far from revealing an excessive employment of bank funds by stockbrokers — transactions both in shares and bonds dwindled to insignificant proportions.

Cheap money is by no means a "bull argument" from the Stock Exchange point of view, because it arises from dull conditions in commerce and industry, and there can be no boom in the securities which represent the nation's business unless mills and factories and railroads are prosperous. There have been more bull markets with tight money, or with money in the neighborhood of 6 per cent., than in cheap money markets of the sort just described. This is not equivalent to saying that a prolonged rise can be conducted through a period of dear money. As a matter of Stock Exchange experience such a condition seldom arises, because the Stock Exchange discounts the future, foresees those economic conditions that spell prosperity for the country, and advances the prices of securities on a money market that has not yet felt the demands of improved conditions.

In June, July, and August, for example, conditions may warrant a hope of bountiful harvests, while general business is dull and idle money abundant. Such a prospect is always discounted, other things being equal, by a rise in securities, and money that is not yet required to market the crops thus finds employment as loans on Stock Exchange collateral. Later on, when reviving business leads the interior banks to call their New York balances, the depository banks meet the demand by calling loans and by advancing rates. The speculative movement on 'Change is then checked or reversed just in proportion to the demand for money elsewhere. It may continue for a while if the discounting process has not been complete, or if there remains a wide disparity between interest rates for money and net returns on securities; or if the independent resources of the city banks are large enough to furnish comfortable interest rates even after the westward drain has commenced, but, generally speaking, "the move is over," to quote the vernacular, by the time business men want their money. Nine times out of ten any monetary strain that results thereafter is not due to speculative operations in securities nor to any other cause attributable to the Stock Exchange.

A word should be said here concerning the Stock Exchange Clearing House, because just as the Clearing House of the associated banks ascertains and pays the balances of its members with a minimum outlay of coin and legal tender notes and with great economy of time and labor, so the Stock Exchange Clearing House stands the strain of an enormous business, reduces the volume of checks and deliveries, and relieves both the banks and the stockbrokers of an amount of risk and confusion that would be well-nigh intolerable.

In order that the layman, for whom these pages are written, may understand what this means, it may be said that if 500,000 shares of stock are sold in a day on the Stock Exchange, and if we assume the average price of these stocks to be 50, the checks paid out on that day would be $25,000,000, and in a year at that rate certifications would be necessary involving the stupendous total of $7,500,000,000. This clumsy if not impossible method the Clearing House was designed to avoid. Moreover, the actual daily transfer of such a volume of securities is largely obviated by the Clearing House system, and thus another and highly important economy is effected.

The Stock Exchange Clearing House is managed by a committee of five members of the Board of Governors of the Exchange. Each day the seller of stocks sends to the office of the buyer his "deliver" ticket, and the buyer sends to the seller his "receive" ticket, this transaction constituting a "comparison" by both parties, and an evidence that the transaction has been entered on their books. Before 7 P.M. of that day these tickets, and the sheet comprising the record, are sent to the Clearing House. This sheet contains a "receive" and "deliver" column, with all the transactions in each security grouped together, and with a balance — i. e., a debit or credit, struck at the bottom. If there is a credit, a draft on the Clearing House bank is attached; if a debit, a check for the balance accompanies the sheet.

When the Clearing House receives this sheet a simple and a very ingenious process ensues which relieves the broker of a great deal of trouble, risk, and labor. If he has bought and sold, let us say, an equal amount of stock, comprising numerous transactions, instead of having to draw checks for all these separate trades, the Clearing House settles the whole day's transactions by a single eheck for the actual balance. If his numerous purchases and sales do not balance, and if there are various lots of stock to receive and deliver, the Clearing House eliminates a host of intermediaries and puts him into direct touch with one firm to whom he delivers, and with one from whom he receives. He may have had no transaction with the firms thus arbitrarily assigned to him; that makes no difference. The books of the Clearing House always balance; somewhere a firm is entitled to a receipt of stock, and somewhere another firm will be found to deliver it to him.

Nothing could be simpler and more economical than the manner in which the two are brought together. In such a system, the number of shares actually delivered is reduced by the Clearing House to one third of the number represented by the broker's actual transactions, while the amount of money which he must command to meet his daily engagements represents, on an average, only 25 per cent. of the actual capital that would be required were it not for the excellent system thus afforded him. Persons who wonder at the magnitude of Stock Exchange transactions, and who jump to hasty conclusions as to the actual capital involved, may well reflect upon the manner in which this method reduces to a minimum the stockbroker's drafts upon the banks.

In a larger sense, if the critic in these matters affecting the relationship of banks to stockbrokers feels aggrieved at what he thinks is an improper diversion of funds, he must remember that the comparative scarcity of capital to-day — which is at the bottom of his complaint — is not due in any sense to Stock Exchange speculation, for there has been almost no extensive speculation in this quarter from 1907 down to November, 1912. To find the cause of the scarcity of capital — and it is unquestionably scarce — he must consider the immense destruction of tangible wealth in the last decade, and the extraordinary tendency to convert floating forms of capital into fixed and immobile forms.

The amount of money expended in State

roads since automobiles came into popularity is probably ten times more than it was before; at the election in November, 1912, a fresh total of $50,000,000 was voted for "good roads" by the electorate in New York State. The building of the Panama Canal has cost or will cost about $365,000,000; all over the country large municipal or state works are under construction; here in New York the contract for the Erie Canal calls for $150,000,000, and for the city's new water-supply system — the Ashokan basin and the Kensico reservoir — $177,000,000, each contributing a share to the depletion of the normal supply of working capital. Meantime, to cite another instance, Congress appropriates $160,000,000 to pensions in a single year, and $40,000,000, as a recent writer puts it, "for that particular form of graft which consists in giving a $30,000 post office to a thirty-cent village." The railroads of the country alone require to-day sums of money equivalent to the working capital represented by all our bountiful harvests of 1912.

Aside from these matters the critic should remember, in fair play, that the currency famines which occur with periodic frequency in our country are due in large measure to the non-elastic nature of the currency, to its persistent absorption by the Treasury, and to the rigid restrictions which these abnormalities impose on the volume of banking credit. Conditions such as these contributed in no small measure to our last great panic, and led to a premium on currency that made us a laughing-stock among the nations. There has been no such money delirium in England since the Napoleonic wars; no such condition in Germany since the empire was founded, and nothing approaching it in France, even in the commune and the war with Prussia. Yet in America we go on wobbling uncertainly under the makeshift act of 1908, with its currency associations and its emergency measures, and with the added fear of what may come when the Act expires in 1914.

The situation in America is substantially this: Business drives ahead at a tremendous pace, with perils on every side, chiefly anxious to be undisturbed. Matters run along smoothly for a while; then something happens — there is too much optimism or too much confidence — and a smash. It is not due to speculation in securities, because, as in 1907, the stock markets are the first to see what is coming and to discount it. But speculation in lands, or in manufacture, or in railroad construction go on and on; there is too much work for the dollar to do; the currency system breaks down; here and there a financial institution closes its doors; public confidence is shattered, and the whole credit system is disturbed.

Then there arises a noble army of critics who, with the best intentions but with insufficient knowledge and study, set to work to remedy conditions they do not understand by methods untried and unpractical, that only add to the general confusion. More harm than good results when the physician, brusquely entering the sick-room, tells the patient he is a very sick man, denounces the lobster that poisoned him, and departs with a general condemnation of shellfish, but without prescribing suitable remedies. Persons who denounce the relationship existing between banks and stockbrokers are in most instances upright citizens of high character, but until a little patient study of conditions has enabled them to speak with authority upon matters that are necessarily complex and delicate, they cannot accomplish any really useful purpose. "The wicked are wicked, no doubt," said Thackeray, "and they go astray, and they fall, and they come by their deserts; but who can tell the harm that the very virtuous may do?"

The three leading groups of banking interests in Wall Street are said to represent $500,000,000 of available capital each; the deposits in what are called the "trust banks" amount to between

$700,000,000 and $800,000,000, while the banks of the whole country hold deposits of $16,000,000,-000. The savings banks now hold $4,450,822,522 which is owned by 10,009,804 depositors.*

As we have not yet reached the point of abolishing property altogether, we may concede that these great combinations can do for individual business and for the country at large what cannot be done without them. They furnish the large sums which, from time to time, are required by the Government, the State, the town, the manufacturer, the tradesman, and the speculator, and to each of these — especially the speculator — the tremendous develompent of this country is due. Because of speculation in securities, the 26,000 million dollars' worth of capital represented on the New York Stock Exchange by the stocks and bonds of railroad and industrial corporations have found a public market through which necessary capital has been raised, and the total increases yearly by about one billion dollars. This is "big" business, to be sure, but it is the bigness of the whole people, for the welfare of each is the welfare of all.

Such large affairs naturally set people thinking; men want light; they want to know, entirely aside from the doctrines of political platforms and stump

* Report of the Comptroller of the Currency, October, 30, 1912.

orators, to what extent the relation of capital to business meets the test of proved effectiveness and economic worth. Especially do they seek information in this oft-discussed matter of speculation in securities and of the bank's relationship to it; and here, fortunately, there is no lack of results by which that relationship may be tested.

Pragmatism tells us that as phenomena appear, become mighty, and persist in accordance with natural processes, so they demonstrate their ultimate good and their obvious usefulness. In its especial application to the matters we have discussed, pragmatism teaches us to wait for results in estimating a particular business method, and then to study it in its relation to *all* business. Applying this test to the use of loanable bank funds by those who deal or speculate in the things that represent American enterprise, we find that the very existence of these enterprises depends upon the maintenance of these methods. Finally, both the banks and the Stock Exchange are the trustees of the property of others, and in that capacity their reciprocal relations are certain to be attended by greater caution than if they dealt in a freehanded way with their own property. The magnitude of their undertakings spells responsibility, and responsibility breeds sobriety.

CHAPTER V

PUBLICITY IN EXCHANGE AFFAIRS; CAUTIONS AND PRECAUTIONS

CHAPTER V

PUBLICITY IN EXCHANGE AFFAIRS; CAUTIONS AND PRECAUTIONS

IF A list of "don'ts" were compiled for the public that is interested in the Stock Exchange, the first prohibition would be "don't believe all you read in the newspapers"; at least do a little independent thinking before jumping at conclusions. The relationship between the Stock Exchange and the metropolitan press is, with perhaps one exception, cordial in the extreme. The newspaper man is a thinking person; if he were not he could not hold his job. He knows, for example, that the Stock Exchange is an indispensable part of the machinery of modern business; he is aware of the fact that it maintains a high standard of probity. He would be the last man to attack the institution unfairly, and he is the first to defend it, editorially, when misconceptions and unfounded suspicions are rife.

But on the other hand, newspapers want news; their circulation and the popularity of their advertising columns depend upon the skill and ability with which they parade before the public everything that happens. If a politician or a clever and ambitious lawyer makes a startling charge against an institution that occupies a conspicuous place in our affairs, that is news, and the newspaper must print it. In order to make the news attractive to the jaded palate of its readers the dry-as-dust parts must be skimmed off, and seasoning added in such peppers and vinegars as the occasion permits, with a final dash of spice in the shape of pungent headlines that will arrest and hold the appetite.

Somewhere off in the dim recesses of the editorial page there may be a sober (and deadly dull) analysis of the matter, revealing the politician or the notoriety-seeker in his true colors, but this is often ignored by the reader. What he wants with his morning coffee is his daily thrill, and he finds it under blatant headlines on the first page. Because he wants it, and because he won't be happy till he gets it, the newspaper gives it to him on a generous scale. Until we arrive at a Utopian state in which art, religion, and kindred abstractions satisfy the mind to the exclusion of fires, riots, suffragettes and Stock Exchanges, we cannot blame the newspapers for giving us what we want, nor the politicians for helping the good work along.

And yet, as Mr. Bryce pointed out in his lectures at Yale on "The Hindrances to Good Citizenship," this willingness to accept as conclusions the scare-heads in newspapers which are not, and never were intended to formulate serious opinions, lays us open to the charge of indolence; "the neglect to think" thus becomes a serious phase of a deficient sense of civic duty. In countries where men are imperfectly educated, or in rural districts where means of acquiring knowledge are small and scant — where men lead isolated lives out of reach of libraries and learning — they ask advice of the priest or the village schoolmaster, and thus vicariously discharge the duties of citizenship without any real knowledge of the problems before them and without contributing to the solution of those difficulties to which the ever-increasing complexity of our civilization gives rise.

Now if we apply this line of thought to the study of such economic problems as arise in our country from time to time, we find that the same conditions apply. We fancy ourselves immeasurably better off than the uncultured frontiersman who must rely for his information upon the priest or the schoolmaster, but in our dumb submission to the rant of the hustings and the scare of the headlines are we really discharging the functions of good citizenship? Are we not indolent? I can have a lively sympathy for the half-breed in the Canadian woods seeking information as best he may, but for the man in our populous and cultivated communities who is too lazy to turn to our great public libraries for light on the vexed and vexing economic problems of the day, contenting himself with the half-baked opinions of demagogues and quacks — for such a man it is difficult to say a good word. There is hope for the one; the other is the most menacing and discouraging type in our citizenship.

Take up the morning newspaper almost every day and we find the crude essence of this misinformation paraded in a way that makes us sorry for a public that cries for such stuff. A custodian of public funds, collected for the purpose of erecting a monument, is found very recently to have squandered the money entrusted to him. One of his co-trustees, who must have been somewhat lax in his duties, bewails the loss and seeks to enlist sympathy for himself by hazarding the opinion that "the money *must have been* lost in speculation in that hell-hole, the Stock Exchange."

This from a former army officer and a gentleman, who subsequently states that he has no idea what became of the funds, but "cannot think of any other explanation." "Hell-hole" and the "Stock

Exchange" constitute a good repast; the headline artist contributes his quota to the feast, and so a portion of the public that feeds on this meat arises from the table with the satisfying conviction that another awful indictment has been leveled at the Exchange, notwithstanding an utter absence of proof or evidence of any kind tending to show that the delinquent trustee had lost a dollar in Wall Street. And suppose he did so lose it, what then? Is the Stock Exchange or any other market-place a "hell-hole" merely because a thief whom nobody suspects squanders his money there? Suppose he had spent it in automobiles, or in real-estate speculations, or in campaign contributions, or in foreign missions, would the same amiable characterization apply?

Another familiar instance of making Wall Street the scapegoat is seen in the "explanations" of defaulting bank clerks. "When a young bank employee," says a financial journal, "with a wife and two children in Flatbush, and a salary of something less than $2000 a year, takes to entertaining angels, more or less unawares, in the Great White Way, and matching his trained financial mind against 'bankers' of another kind, he always blames Wall Street when the inevitable smash comes. He has been 'speculating in stocks,' he says. He thinks, and a great many people equally silly agree with him, that he thereby shifts the blame for his extravagance and folly to other shoulders. Entirely well-meaning people, without the slightest conception of the real purposes for which the financial centre of a nation exists, say: 'Here is another indictment against sinful Wall Street. Let us kiss away the tears of this misguided young man, who now promises to be good.' They never think of asking the misguided young man to show documentary evidence of his losses, which of course every broker must necessarily provide, and must keep in duplicate as a matter of record."*

A police officer whose salary has never exceeded $3000 a year is arrested, and it is shown that he possesses a fortune of $100,000. Where did he get it? Why, he made it in the course of nine months of remarkably successful speculation in Wall Street, and one of his henchmen, too stupid to know that everybody in Wall Street keeps a set of books, promptly came forward to endorse this explanation. Proofs were sought by the authorities, and the lie was, of course, exposed, but the readiness with which the frugal officer sought to fall back upon this hoary explanation shows that it is a permanent fixture of the crook's property-room, and that in the stage-setting for his sordid

* The *Wall Street Journal*, August 31, 1912.

accumulations there must be the familiar Wall Street background.

Another notorious pastime, that seems to be well known to every one but the officers of the courts, consists in the practice of fraudulent bankrupts in producing in court a mass of worthless securities as evidence that the bankrupt's money has been "legitimately" lost in speculation. The certificates thus exhibited are beautifully engraved memorials of defunct mining concerns, sold at so much a pound by well-known dealers. It is related that a person who wished to keep ever before his eyes a lesson and a warning once papered the walls of his house with a wagon-load of this junk, which he was able to purchase at less than the price of ordinary wall paper.

Any scamp who intends to "lie down" on an uprofitable contract can buy $1,000,000 nominal of the stuff at waste-paper rates. He is assured of the sympathy of his family and friends, and, if it does not occur to the lawyers to inquire who his brokers were, and when, where, and how these purchases were made, he stands a good chance of going the way of all undetected swindlers, notwithstanding the fact that documentary evidence of his purchases, if there were any, is always available. In this way another indictment is framed against Wall Street in the minds of thoughtless people. They seem to ignore the obviously improbable nature of the story, preferring rather to make Wall Street the scapegoat, and by "Wall Street," in the majority of cases, they mean the Stock Exchange, yet the Stock Exchange had no more to do with it than Trinity Church, at one end of Wall Street, has to do with a stevedore's crap-game at the other end.

So far as concerns the case of the crooked bank clerk, it is perfectly well known, or at least it should be, that no member of the New York Stock Exchange is permitted under its rules to have any speculative or investment relations whatever with employees of banks or trust companies, or of other brokerage houses. The Exchange authorities enforce this rule to the letter. Disgrace and expulsion faces the man who would attempt it. More than that, members are unusually careful in investigating customers' accounts for reasons involving their own safety in actions that may be brought in the courts; so rigorously is this care exercised that accounts are repeatedly refused where the bona fides of the customers are not fully understood by at least one of the firm's partners.

Furthermore, any negligence on the member's part in this important matter, or in other matters affecting the general welfare of the Stock Exchange, places him at once within the all-embracing grasp of that one of the Exchange's by-laws which has to do with "any act detrimental to the interests of the Exchange." This is a large order, and its importance is well understood by the members. They know, and all those who so freely criticise the Stock Exchange could find out if they inquired, that the power of the Board of Governors to supervise every action of its members is vastly greater than any power that could be vested in the courts. There are constitutional limits to the authority of common law; there are no limits whatever to the powers of the governors in dealing with members.

This leads us to consider another popular criticism of the Stock Exchange, based on its unwillingness to abandon its present organization and incorporate under State regulation. The public seems to feel that this reluctance to submit to State or Federal control shows that the institution is trying to conceal something, yet nothing could be further from the fact. The Exchange does not incorporate because the interests of the public, which it is bound to conserve, would suffer enormously by such a step. "In its present form," says the *Wall Street Journal*, "the Stock Exchange is a private organization. It can inspect any member's books at any moment.

If it suspects him of wrongdoing it can tap his telephone wire, and has done so in the past. It can terminate his membership for conduct which no legislation could possibly touch. One reason, in fact, for its admittedly high standard of probity is the power, at once democratic and despotic, exercised by the Governing Committee elected by all the members.

"But if the Stock Exchange were reorganized under State supervision, much of this power would be taken away. Members would possess rights which no governing committee could ignore. They could resort to practices legally right and ethically wrong, which under the present system would be visited by swift punishment. Any member of the public, now, who can show the Stock Exchange committee an act by a broker toward him legally defensible but morally wrong, can secure that broker's expulsion from the Stock Exchange. Under State incorporation he could only obtain redress by prolonged litigation. . . . No legislative safeguards are needed. The Stock Exchange now possesses a power of supervision over its members which neither Congress nor the State legislature could give. The only power our lawmakers really possess in the matter is to limit that supervision; and for this, if for no other reason, the Stock

Exchange should fight incorporation to the last, and should take every proper means of publicity to range public opinion behind it."*

An instance in which Wall Street in general, and the Stock Exchange in particular, occasionally comes under the ban of more or less hysterical public condemnation, results from the work of company promoters and swindlers, wholly outside the Exchange's jurisdiction. In spite of the vigilance of the postal authorities and the police, every now and then a swindler finds his way into this forbidden ground, and here he plies his trade. Sometimes it is a land scheme, sometimes it is timber, recently it was wireless telegraphy, often it is a gold mine.

The promoter of these enterprises does not permit himself or his affairs to come under the scrutiny of the banks, the Stock Exchange, or the Clearing House. He fights shy of the curb market as it is now organized, and avoids the watchful eye of the metropolitan newspapers that enjoy the pastime of exposing frauds. His ways are ways of darkness. His methods are mailing lists; his victims are that numerous progeny born every minute; the lure is the engraved letter-head with its "Wall Street," its list of "Directors," and its subtle assurance that this

* December 7, 1912. Consult also p. 235.

precious property now literally "given away" bears the endorsement of the elect, and is known and approved by the whole financial community.

Whenever he can do so, the artful gentleman behind this bait contrives to have a market for his wares. He cannot do this anywhere in New York, for the curb market, once the refuge of the swindler, is now closed to him, thanks to the improved morale of the curb brokers themselves, and to the recommendations of the Hughes Investigating Committee. Consequently the dishonest company promoter is forced to manufacture his market in another city, where fluctuations in the price of his wares are made to order, usually on a rising scale, without interference by the authorities.

More often still, this market and its rising prices do not exist at all; in any case it is only a fraudulent attempt to excite the cupidity of speculators into the belief that there is active trading in the particular stock offered for sale. "The mines," says the Chairman of the Hughes Committee in discussing these swindling operations, "are situated in distant places, as Nevada, Alaska, Canada, Mexico, and even in South America. In proportion as they are remote, inaccessible, and subterranean, they are attractive to the class whom Tacitus had in mind when he said: "*Omne ignotum pro magnifico.*"*

The halcyon days of these enterprises are now drawing to a close. Their field of operations is becoming more and more limited, the postal authorities are redoubling their energies, the newspapers are closing their advertising columns, and the victims who have birthdays every minute are, it is hoped, growing wiser. In any case immense losses have been incurred, and immense harm done. To appreciate the extent of it, one has but to look over the circle of one's own acquaintances, and count the worthless specimens of the engraver's art that have found a resting-place — permanently, I fear — in homes ill-prepared to house them. Each one of these chromos has left its sting—each one has excited a bitterness and resentment that, in the misdirected anger of losers who will not see their own folly, is too often flung at Wall Street and at the Stock Exchange.

The bucket-shop method is better known and easier to detect — hence it is rapidly being exterminated. "Bucketing," as it is called, usually flourishes in small towns at a considerable distance from New York. Formerly it thrived in the larger cities, even those adjacent to the Metropolis,

* "The Hughes Investigation," by Horace White, *Journal of Political Economy*, October, 1909, pp. 537–8.

but it has now been driven from these places. It professes to trade in stocks for its customers, and its office windows are usually decorated with signs that indicate, though they do not always say so plainly, that the house is identified with "the Stock Exchange."

It allows its customers to trade on what is called "a two-point margin," that is to say, the buyer or seller is "wiped out" when the market has fluctuated two points against the price at which the trade is made. The word of the house must be accepted for the veracity of its prices, which, however, are supplied to it by telegraph from New York. Bear in mind that these prices are not telegraphed to the customer, but to the mysterious persons in the rear office of the shop. They call themselves brokers — this bucket-shop fraternity — but they are not brokers in any sense by which that elastic term is used. They have not even the "redeeming vices" of gamblers; they are swindlers.

The trader in such a place starts with all the odds in favor of the house. To be exact he pays two commissions and the market "turn" is against him *ab initio*. If the stock is 100 bid, 100¼ asked, he buys at 100¼ always. If he sells at the same quotation, he sells at 100. He could not sell in the former case at 100¼, nor buy in the latter case at

100, so he starts $\frac{1}{4}$ per cent. "to the bad." If, then, he bought at $100\frac{1}{4}$, when the price is $98\frac{1}{4}$-$\frac{1}{2}$, his two-point margin is exhausted, although the price has actually declined only $1\frac{3}{4}$ per cent. Thus he is required to bet heavy odds on what is really no better than an even money chance, even allowing that the prices are honest.

But they are not honest, because in the large majority of such transactions the prices are "rigged," that is to say, the bandits who run the shop run it to win and not to lose, and "fix" the prices accordingly. The player is thus required to give odds by laying 3 to 4 not on what the price of a stock will be, which is ruinous enough in all conscience, but on what his opponent will choose to make it! Since we are talking of gambling now and not of any real transaction, we may as well adopt the vernacular of the fraternity and say plainly that the bucket-shop man holds the stakes, cuts, shuffles, and deals the cards, and then telegraphs you what your hand is. And the loser at this joyous pastime thinks he has been robbed by Wall Street.

The game works against the player in yet another sense, as the *Wall Street Journal* points out, for when you buy stock you are entitled not merely to the stock itself, but to all the privileges which it carries, and not the least of these privileges is the effect which your purchase will have on the market. That is to say, if ten thousand purchasers throughout the country should buy even small amounts of a certain stock on a given day, the combined effect of all these purchases would undoubtedly lift its price on the Stock Exchange, and thus we see that each buyer's action carries with it a privilege of no inconsiderable proportions. But the keeper of the bucket-shop does not buy any stock for you at all; he merely makes a bet with you as to what the price will be — and so, having robbed you of your money, he now robs you of the privilege which goes with your money, since the alleged purchase of a million shares of your stock in bucket-shops would not have the slightest influence on its price at the Stock Exchange.

The man who has saved money by his own enterprise and thrift is a fool if he gives his savings to mining "bonanzas" through the itching palms of promoters, or to bucket-shops through the lure of slender margins. The very fact that promotors always play upon the theory that distance will lend enchantment to the view, and solicit their funds solely by means of prospectuses, should be a sufficient warning to the most credulous. A word to his banker, or a letter to any responsible institution in Wall Street, will supply him with the necessary information and save him from the possibility of loss.

As to the bucket-shops, if he is in doubt, he has but to follow the same procedure. The New York Stock Exchange authorities will gladly tell him whether the so-called "banker and broker" is really a member of the Stock Exchange, and the local bank nearest at hand will expose any fraud if it is called upon for information. As to the two-point margin bait, it is a good rule that the smaller the margin asked for, the less strength there is behind the house that asks it, and just in proportion as the margin requirement diminishes so a suspicion of the solvency of the firm should become fixed in the mind of the customer. This warning applies to stockbrokers no less than to bucket-shoppers. If the stockbroker takes from you a ten-point margin, and from somebody else a two-point margin, you may be sure your money is being used to finance the other customer's trade, and you should lose no time in withdrawing your funds from such a house.*

* In his article on "The Hughes Investigation" (*Journal of Political Economy*, October, 1909, p. 539), Mr. Horace White refers to the attempt of the Hughes Commission to devise a means whereby the company-promoter's activities might be curbed. He says: "The British 'Companies Act' forbids the public advertisement or sale of any securities unless the issuing company has been registered in a bureau of the government with information regarding the business to be transacted, the names of the officers and other persons responsible for the statements of fact, etc. Much

I often think that those who so freely criticize the Stock Exchange would have applauded it could they have witnessed the fight between the Exchange and the bucket-shops. In England, because telegraphs are a Government monopoly, the transmission of prices by or to bucket-shops is effectually barred, and the same is true of the telephone. But in this country the transmission of prices by wire is not a breach of law, and the difficulties that have attended the attempt to suppress the transmission of racing news by wire to poolrooms shows that even if it were prohibited there would be great difficulty in its enforcement.

Notwithstanding these obstacles, however, the Stock Exchange labored zealously to close bucket-shops long before the officers of the law became

---

time was spent by the committee in discussing the advisability of adopting the English system, regardless of the fact that it would be operative in only one state of the union, and that it would serve as an obstacle to all securities, sound and unsound, alike. Thus, if the Pennsylvania Railroad Company desired to issue a new lot of bonds it could advertise and sell them everywhere except in New York, without the trouble and expense of registration. Would it be worth while to give to other markets such an advantage over that of New York? The opinion of the governors of the Stock Exchange was sought and was given orally, to the effect that it would be unwise to take the risk unless the benefits to be derived from registration were preponderating and reasonably certain. It was their belief, however, that a certificate from state officials that a company was registered at Albany would be interpreted by the class of investors, who are most liable to deception, as a certificate of the soundness of the securities, in which case the act of registration would do more harm than good. The latter consideration prevailed in the committee, but recommendations as to advertising were made, which, if adopted by the legislature, will add something to the responsibilities of greedy and unscrupulous newspapers, while not going upon the doubtful ground of a censorship of the press."

active, and, while the work thus done was not published broadcast, it was none the less effective. Many a bucket-shop proprietor doing business a few years ago under a high-sounding company title probably never knew what hit him when the raid took place. It was the strong arm of the Stock Exchange working unostentatiously that did it, and in that good work it saved from further losses a large number of innocent people who used the establishment with no knowledge of its real character.

As long ago as 1875, in its contracts with the telegraph company, the Stock Exchange began restrictive measures to prevent its quotations from reaching the bucket-shops. In 1878 still more forcible measures were employed, and in 1882 positive steps were taken by which the Exchange authorities personally inspected the telegraph company's quotation contracts with its patrons. To-day this is carried to such an extreme in the determination to protect the public from the impositions of those who might in devious ways convey these quotations to improper hands that even members of the Exchange may not install wires from their offices to outsiders until the proper committee of Stock Exchange authorities has viséd the application.

Meanwhile, a secret-service has been at work,

silently ferreting the hidden, underground channels in which the bucket-shop is forced to conduct its operations. Thanks to this good work and to that now done along similar lines by the Federal authorities, this form of rascality is rapidly disappearing. Is it too much to hope that at least a part of the unmerited criticism of the Stock Exchange by the victims of bucket-shops may also disappear?

In heading this chapter "Cautions and Precautions," my purpose was not merely to warn the credulous outsider against the news items of the day as related to the Stock Exchange, nor was it solely to point out to him the pitfalls and dangers that exist under the Wall Street mask. I had in mind also a word of caution to Stock Exchange members themselves. That these gentlemen are more sinned against than sinning is, or it should be, apparent to anybody who has taken the trouble to learn the A B C's of the business. Such a man knows that Stock Exchanges occupy an important place in the mechanism of modern business; he knows, too, that just in proportion as their functions enlarge and the scope of organized markets increases, so persons will be found who foolishly or dishonestly abuse the facilities there afforded.

"Reflection," says a recent writer, "seems to

have little part in the intellectual equipment of the assailants of organized markets. The fact that the stock market is sometimes abused by people who know nothing of its purposes or are incapable of understanding the mighty influences which dominate it, is no reason for considering it as a harmful excrescence on the body politic."

This fact established, one who has been a member of the Stock Exchange for many years may, in a spirit of complete loyalty to the institution, comment freely on some of the mistakes within the Exchange itself, errors of judgment or sins of omission that have given to the popular criticism of the day its one supporting prop. Admitting mistakes freely is the surest way of correcting them; frequent reminders of them serve to keep one on guard against their recurrence. The history of deposit banking, for example, has been, like the history of the Stock Exchange, a story of gradual development to meet growing conditions, and this is true also of the history of note issues, joint stock companies, clearing houses, cable transfers and of all the instruments that enter into that economic structure which gives mobility to capital and flexibility to credit.

In the very nature of things the development of each part of this gradually devised machinery has been attended by mistakes, by errors of judgment, and by occasional wrongdoing, yet we do not condemn the national banking system because there were once wildcat banks; we do not utter hasty judgments on stock-companies because in other days they were badly organized and incompetently managed; we do not withhold our support from railways because they once erred by pushing too ambitiously into projects that ruined innocent stockholders; we do not abandon our form of government because there was once civil war. No, but we try to keep all these things in view in order to profit by them, and to see to it that they do not happen again. We say of individuals that no man's vices are sufficient reasons for not admiring his virtues. Why not apply the same code to business?

One of the mistakes of members of the Stock Exchange in the past has been in trying to do too much business on too little capital. This is a subject that calls for plain speaking, since it directly caused two Stock Exchange failures in recent years, failures that were, I am sorry to say, essentially the result of dishonesty. Every Stock Exchange house is looking for business, and a house with small capital sometimes gets more than it should attempt to handle. Such a house borrows from the bank, as all houses do, and allows its bankers a 20 per cent. margin; so far so good. But it accepts business from its customers on a 10 per cent. margin, and this means financing the difference out of the firm's capital. If the capital is large, the business is safe, but if it is small, the house finds itself "loaded up," as the phrase is, and is then in such a predicament that it must either summon enough moral courage to refuse business altogether and so advertise its limitations, or abandon its moral courage, sell its customer's stocks "short" and incur the risk of buying them back cheaper.

The latter course is dishonest; it is in fact nothing more or less than a form of "bucketing," since the customer must lose for the broker to save himself, while, if the customer wins, the broker may not be able to pay. This is not a common practice of course — first, because 99 per cent. of the members are absolutely honest; second, because the majority of those who carry accounts on the books of Stock Exchange houses are wise enough to acquaint themselves with the firm's resources and to withdraw when too much business becomes apparent, and, third, even though a broker were not himself essentially honest, he would not dare expose himself to the expulsion and disgrace that would attend exposure. Nevertheless, the thing has been done, and it may conceivably occur again. How then may it be avoided?

As the Stock Exchange is, as we have seen, an unincorporated body with a set of rules which no legislature and no court could enforce without depriving a man of his constitutional prerogatives, it is obvious that this and all other reforms must come from within; all the many reforms that are constantly lifting the Exchange to a higher level come from that quarter. There are 1100 members of the Stock Exchange and perhaps 600 of these are engaged in active commission business. A committee of the governors can enter any member's office at any time, and demand every book or record without reserve. It has absolute power to compel him to do anything that in its wisdom seems desirable. If he is doing too much business on too little capital, he can be forced to restrict, or to retire from business altogether. Failure to comply immediately means expulsion and a peculiarly stinging disgrace. Naturally in the face of these despotic powers any plan of mutually guaranteeing brokers' accounts, such as that employed by Lloyds in London, or by the *Agents de Change* on the Paris Bourse, would seem unnecessary.

The remedy lies, first with the members themselves in striving to attain continually to a higher standard of business morality, and second with increased watchfulness by the committee having this matter in charge. In point of fact it is apparent that both these solutions are now being employed to a greater extent than ever before. The two failures that occurred some years ago as a result of this iniquitous practice hurt the Exchange, and stung the members to the quick. It can never happen again if the vigilance of the governors can prevent it, and yet every now and then a bank fails even under the watchful eye of the bank examiner. No committee and no group of committees can watch the books of 600 houses engaged in a business in which the dividing line between sound and unsound business may be crossed and recrossed with surprising suddenness many times a day. The members themselves must look to this, and that is what they are doing to-day, as never before, with an earnestness begotten of real pride in their great organization.

If they do not do it, if they relax in any degree the vigilance upon which the proper conduct of their business depends in this important respect, they will be forced sooner or later to resort to the plan of guaranteeing the accounts of their fellow members, or to submit to that form of government incorporation or regulation which must impair, if it does not actually destroy, their usefulness. Members must also see to it that manipulation in its improper forms is driven out of the Exchange, and that every conceivable precaution is taken in the listing of new securities. These matters I shall discuss elsewhere. Meantime it is cheering to note that Stock Exchange failures, whether arising from this or any other cause, are diminishing in number. In London, at the account day immediately following the failure of the house of Baring, thirty Stock Exchange houses announced their inability to meet their obligations. Certainly the New York Stock Exchange has not witnessed so many failures in ten years.

One of the many excellent results of the work of the Hughes Committee from the standpoint of the Stock Exchange was the publicity that came of it. Critics of the institution had long found fault with it because of its atmosphere of aloofness, the air of mystery that seemed to surround it, its silence under attack, and its apparent unwillingness to defend itself from adverse comment. This reticence, however, while it did harm, was more apparent than real. In so far as the Stock Exchange is concerned the advantages of publicity have long been recognized. The difficulty has been in having its purposes and its methods properly attested by competent authority in a way that would enlighten the public and carry conviction. Members and friends of the Exchange feel very strongly that in this day and age, when the spirit of publicity is in the air, the Stock Exchange should fall in line with a resolute determination to assert itself and make itself heard on all proper occasions.

If a sub-committee of Congress retains as counsel a shrewd lawyer who by devious ex-parte methods reads into the record and thence into the newspapers only such biased and prejudiced information as will do harm to the Exchange, while rigidly excluding all that properly belongs there by way of refutation and explanation, energetic steps should be taken to remedy this obvious injustice by invoking that spirit of fair play which is essential to any judicial inquiry. These are not the days of the Inquisition. We have progressed beyond the point of the Star Chamber. Members of the Stock Exchange know that they will receive fair play from the newspapers whenever they seek it, but they cannot expect to find their side of the case stated unless they themselves take the necessary steps to secure its presentation. And the way to do this is to proceed with energy and determination against every avenue from which the malicious slander or the insidious suggestion emanates.

The time has passed to sit supinely under every

sinister attack and imagine that a consciousness of rectitude will suffice as an answer. Let the Exchange bestir itself. If, as happened very recently, a judge on the bench can so lose his poise as to say to a common thief at the bar, "You have committed a petty theft and you must go to jail — but had you gone down to the Stock Exchange and stolen a million you would go free" — such an unworthy utterance should be handled promptly and without gloves by the Exchange authorities, and the same course of treatment should be applied vigorously to every thoughtless minister of the gospel and every cheap politician who, because the Exchange has so long remained silent, may think that such silence entitles him to utter any libel that comes to mind. The newspaper that publishes the original utterance of this judge or that preacher will publish also the steps taken by the Exchange to bring him to book, and even though the slanderer may escape the consequences of his act through the technicalities of the law, or otherwise, the knowledge that the Exchange is at last aroused from its lethargy and in a fighting mood will serve to deter others from similar indiscretions. I violate no confidence when I say that henceforth the Stock Exchange will be found defending itself manfully, and I venture to remind all noisy seekers of notoriety that "thrice is he armed who hath his quarrel just."

The Stock Exchange has felt, since the report of the Hughes Commission in 1909, that such a report, by such a body of men, would inevitably stay the hand of many of its detractors by showing them just what the Exchange is trying to do, and just how the work is done. "The committee," says its chairman, "was in session about six months. Its expenses were paid by the members themselves, and since frugality was a necessity the services of the stenographers were dispensed with, the members taking only such notes of the testimony of witnesses as each one deemed important to the matter in hand. The officers of all the Exchanges in New York City were invited to appear before the committee and answer questions both orally and in writing, and all of them responded promptly and courteously, as often as they were asked to do so. Many volunteer witnesses, citizens of the State, were heard. None such was refused a hearing. Citizens of other States were not called, or accepted, as witnesses unless they had given evidence, by published writings or otherwise, that they had something of value to contribute to the discussion."*

* "The Hughes Investigation," by Horace White, *Journal of Political Economy*, October, 1909, p. 529.

This committee was composed of Horace White, Chairman; Charles A. Schieren, David Leventritt, Clark Williams, John B. Clark, Willard V. King, Samuel H. Ordway, Edward D. Page, Charles Sprague Smith, Maurice L. Muhleman.

Nobody who read these names doubted the independence and public spirit of its members. It was precisely the sort of committee that all fair-minded men welcomed. The high character of the members carried assurance of their good faith; their wisdom and practical experience meant a critical analysis of the subject; their independence of spirit made a whitewash impossible. Here then was the long looked for solution.* If there were abuses, nobody was more anxious to know of them and of the remedies for them than the members of the Exchange; if indefensible conditions existed nobody stood readier to correct them. It was felt that this was the first and greatest step toward publicity under the right conditions, and that a valuable contribution to the popular knowledge of an intricate and greatly misunderstood subject would result. There was nothing ex-parte or one-sided about the committee's deliberations; everybody with a grievance might state it, and both sides were accorded

---

* The report of the Hughes Investigating Committee is published in full in the appendix to this volume.

fair play. But, *mirabile dictu*, the very fact of its fairness is found, three years later, to afford a reason for flouting it at the hands of counsel for a congressional sub-committee that will not hear both sides! Is there anything just or equitable in the proceedings of such a body, or in the prejudiced emanations of its precious lawyer? Is it conceivable that the law-making branch of our government will give serious heed to a report thus conceived in bias and born in inquisition? I think not.

Passing to more agreeable topics, the late Addison Cammack is said to have remarked on one occasion that publicity was ruining the business of Wall Street and the Stock Exchange and would ultimately drive it all away. Those were the days of inadequate and unreliable balance sheets, of suppressed reports of earnings and assets, of accounts that were never subjected to independent audits, and of a general atmosphere of mystery that led to financial abuses of all kinds. As a result of those conditions there was created in the public mind another vague aversion toward the Stock Exchange, and a popular prejudice which has been hard to dispel. Cammack had been brought up in the old school; he saw what was coming, but he mistook causes for effects. He would probably turn in his grave could he see the new conditions and contrast them with the old. As a matter of fact nothing could be more democratic in principle than the way the business is conducted nowadays. The rights of stockholders to information, the reports and balance sheets submitted to them, the mass of Wall Street financial material in the magazines and journals, the stock ticker, the news ticker, the printed news bulletins, the card index system, the statistical manuals and the quotation lists published in the morning and evening newspapers, together with the market letters constantly circulated by brokerage houses, these are evidences that the public is entitled to full information and that many avenues by which it may safeguard its interests are always open.*

It has long been known that investors and speculators in America enjoy vastly more safety in their market operations through these various avenues of publicity than do investors and speculators abroad. There are no tickers worthy of the name across the water, and the daily list of business done, as published in our newspapers,

* One of the witnesses before the Hughes Committee actually recommended that the stock ticker be suppressed. Such a suggestion is silly and would lead to great confusion and many complaints from the public. The ticker is essential to publicity and offers the very protection which the Stock Exchange seeks to extend. Speculation was never so unscrupulous and wrongdoing never so abundant as in the days before this instrument was invented.

with bid and asked prices and total transactions in detail, is unheard of among all the Bourses of Europe. The eminent French economist, Paul Leroy-Beaulieu, speaks very earnestly of the superiority of our New York Stock Exchange system in this matter; he says the need for a similar method in France is "very urgent," that the information thus spread broadcast is "very instructive," that the pledge of publicity "is better assured in the United States than in any other country of the world," and that an immediate reform along these lines is "absolutely necessary" in Paris in the interest of the public.*

This leads to another word of caution suggested by the fact that the public, despite what is done for it, does not always avail itself of these safeguards. Men buy worthless mining stocks without bothering to inquire into their bona fides. They put their savings into new and untried enterprises and they neither read the balance sheets nor attend the meetings. A thousand stockholders will attend a meeting in London and they will have their questions answered whether the majority in control likes it or not. In New York almost nobody attends these meetings. The stockholder's right to information is absolute, but he does not go and get it, and so finally when

* *L'Economiste Français*, Paris, October 5th.

something goes wrong he writes angry letters to the newspapers and damns both Wall Street and the Stock Exchange because he has been burned, although the fire escape and the extinguisher were always at his hand. "It is all very well" says the *Wall Street Journal*, "to talk about what the law, the newspaper press, and the Stock Exchange can do to protect the investor, but the investor himself can do more than all his protectors put together. His investment, however conservative and secure, carries responsibilities as well as privileges, and it is his duty to discharge the one in order to safeguard the other."*

---

* When the first issue of Union Pacific convertible bonds matured, so many people had failed to notice that their bonds could be exchanged dollar for dollar against the stock, selling at much higher price with greater yield, that the company extended the time for conversion. It would have been entirely warranted in paying off such bondholders at par, but it spent considerable sums in advertising them of a privilege they should have known all about. In the face of all this, bonds came in for conversion many months after the extended time, and the bondholder sincerely believed that he had a grievance because his bond was redeemed at par.

The same thing happened in the case of the old St. Paul 7's, which were convertible into preferred stock. Bondholders allowed themselves to be paid off at par for a bond which had been standing at 170 and apparently had never read the terms of their own mortgage. What can the law, the press, or the banker do against such criminal negligence as this? And if bondholders are remiss, what shall be said of the average stockholder? He is improving undoubtedly, but he has still a great deal to learn. His right to information is unquestionable, but he fails to exercise it in anything like the degree he should. It is to be feared also that he does not take a great deal of trouble in learning to analyze such reports and balance sheets as may be submitted to him.

A stockholder should never hesitate to write to the officers of his company for information. He should do it often, and he should get other stockholders to do the same thing. One stockholder writing frequently may be regarded as a nuisance. Ten will be treated with respect, and it will be a very autocratic control which will venture to deny information to a

He must learn to make inquiries, to discriminate, to use his wits, to read mortgages, to study sinking funds and operating ratios. He must eschew the financial columns of questionable newspapers and confine his attention to those of established probity. He must not put all his investment eggs into one basket. The Stock Exchange cannot do all this for him, but it is always ready to help him, and the information he requires may be had for the asking.

In a recent public address the president of a great American railway sounded an encouraging note. "We railway men," he said, "have been in a practical school, having taken a thorough course in working economics. We have learned that a railway can thrive only as a result of the prosperity of the community it serves, and that the best policy, from the viewpoint of permanent railway interests, is one of co-operative helpfulness."* The New York Stock Exchange has learned the same lesson, in a similar school. As an institution it realizes that if it is to grow in prosperity the public must grow, and that as

hundred stockholders, taking a legitimate step to protect their own proper interests. The newspapers are glad to furnish any information in their power, but if the stockholder would write to the company first and the newspaper afterward, he would probably derive more ultimate advantage. — *Wall Street Journal*, September 22, 1909.

* Address by President Finlay of the Southern Railway, before the Transportation Club of Indianapolis, October, 1912.

the public is attracted to investment and speculation by the soundness of the institution through which it deals so it requires and must receive full information and an assurance of fair play. "Co-operative helpfulness" is the only way. Members of the Exchange who become discouraged now and then must bear this in mind. In the face of every harassing annoyance they must never cease their work of keeping their house in order, and of inviting that portion of the public that is open-minded to lend a hand. Their labors resemble the task of Sisyphus; like him they must cultivate the spirit of "everlasting hope," and when unworthy assailants seek to prejudice the popular mind, they must stand forth, give blow for blow, and never say die.

Pessimists may blind their eyes to the manifold evidences of material progress on every hand, but just as the workshop, the farm, the school, the hospital, and the bank, each supplies proof of continuing improvement, so also in its sphere of usefulness does the Stock Exchange. Within a few years, for example, it has rid itself of the unlisted department, and this may very properly be mentioned as a distinct progression. Under the old system a limited number of industrial corporations were permitted to obtain a market on the Exchange for their securities, although they furnished but few figures to the Listing Committee in return. This was a practice wholly at variance with the duty of the Exchange to protect the investor, since it practically assures him that corporations admitted to the Exchange have demonstrated their worth to the authorities. That character and countenance should be given to the so-called "unlisted department" was a mistake, and it has been abolished.

In this reform the Listing Committee accomplished a twofold blessing in setting the Exchange right with the public by ridding their institution of anything approaching the blind pools of early days and at the same time forcing certain wealthy corporations to abandon their policy of concealment or lose the privilege of the floor. Certainly if the country's leading steel corporation can afford to take its 150,000 stockholders and its 250,000 employees into its confidence and treat the whole public, including its competitors, with entire frankness, there is no insuperable difficulty about the others. In any case the desire to protect the investor, which is the controlling motive of the elaborate restrictions imposed by French and English laws in new security offerings, has advanced far in this country within the last few years, and the farther it goes the more popular it becomes.

That there is still work for the Listing Committee to do goes without saying. One of the most promising improvements that comes to mind at the moment is the one employed in London, where shares of new companies are not admitted to the Board unless a sufficiently large allotment has been made to the public. This is also the rule in New York, but perhaps we may add to its effectiveness by increasing the size of the public allotments. Another praiseworthy feature of the London system is that which has to do with vendor's shares, which are not listed until six months after the admission of the company's securities. Under this plan if one or more individuals secure a block of stock in payment for properties in the concern, they are prevented from unloading those shares on the public until a sufficient time has elapsed to determine the merit of the property.

Another instance of progress made in recent years in the internal mechanism of the Exchange, is the abolition of fictitious transactions or "wash sales," utterly indefensible transactions not enforcible at law. These were always prohibited under the rules, yet despite this a flagrant instance of a violation was discovered in which the guilty were made to suffer. So far as I am aware it was the only case on record in which obvious collusion between buyer and seller in a Stock Exchange transaction was shown. The broker in this instance must have known that the Committee would demand his books and that it would appear that no genuine bargain had taken place. If he did not know it, he knows it now. The example made of him will, I fancy, prevent a recurrence of the episode.

This leads to the subject of "manipulation," as it is termed, or the uses to which the facilities of the Exchange are sometimes put to give certain stocks an appearance of activity out of proportion to their normal movement. Now we must assume as our major premise in discussing this matter that any artificial interference with the natural operation of supply and demand is pernicious; from the standpoint of economics it is harmful. The Stock Exchange has nothing to conceal, and it recognizes not only that manipulation exists, but that at times it assumes the proportions of a real evil. Therefore it is doing what it can to stop it, and it will continue to do so. Whenever unwonted activity arises nowadays in a security long dormant, as happened very recently in the stock of a certain gas company, the governors of the Exchange entrusted with such things take the matter in hand and put a stop to it if obvious manipulation can be shown after investigation. The public and the newspapers know nothing about it; the vial of their criticism is poured forth only when something escapes the watchful eye of the Exchange authorities, as must inevitably happen now and then. But if these critics could know how indignant the members of the Exchange became when the Hocking Coal episode occurred, and if they could see the resolute determination of all hands to prevent another such occurrence, they would at least give the Exchange credit for faithfully attempting to suppress manipulation of the flagrant sort.

The fact is that all forms of manipulation are by no means improper; some of it performs a useful service and is a necessary and legitimate part of the functions of the Exchange. To understand how true this is let us consider, for example, the case of a corporation that has been organized, let us say, to develop a group of recently discovered coal properties in new territory. This is legitimate endeavor as applied to American enterprise; in a broad sense it is the spirit of adventure and speculation that has made our country commercially rich and powerful.

Now, in order to develop this enterprise, it is necessary to ask the public to buy its shares or its certificates of debt and thus become partners in the undertaking. In that way our great railways were built and our Western country opened to progress. But the public will not support the new enterprise until it knows something of its merits, and accordingly the company introduces its property through the medium of that great central market-place — the Stock Exchange — furnishing the Exchange authorities with its credentials in minute detail.

At this point the so-called manipulation takes place. The securities are new, the company may wish to advertise them, attract attention to them, and solicit a public interest in the laudable enterprise that lies behind them, all of which is as right and proper as it is for any merchant to establish a market for any new article on his shelves. To accomplish his purpose the merchant must first fix an arbitrary price; if the public will not buy at that price he must "manipulate" a lower price, and in all his subsequent dealings there must be manipulation of one form or another designed to conform to the supply and demand in that particular article.

The men behind the coal company in question must do the same thing. They fix a price at which their shares are introduced in the market-place; let us say this price is $100 per share. This is manipulation. It may happen that the public will not buy at that price, in which case the price is lowered, let us say, to 80. This also is manipulation. But is it improper? Is it subversive of good morals? Is it an unhealthy interference with natural laws of supply and demand? Is it anything less than a legitimate method of attracting capital into worthy enterprises?

Critics are invited to remember that the Stock Exchange does not buy or sell anything; it merely acts as a market-place through which, among other things, capital may be directed from channels where it is least needed into those where it may be most beneficially and profitably employed. If, therefore, an oil company or a coal company or any other enterprise whose ultimate success cannot fail to enrich the community seeks to market its wares—i. e., its securities—and thereby enable itself to do business, where else is it to turn save to the Stock Exchange, and how is it to fix an attractive market price at the outset save by what is termed manipulation? Nobody is compelled to buy; as for selling, any holder of 100 shares or any other number of shares can sell them at will, and no amount of manipulation can prevent him from a free exercise of this privilege. You may depend upon it, Mr. Critic, that the Stock Exchange will take pains to suppress all forms of manipulation that are unsound and harmful, but until you or some other gifted student of economics can devise a method by which capital may be attracted to excellent channels other than through the medium of an Exchange, manipulation of the sort just described must continue or enterprise must stop. Strike out the word "manipulation," and substitute "establishment of values" in transactions of this sort, and the practice seems to become, as it really is, in keeping with the finest traditions of the market-place.*

* "If there is one man who really understands the nature of the transactions in the New York Stock Exchange from day to day, it is Robert L. Doremus, the chairman of the Stock Exchange Clearing House Committee, which has the power to lay bare the character of any broker's business. His reputation for veracity is of that high character which Wall Street demands from the men in its responsible positions. When he says that the main influence in any day's trading is a legitimate and widespread demand for sound securities, in lots small enough to be within reach of the investor of moderate means, he is talking facts and not theories.

"Our politicians, however, are legislating for a Wall Street of twenty years ago. The stock market is not controlled by large speculators creating deceptive prices by manipulative orders. That kind of business is passing away, and it may be said that another kind, that of the purely gambling accounts carried on the lightest of margins, has practically gone, and is not likely to return. The few houses whose business is still of this character are dying of dry-rot; while the active houses who are doing the real business of the stock market report their speculative accounts so broadly margined as to be of a semi-investment character.

"What is still more satisfactory is the wide diffusion in the ownership of industrial and railroad stocks. This is not new. The Illinois Central's great strength for forty years was in the small stockholder, who made his voice heard to some purpose when "strike" legislation developed in his State legislature or in Congress. But the ever-widening character of the investment area, the recognition of the convenience and convertibility of Stock Exchange securities, safeguarded by sound management and full publicity, is a growth of the most hopeful character. It indicates a force of enlightened conservatism of the greatest value to the country."— The *Wall Street Journal*, October 22, 1912.

It is a difficult matter for the Stock Exchange authorities to suppress all forms of manipulation that are plainly and admittedly improper. Such things do exist; the difficulty is in devising ways and means of preventing them. Mr. Smith, a non-member of the Exchange, may be interested in a certain security to which he wishes to give an appearance of activity. He calls Brown, a stockbroker, and instructs him to buy 5000 shares "at the market." Then he telephones Jones, another stockbroker, to sell 5000 shares. Brown and Jones are each in ignorance of the other's order, but they meet in the crowd where this stock is dealt in, and their orders combine to give the market an appearance of animation. The governors are as determined to stop this sort of thing as the most energetic critic could wish; they send for the two brokers and the facts are revealed. But as each was entirely innocent of wrongdoing, and as no rule of the Exchange and no law of the land has been violated, what is to be done?

They may caution both brokers against accepting any more business from Smith, but Smith is not a member of the Exchange, and hence he is not amenable to its discipline. When his next orders are refused he gives them to some one else, and if the entire Stock Exchange refused to accept business from him he would and could with perfect propriety ask his bank, or a trust company, or an individual to give out the orders under their own names. Finally, if the Exchange authorities were so sagacious as to be able to close to this man every conceivable avenue by which he might approach the Stock Exchange in New York, there would still be left open to him the market in Boston, or Montreal, or London, or any other centre in which the security was listed, and the pernicious effect of his manipulation in these cities would be felt in New York just as promptly and just as harmfully as if they had originated here. I mention this case, a purely hypothetical one, to show how easy it is for manipulation of this sort to find employment, despite all that may be done to suppress it. Perhaps somewhere in the noble army of critics there may be one who can devise a means of meeting this issue. If so, let him stand forth and speak. The Stock Exchange, root, stock, and branch, will be glad to hear from him.*

Counsel for the Congressional Committee that

---

* It is truthfully declared by Courtois, in his *Traité des Opérations de Bourse et de Change*, that a fictitious movement, even on the part of the most powerful operators, cannot overcome the natural tendencies of values, and that the most that can be accomplished is sometimes to hasten or retard slightly the certain effect of a foreseen event. "Wall Street and the Country," by Charles A. Conant, p. 88, G. P. Putnam's Sons, New York, 1904

is in session as these lines are written seeks to raise another dreadful ghost with which to frighten ignorant people in his alleged "discovery" that a great part of the business done on the Stock Exchange is speculation. He parades through the newspapers the fact that the number of shares bought and sold often largely exceeds the number transferred on the companies' books. In a chapter on "The Uses and Abuses of Speculation," I have attempted to show that the more speculators there are in a market, the better and safer the market, and I rest this dictum on the authority of every student of modern markets. In this connection let us consider the opinion of a thoughtful newspaper writer. "There is no doubt," he says, "that the committee will find that there is speculation in Wall Street, just as there is speculation elsewhere, and in commodities other than in stocks and bonds. The instinct has always been a pronounced human characteristic, being a part of human progress, and the manifestation of it is one sign of the difference between man and the lower sorts of creatures. It is doubtful whether the general gambling impulse can be entirely wiped out, even if the mighty power of an act of Congress be called into requisition. If Mr. Pujo and his committee can abolish speculation in Wall Street (to say nothing of gambling, which is not the same thing), they may be asked to abolish every commodity market throughout the land, for there is plentiful speculation in all of them.

"What seems to bother some representatives of the Pujo Committee is that the number of shares traded in on the Stock Exchange exceeds largely the number actually transferred. It is true, for example, that the number of shares of United States Steel common sold during last year were largely in excess of the number of shares outstanding, the sales amounting to 31,266,208 shares, while the entire number outstanding was only 5,084,952. The ratio of six to one suggests healthy activity in the market for steel stocks. It is conceivable that a block of stocks may pass through many hands before it arrives at its ultimate owner, just as a crop of potatoes passes through a long chain of handlers and buyers and dealers before it reaches the ultimate consumer. Meantime, the number of potatoes has neither increased nor diminished.

"But the potato crop, which easily changes hands six times in a year, is finally eaten. The stocks go on forever. The legitimate holder is not injured if they change hands not six, but sixty times, provided he is secured by proper publicity, which the Stock Exchange assures. The free speculative market is in itself an element of value, and if it were destroyed the investor would be chiefly injured, while future capitalization for the development of the country would be paralyzed."*

At the outset I began by cautioning the reader not to cry out in alarm over the utterances of newspaper statesmen bent on justifying their existence, and determined to make the punishment fit the crime. Stocks will always be bought and sold, they will pass from hand to hand just as horses are traded and lands are exchanged. The modest dollar, too, will continue to pass from pocket to pocket, having a thousand owners and performing a thousand functions many of which may alarm a timid and unsuspecting lawmaker, but which to you and me may seem natural enough.

When you read that a great Congressman is determined to put the Steel corporation into bankruptcy and throw its 250,000 employees out of business, depend upon it he is only trying to justify his job for the benefit of this constituents. When somebody else seeks to mend his fences by the noisy announcement that the Stock Exchange reeks with improper manipulation, that speculation is wrongful, and that the criminal nature of an

* The *Wall Street Journal*, December 7, 1912.

institution is directly proportionate to its size, remember that the votes of your fellow-citizens put this man in office and that you and they must foot the bill, since it is your money that pays for all these junkets, all these investigations, and all these political excursions. More than that, you must pay your share of the $160,000,000 for pensions, of the $40,000,000 for post-offices, and of the countless millions for rivers and harbors, and these, too, are voted with amiable frugality by the gentlemen who see nightmares in banks, Clearing Houses, and Stock Exchanges.

Finally, try to investigate and study all these matters for yourself. Read the men who have spent their lives in the study of economics. Compare the results attained by our great financial institutions with those reached in similar lines abroad. In the particular application of these studies to the New York Stock Exchange, you will find that charges such as we have been considering could be brought against any institution that has stood the test of time and made the mistakes that fallible human beings must make. You will find that if changes and improvements seem to come about slowly it is not because of the unwillingness of the Exchange to remedy these conditions, but because of the gravity and deliberation with which they must be considered in the light of the future as well as the present.

The management and control of a great public business, especially one that has long survived public criticism, is no light matter. It requires more than common industry, and more than common ability. What the Stock Exchange asks of you and of every thoughtful citizen in the land is a recognition of these matters, and a patient survey of all that enters into them. The critic in "The Vicar of Wakefield" laid it down as a good rule that you should *always* say the picture would have been a better one if the artist had taken more time. Criticism offered in this spirit the members of the Stock Exchange can bear with good humor. What hurts them on the raw is the critic's failure to study and investigate, or, getting back to the text of Mr. Bryce's sermon, "the neglect to think."

CHAPTER VI

PANICS, AND THE CRISIS OF 1907

CHAPTER VI

PANICS, AND THE CRISIS OF 1907

A PANIC is a state of mind. It cannot be regulated by statute law nor preached down by press or pulpit. At such times, suspicion, apprehension, and alarm take possession; reflection and sobriety are crowded out; men do and say irrational and unreasoning things; incidents trifling in themselves are exaggerated into undue proportions; all kinds of difficulties are conjured into the imagination. The best that can be said of such a phenomenon is that it is of brief duration.*

In Wall Street, where men are accustomed to looking forward at all times, the question is ever in mind as to the next panic. The last one left its sting; we are interested now in knowing about

* The distinction between "panics," "crises," and "depressions," are clearly stated in the opening chapter of "Financial Crises and Periods of Industrial and Commercial Depression," by Theodore E. Burton, D. Appleton & Co., N. Y., 1902. In the following pages, I use the terms as they are commonly applied in Wall Street, although this application is not always governed by sound etymology. Thus in Wall Street we speak of "the panic of 1907," meaning broadly the events of that entire year. Strictly speaking a "panic" is the brief period of a day or an hour of unreasoning fear, brought about by the "crisis" of a money scarcity which preceded it. The period of commercial and financial suffering, which continues after the panic and the crisis have passed, is the "depression."

the future. Have we learned how to avoid these difficulties? May we hope to diminish their force and mitigate their terrors? May we rely upon the superior organization of business and the greater quantity and quality of capital to soften the effect of the next shock? I think not. We may lull ourselves into a coma of fancied security as we reflect upon experience and its expensive lessons, but we deceive ourselves if we think that we shall finally arrive at a point where these convulsions shall cease.

Nothing of that sort can come about among people strong with health and vigor, confident and full of energy, and impatient for action. With such a people life is incessantly mobile; a constantly increasing volume of creative activity impels them onward. Panics are unknown in dead countries and in countries that have not yet heard the call of progress; in all other countries the violence of these shocks is directly proportionate to the enterprise of the people. The more civilization there is, the greater the creation of wealth; the more wealth there is, the greater the volume of speculation that creates wealth. In such circumstances it is idle to talk of a time when panics shall cease, because confidence and enterprise must ever push onward, speculation in material things must accompany them, supply must overtake demand, and human nature with its moods and caprices must finally pay toll.

Vast industrial, commercial, and credit expansions lie somewhere ahead, and somewhere ahead excesses and indiscretions the world over must play their part and exact their penalties. We should cease to be surprised at these vicissitudes, for, "paradoxical as it may seem, the riches of nations can be measured by the violence of the crises which they experience."* Moreover, panics are rarely such unmitigated calamities as they are pictured by those who experience them. At least they serve to place automatic checks upon extravagance and inflation, restoring prices to proper levels and chastening the spirit of over-optimism. In a world of swift changes they are soon forgotten.

We may seem to be prepared for these periodic set-backs, and there may be men amongst us of sober reflection who are really wise enough to foresee the top to a normal movement, yet the accidents that have happened will happen again, — bad harvests, war, sudden failures, earthquakes, — these are not easily discerned in advance. Sanguine and ardent merchants will make the same old mistakes; good times will engender the same old hallucinations; people who see, or think

* "Des Crises Commerciales," Clément Juglar, Paris, 1889, pp. 44–5.

they see, wealth being created all around them, will always rush in and buy at the top; there will be too much work for the dollar to do — and after that the deluge. Finally, in order that we may not become pessimists, let us remember the words of the greatest of American philosophers: "The changes that break up at short intervals the prosperity of man are but advertisements of a nature whose law is growth."

Another phenomenon quite as curious as that of panics, and one that is similarly psychological, is the unhesitating, slam-bang zeal with which we place the responsibility for these misfortunes on the shoulders of others. We, as a people, have brought the disaster upon ourselves by reason of our indiscretions. We have lost our heads and entangled ourselves in a mesh of follies. But we do not admit such reproaches, even in our communings with self. Not at all. The fault lies elsewhere, and it is balm to our bruises to place it elsewhere with indignant energy. It will not do to preach at such times about currency systems, laws of supply and demand and kindred generalities, for these are abstract and vague to a mind inflamed by losses. What such a man wants is a head to hit; something concrete, a target for his exploding wrath. And he never hesitates. He says Wall Street did it. His fathers said the same thing, and his children will follow suit.

Now here is a strange thing. After a man has said, "Wall Street did it" over and over again, he believes it, just as he believes or takes for granted a similar tedious reiteration by the humble katydid. To such a man, the thing he *wants* to believe, when stated over and over again, comes by repetition to fix itself in the mind as a demonstrated truth, notwithstanding an utter absence of proof or of reasoning. He says "Wall Street," or "the Stock Exchange," until he can think of nothing else. It is a catch-phrase, short and sweet, which he hammers home to his own ineffable satisfaction, and he thinks it and broods over it to his heart's content. The politician then comes along with his cures for all the ills of society, and, finding Wall Street a convenient means of perpetuating his accidental notoriety, his voice joins the harmony. The indictment is then complete.

Take the panic of 1907 as the last and most conspicuous example. The financial losses involved, and the extent of the disturbance of the machinery of credit, made it the worst panic of this generation. As it burst upon the country at a period when to the outward eye prosperity reigned throughout the land, men were at a loss to explain it. They could not understand how such appalling conditions could occur in such apparently cheerful surroundings. As everybody was affected by it in greater or less degree the whole country was full of people with a grievance. They were themselves directly to blame for it, but they looked elsewhere for the responsibility for their folly.

That sinister influences were at work was, in the popular mind, undeniable; and by that same token we are pretty close to "Wall Street" when we talk of things sinister. At about that time a member of Congress made a speech in which he asserted, with all the art of katydid repetition so dear to the heart of the true believer, that the Stock Exchange was the cause of the panic. Rich men broke the market and "held the bag," he said, while panic-stricken owners of property poured the invested savings of a lifetime into that capacious receptacle. Nothing could be simpler. Newspapers must print such things, and the public found what it wanted on the first page. Even to-day, five years after the fact, this delightful explanation of the 1907 panic blossoms like the rose as a political campaign progresses. The voice of the hustings "knows its business."

Mr. John Burroughs warns us that it is one thing to treat your facts with imagination, but quite another thing to imagine your facts. Sufficient time has elapsed since 1907 to soften, somewhat, the bias and prejudice created by the events of that year, and perhaps there may be among us minds open to reason. The New York Stock Exchange feels, honestly, that a great injustice was done it by the criticism and abuse so generously poured out in the first shock of that event. Far from causing the crisis, its members assert that the institution fulfilled one of its most useful functions in giving ample warning of its approach, and that, when those warnings were disregarded, it concentrated all its machinery on the task of restoring order from chaos. They speak feelingly when they say that never in its history has the Stock Exchange been called upon to deal with so great an emergency, and never has it demonstrated so admirably its fundamental purposes. When they make these statements they offer to prove them. Let us examine the proofs.

The panic of 1907 was not unlike many preceding financial disturbances. The opening months of the year had witnessed a general liquidation on the Stock Exchange, brought about naturally, and in simple, automatic compliance with economic laws and precedents. There had been overexpansion in all lines of business; careful students saw the portent; able men of power and influence heeded its warning and set corrective forces in motion months before the shock came. Total transactions in shares sold on the Stock Exchange had risen from 187 millions in 1904 to 284 millions in 1906, while the value of the securities thus sold increased from 12,061 to 23,393 millions of dollars respectively. This was too rapid growth, and the general liquidation that had been under way for months effectually corrected it, since New York City bank loans secured by Stock Exchange collateral declined, as shown by the Comptroller's report, from $385,652,014 in August, 1905, to $251,867,158 in August, 1907 — a corrective force represented by $133,784,856.

The Stock Exchange has been defined as "a barometer of future business conditions," and never did a barometer give clearer warning. It said in effect to all the banks of the country and to business men generally: "There has been a widespread over-expansion of credit; it must stop; we are doing our share here in New York to correct it; you must do likewise." And, in order that there might be no failure to understand what was meant, New York City bank loans were reduced with drastic emphasis, months before the panic came, by nearly 35 per cent. "Without an exception," writes Prof. S. S. Huebner, "every business depression in this country has been discounted in our security markets from six months to two years before the depression became a reality."* Senator Burton, another authority, emphasizes the point further: "In addition to other influences which promote an earlier rise and fall, there must be mentioned the more careful study and attention to the financial situation which is given by dealers in the stock markets and in great financial centres. They often forecast the grounds for a rise or fall in prices before the general public is awake to the situation."† This, then, was the situation in the summer of 1907. The Stock Exchange had "cleaned house," and had liquidated thoroughly, warning the country to go slow.

Why was not this warning heeded? I recall vividly the daily expression of surprise, on the floor of the Exchange, and throughout the financial district, in the months that elapsed between our March liquidation and the outbreak of the October panic, that the country should pay so little attention to "Wall Street's" admonition; that it should continue its unprecedented boom despite the plain intimation that the funds to support it were exhausted, and despite the general

* "Annals of the American Academy of Political and Social Science," Vol. XXXV, No. 3, May, 1910, p. 13.

† "Financial Crises and Periods of Industrial and Commercial Depression," Theodore E. Burton, New York, 1902, p. 234.

knowledge of every tyro in business that future conditions are discounted in Wall Street as freely as promissory notes.

Had the business interests of the country so much as inquired into that warning they would have found by turning to the Comptroller's reports of the loans of national banks for the entire country that such loans had expanded from $3,726 millions in 1904 to $4,679 millions in 1907. They would have seen that whereas the New York City banks *contracted* their loans by nearly $134,000,000 from August, 1905, to August, 1907, loans and discounts by the banks of the whole country in that period actually *expanded* $700,000,000. Surely it will not be urged that Wall Street or the Stock Exchange had anything to do with bringing about this expansion. On the contrary, it shows that speculation in commercial lines, in new enterprises, in lands and in all the various forms that "out-of-town" banks are expected to finance, went on and on in vastly increasing volume long after the danger signal had been hoisted on the Stock Exchange, and in utter disregard of the warnings those signals conveyed.*

---

* The report of the New York State Superintendent of Banks for the same period emphasizes this point by showing a steady *contraction* of loans by State banks and trust companies of New York City during the period quoted, while all other authorities reveal a steady *expansion* in loans by similar institutions outside the city.

As the summer of 1907 advanced, speculation throughout the country continued in rapidly increasing volume, while on the Stock Exchange there was an almost complete cessation of activity. Business men of the West and South seemed to feel that as there had been no serious failures, and as the decline in the stock market had restored values to an attractively low basis, there would be a normal recovery similar to that which followed the panic of 1893. They felt that the trouble, whatever it was, had now been corrected, and in this fancied security they went about with further expansion of their business enterprises, confident that no serious difficulties were in store. The Stock Exchange was often cynically referred to in that period as "the only blue spot on the map." Its members were cheerfully invited by a Western newspaper to "shake off their torpor and join the Sunshine movement."

It is only fair to say that there was some force in the buoyant if superficial viewpoint of the country at large, for in the autumn of 1907 we were blessed with all the kindly fruits of the earth in abundance. The average crop of our agricultural products gathered that year was enormous, and behind it lay large reserves of wealth that had accumulated from a series of good crops in the years just preceding. There was, moreover, a partial failure of foreign crops that brought about heavy foreign requirements, thus assuring rich returns to American producers. Our railroads, which in the previous panic of 1893 were so affected by declining traffic and by the unproductiveness of new territory into which they had ventured that bankruptcies became general, were early in 1907 in better physical condition than ever before. Their gross earnings were at a maximum; their surpluses fat with the profits of recent years; their credit high. A long accumulation of foreign-trade balances had made the inherent strength of the nation greater than ever before. Finally there was the great essential difference between 1907 and former years in that we were now, by statute law as well as in fact, on a gold-standard basis.

And yet, without one unsound basic factor visible to superficial observers, we were suddenly plunged into a grave disaster — a panic which in actual money losses surpassed any of its predecessors. It came, this cataclysm (as the Stock Exchange had vainly predicted six months earlier), at the worst time it could possibly come, just when the banks were called upon to furnish $200,000,000 to transport and market the crops. Small wonder that in the face of such an optimistic outlook men stood aghast at the violence of the panic. As they had not understood the warning, so they could not understand its swift fulfilment. In all the long processions of panic-stricken people who stood in line at the banks in those trying days, not one in a hundred could understand how an institution could be solvent and yet be forced to suspend. Later on, smarting from losses, this bewilderment gave way to distrust and suspicion, as is often the case, humanly speaking, when men look elsewhere than to their own folly for the sources of their misfortunes. They were in a receptive mood when the charge was made that "Wall Street and the Stock Exchange" had brought about all this misery; they believed it to be true, and many still believe it.

The charge was so widely circulated and was fraught with such possibilities of mischief that there was danger of ill-considered legislation directed against the Stock Exchange and supported by ill-advised public opinion. Thus it happened that Governor Hughes of New York, doubtless moved to forestall hasty law-making, appointed a committee to investigate the Stock Exchange. In another chapter we have reviewed the work of this commission; meantime, the words of its chairman are quoted, in passing, as a sort of *ex post facto* reply to the outcry that "Wall Street did it."

"The immediate cause of the panic," he says, "was a simultaneous rush to sell securities, by holders who perceived that there was trouble in the money market, and who wanted cash to meet maturing obligations. These holders were not Wall Street men merely, but people in all parts of the country who had invested some of their savings in stocks and bonds. The very *raison d'être* of the Stock Exchange is to supply a market where invested capital can be quickly turned into cash, and vice versa. The remoter cause of the panic was a long course of speculation in all kinds of property, real and personal, that had pervaded all parts of the country, and many parts of the Old World, and had now reached its climax." Governor White here adds in a footnote that it has been "*shown conclusively that speculation on the Stock Exchange was not the chief contributor to the collapse of 1907, but that speculation on a much wider scale, through the length and breadth of the land, was the exciting cause.*"*

I have said it was not surprising that the public failed to observe signs of disturbance in the happy conditions that seemed to prevail before the panic.

* "The Hughes Investigation," by Horace White, *Journal of Political Economy*, October, 1909, pp. 528–540. Governor White quotes in this connection an article on "The Panic of 1907," by Eugene Meyer, Jr., *Yale Review*, May, 1909, from which many facts in this chapter have been taken.

The blindness of the mass of the people to these impending catastrophes is, indeed, a marked characteristic of all similar epochs. Let us digress for a moment and consider the history of other great disturbances. In 1825 the King's Speech as read by the Lord Chancellor dwells on "that general and increasing prosperity . . . which, by the blessing of Providence, continues to pervade every part of the Kingdom." This was in July; in December of that year the whole country was torn by a devastating financial crisis. The London *Economist*, in 1873, dwelt at length on the "astounding" progress of the Austrian States, and said, "All over the rich countries of the Danube, capital and labor are vigorously at work in the discovering and turning to profit the amazing resources which have been lying unheeded for centuries." This was written in March; the Bourse at Vienna closed its doors May 9th, and a panic of exceptional severity was followed by long and continued depression. On December 31, 1892, R. G. Dun & Company's *Weekly Review of Trade* said: "The most prosperous year ever known in business closes to-day with strongly favorable indications for the future," and yet four months later the storm burst.*

These instances go to show how the elect may

* *Cf.* Burton, *supra*, pp. 49-50-51.

err in estimating conditions, despite the fact that in two of these three memorable crises ample warnings of an impending catastrophe were proclaimed in the stock market long before these prophecies of continued expansion were printed. In each instance the portent was ignored; in each the ultimate penalty was paid. So it was in our own great crisis of 1907, and so it will always be.

There was a panic throughout the United Kingdom in April and October of 1847, yet the early response to changing conditions took place two years before, when stocks began to fail in July and August, 1845. In the year 1857 commerce and industry expanded throughout America in increasing volume up to the very eve of the August crisis, yet the stock market in the summer of the preceding year gave clear warning of what was to occur. One year before the panic of 1873 a similar "slump" foretold what was coming, and the same was true of the year preceding the panic of '93.* Previous to the last-mentioned crisis stocks began to fall, with unmistakable emphasis, early in 1892. Of seventeen of the most active, five reached their maximum price in January, 1892, three in February, four in March, two — Lake Shore and Michigan Central — in April. And as we have seen, identical preliminary warnings de-

* *Ibid.*, pp. 237–8–9.

veloped on the Stock Exchange from one year to six months before the last great panic of 1907.*

The panic that hit the Paris Bourse in October, 1912, causing a disturbance not equaled in violence since 1870, was brought about by sowing the wind through an immense public speculation based on two fine harvests in Russia and a feverish revival of commercial and industrial activity all over Europe. Up to this point all the indicia of the movement — such as bank loans, building operations, public and private extravagance, and

* The panic of 1837 was caused by a great expansion of banking and bank credits, and an intense speculation in real estate. In 1830 there were 329 banks in the country with a capital of $110,000,000. In 1857 there were 788 with a capital of $290,000,000. When the crisis was subsequently examined it was found that there had been an actual shrinkage of $2,000,000,000 in the value of the assets of the country, and that $600,000,000 of indebtedness had been wiped out by bankruptcy.

The panic of 1857 was due primarily to the influx of gold from California after its discovery in 1848, and to the intense passion for speculative gain which attended it. Suspension of specie payments by the banks lasted fifty-nine days. Complete recovery to the normal standard did not take place until 1860, when it was again interrupted by the events antecedent to the Civil War of 1861.

The antecedents of the crisis of 1873 were identical with every other commercial crisis — namely, speculation — the act of buying with a view to selling at a higher price, and overtrading, or the act of buying and selling too much on a given capital. Most commonly these two elements are accompanied by two others, viz. — the destruction or loss of previously accumulated capital, and the rapid conversion of circulating into fixed capital. Speculation and destruction of capital usually go together in preparing the way for a crisis. — Horace White, *Fortnightly Review*, Vol. XXV, p. 819.

The panic of 1893 was distinctly a currency panic. By a curious paradox it came at a time when the volume of currency was unprecedentedly large and constantly increasing. But the inception of the disaster had to do with its quality rather than its quantity. The repeal of the silver purchasing clause of the Sherman Law, November 1, 1893, restored confidence by assuring the commercial world that the existing volume of silver coin would be maintained on a parity with gold.

a blind infatuation for speculation by a normally prudent nation that had not speculated on a large scale since the Panama débacle of 1894 — corresponds exactly with conditions in America just preceding the 1907 crisis. The similarity between the two incidents goes even farther, for early in September of 1912 the French bankers and *Agents de Change*, recognizing the strained condition of credit, had deliberately put in motion corrective agencies designed to stop the rise with the least possible derangement of confidence.

They would have succeeded, no doubt, and the situation would have exactly paralleled our own discounting processes of March, 1907, but for the unforeseen Balkan difficulty which, coming out of a clear sky, upset the plans of the conservative financial forces and precipitated a panic. It came, as a French banker explained, a week too soon — by which he meant that, given a little more time, the worst phases of the disturbance would have been avoided through gradual and orderly liquidation. As it stands, the panic will no doubt go down into French financial history as "the Balkan panic," just as our disturbance of 1907 is ascribed, *faute de mieux*, to Wall Street wickedness; but in reality both the French and American crises had their origin in precisely similar causes. The Balkan news in

Paris only precipitated what the French Bourse had planned to accomplish in an orderly manner, just as Wall Street and the Stock Exchange had done five years earlier in a similar emergency. The essential lesson of both instances is that the same causes which generate prosperity will, if pushed far, generate an equivalent adversity.

The details of the panic of 1907 are still fresh in mind, and need be but briefly referred to. Banks and trust companies closed their doors and suspended payments to depositors. Cash and credit became almost unobtainable; we were face to face with demoralization. Clearing-house certificates were resorted to at practically all banking centres throughout the country; there was a general requirement of time notices for withdrawal of savings bank deposits; all normal credit instruments were impaired. The Secretary of the Treasury was forced to exercise heroic discretion in the matter of security for government deposits and for the very necessary increase of a note circulation that was then suffering from a spasm of contraction. There was an immense hoarding of funds and a consequent drying up of fluid capital, while from one end of the country to the other, there was liquidation, business contraction, retrenchment, panic, and ruin. "Wall Street" and the Stock Exchange had foreseen that the chain was only as strong as its weakest link, and had done what it could to prepare the public for the break. To assert at this late day that it did aught but its full duty is humbug *in excelsis*.

I have already cited one instance, the country's expanding bank loans as contrasted with "Wall Street's" contraction, to show how plainly the warning was conveyed. As another instance, take the immobilization of capital tied up in the enormous real-estate speculation then prevalent. In New York City alone the increase in mortgages recorded jumped from 455 millions in 1904 to 755 millions in 1905, an increase over the previous years of 32.7 per cent. and 66 per cent. respectively.* The figures showing the increase in building permits are similarly significant, revealing the fact that in 1905, 1906, and the early months of 1907, money was pouring into new construction at a rate without precedent. In Greater New York alone, not including Queens County, building permits granted in 1904 amounted to $153,300,000, and in 1905 to $229,500,000, and in the face of disaster this rate of increase continued up to the very eve of the panic.†

* *Real Estate Record and Guide*, 1906–7.

†Consult *Bradstreet's*, 1907; the *Construction News*, Chicago, 1907; the *Engineering News*, 1907.

Outside of New York the expansion in building operations was equally rapid and equally ominous, showing an *increase* in twenty-five cities alone from $201,300,000 in 1903 to $234,200,000 in 1904, to $280,400,000 in 1905 and to $307,800,000 in 1906 — all this but a small part of the actual funds thus locked up throughout the whole country.* We thus find that one of the most important and inevitable causes of the panic was the absorption of exceptionally large amounts of capital in enterprises that required a considerable time for competition, or which, when completed, were not immediately profitable; and to them may be added factories and extensive public and private works of every kind. This form of expansion, as Senator Burton points out, when carried to extremes almost invariably brings about a disturbance.

Now let us consider. Does all this expansion of bank loans outside of New York and all this tremendous increase of building operations show that the Samsons of "Wall Street" were pulling down the temple on their own heads in order to slaughter the Philistines, as alleged, or does it show an indifference and lack of readjustment to the growing stringency of money, as revealed by

* "The New York Stock Exchange and the Panic of 1907," by Eugene Meyer, Jr., *Yale Review*, May, 1909.

the Stock Exchange in its liquidation of March and April? "As a rule," said John Mill, "panics do not destroy capital; they merely reveal the extent to which it has been previously destroyed by its betrayal into hopelessly unproductive works."* There would have been no such "betrayal" had judicious reflection and a measurement of facts followed Wall Street's warnings.

A shrewd man, one of the old school of New York City wholesale merchants, who has nothing whatever to do with Wall Street or the Stock Exchange, yet whose trade arteries extend to many parts of the country, has long governed his business by the published reports of Stock Exchange transactions. If he sees there revealed a wholesome, normal, and conservative expansion in all lines of business and a money market that betrays no uneasiness as to the future, he presses on into new lines of endeavor, confident that the immediate future is serene. If he finds an urgent liquidation on 'Change, with the coincident phenomena of impaired credit instruments, he draws in his lines and waits. It makes no difference to him who is rocking the boat, nor why; experience has taught him that if it rocks, the time has arrived to go ashore. And this steady

* "Credit Cycles and the Origin of Commercial Panics," Manchester Statistical Society, December 11, 1867.

old merchant, I have no doubt, is but one of a numerous type.

Those who ignore the economic tides that ebb and flow through the medium of the Stock Exchange as they did in 1907, do so because they do not understand that these great market movements are really but expressions of natural laws. If there is a rising tide — a boom — it is attributed by thoughtless people to speculation and gambling. If there is a bad break, it is caused by panic-stricken repentant sinners, or by the activities of the bears. The essential point that is missed here lies in the fact that, while bulls and bears alike may have their brief hour, sooner or later, regardless of them, the market responds to actual conditions and discounts the future of those conditions.

Booms are not made on the Stock Exchange; they are made in the country's fields and forests and workshops. Panics are not created there; they have their origin in mistakes and excesses throughout the world, and in psychologic conditions which stock markets cannot hope to control. The pendulum may swing far, but it comes back. Sooner or later the movement of prices tells the exact story of future business, and of credit, and of all the economic agencies that enter into them. This was not well understood in 1907, and, as I said at the beginning, I doubt if it will ever be understood in the sense that it will avoid a recurrence of panics. All that we may hope for is that periods of depression, which are inevitable, may not be attended in future by such a loss of the reasoning faculties as that which brought about the affair of 1907.

Now let us consider another cause of the panic — the currency system, always bearing in mind the fact that the first and greatest cause of the panic was the over-expansion outside of New York that has just been described. The causes which we are now to consider were of minor importance when measured by this overshadowing matter; nevertheless they played their part and must be considered accordingly.

Not all panics, to be sure, can be prevented by a perfect currency system, yet this one could have been measurably prevented, and "Wall Street" and the Stock Exchange had labored for years so to prevent it. At the gatherings of the Chamber of Commerce, at the bank meetings, at all the meetings of merchants and manufacturers for years preceding 1907, the mischievous effects of our currency system were proclaimed and the ultimate outcome predicted. Congress was petitioned again and again to remedy those intolerable conditions, and to permit national banks to expand their circulation under proper safeguards, but without avail.

When the storm burst, a most impressive object lesson in practical finance resulted. What was at worst but a normal stringency of the circulating medium developed, when added to abnormal demands from the country at large, into conditions that created great alarm. There was no way by which the banks of the country could use the resources which they actually possessed to meet the urgent requirements of the hour. A great nation of enterprising people found itself — and still finds itself — compelled to do a banking business differing in degree, but not in kind, from the old-woman-and-her-stocking system of finance. The way our bankers got down on their knees to London and Paris in that emergency, frankly admitting their inability, under our old flint-lock laws, to handle a situation which foreign bankers meet without difficulty, is a subject at once painful and humiliating. Literally our bankers begged for help and got it. Some day we shall have to beg again.

Had the national banks of New York City enjoyed the right to expand their circulation in the manner provided by the plan of the American Bankers' Association, at least a part of the débacle would have been avoided. "The banks and trust companies of this city have in their vaults the largest store of good credit that can be found in any city in the world," said one of America's foremost economists as the panic raged, "but much of it is utterly unavailable because of our currency system. One of the trust companies that closed its doors has in its possession live assets amounting to over $50,000,000. All this credit is dead. It cannot do the work of a single dollar in the paying-teller's cage. What is wanted in a time like this is freedom to convert the credit of banks into a medium of payment that will satisfy the people."*

True enough, and just what the whole financial community, including the Stock Exchange, had been repeating for years. Currency issues which do not provide for *all* situations, including not only ordinary demands, but also such exceptional cases of shrinkage as this one was, can never be called perfect, nor even safe. There is no health in them.† The most effective and the most rapid means of regulating and protecting the general credit situation is by increasing or diminishing the volume of outstanding bank-note currency not

---

* Remarks of Joseph French Johnson, dean of the New York University School of Commerce, at the American Institute of Banking, October 25, 1907.

† Consult Burton, *supra*, pp. 109–110; Muhleman. "Monetary Systems of the World," pp. 128, 130, 135, 140.

covered by a reserve of gold or other lawful money. This method is employed successfully both in France and in Germany. The Bank of France and the Imperial Bank of Germany to some extent regulate credit conditions by acting as central banks of discount; but their most effective action is by increasing or diminishing the uncovered amount of their outstanding notes. When additional currency is needed as a circulating medium they supply this currency by issuing notes. When contraction of currency, or a check upon the further expansion of bank credits is desirable, they accomplish the result by diminishing the volume of their outstanding notes and by raising the discount rate. This system is as nearly perfect as any yet devised.*

Whether we shall ever succeed in adopting it, or something like it, in America, is the burning question in our banking offices to-day. Until something is done, the layman who distrusts the plan of a central bank and looks upon Wall Street with abhorrence, may find satisfaction in knowing that the average New York banker is the most worried and harassed man in American business life. With millions of other people's money in his possession subject to withdrawal

* "The Banking and Currency Problem in the United States," Victor Morawetz, New York, *North American Review* Publishing Company, 1909, pp. 87, *et. seq.*

by check at sight, and with millions of the best security in the world in his vaults lying absolutely idle and worthless so far as raising currency is concerned, he stands between the devil and the deep-blue sea. Anything that frightens his depositors, or even remotely suggests panic, gives him a cold chill. People who talk of manipulation by New York bankers as a cause of the panic of 1907 or any other panic are blind to the fact that any disturbance of normal conditions is the one thing that bankers would avoid as they would avoid the plague.

There was a third cause of the panic in the course pursued by the President. In some quarters it is still termed "the Roosevelt panic," and there exists a belief that the President by his actions and speeches played a large part in bringing about the crisis. Personally, I feel that this has been exaggerated. There had been, unquestionably, wrongdoing by certain corporation managers. The President, with a characteristic vigor not unknown to politicians, seized upon it as a theme for his speeches, and the "evils," the "malefactors," the "corruption" and "dishonesty" with which he bruised the air, raised a suspicion in many quarters as to the status and security of the whole financial situation and undoubtedly contributed to the frightened liquidation of the day. The impression these utterances produced abroad, where American securities were popular, was painful, and led one returning tourist to remark that Europe was acquiring the idea that we were "a nation of swindlers."

All panics are largely psychological, and this was no exception. The President's public speeches came at a time when emotion, apprehension, and alarm filled men's minds; and at a time when those irrational moods were most likely to exaggerate the difficulties that existed, and to conjure up difficulties that did not exist. Panics *seem* to come from lack of money, the real difficulty is lack of confidence, and it was to this that the President's course directly contributed.

I am of the opinion that, judged by his public utterances, especially his October speech at Nashville, Tenn., the President had not the remotest idea that such an awful shock as the panic of 1907 was imminent. He was not a student of economic conditions; he had no familiarity with crisis-producing phenomena; he had never seen a panic at close quarters. His speeches did not cause the panic, for that disturbance was foreordained; they served, however, to hasten it, to intensify it, and to keep it alive. Perhaps I may add that the sparks beaten by him from the anvil of political expediency at that unfortunate moment threw more light upon the President himself than upon the evils he condemned. Perhaps, too, that was what the President most desired. In any case, the fact remains that just as there is too much confidence in times of excessive expansion, so there is too little in times of unreasoning depression; and that the President's attitude aggravated the latter situations is undeniable.

But by what stretch of the imagination can the Stock Exchange be credited with playing any part in this third cause of the panic? If temporary depression results from exposure of wrongdoing among railroad, industrial, or financial institutions, nowhere in the land is execration poured forth upon the evil-doers more vigorously than within its four walls. Far from complaining, the Stock Exchange and the whole investment community welcome such exposures, despite their effect on the market, for the precise reason that their own protection and benefit, if nothing else, is promoted by it.

There was yet another reason for the panic, closely related to the attitude of the President. I refer to the predicament of the railways of the country as 1906 passed into 1907. Staggering under a load of traffic which sorely taxed their equipment, the managers of these properties cried aloud to the investing public for funds. But capital was not to be had. Tied up in real-estate speculation and in quarters whence it could not be easily recovered, the normal supply of capital was immobile and inert. What was worse, encouraged by the attitude of the President, an epidemic of radical anti-railroad legislation became manifest in the several States, new and onerous burdens of taxation were imposed, and a wave of distrust and suspicion regarding railway investments was created. Simultaneously the cost of wages and materials advanced — both characteristic phenomena indicating trouble — and, as a consequence of all this blockade, the ratio of net to gross in the matter of increased earnings fell from the normal proportion of about 40 per cent. in the first nine months of 1906, to less than 10 per cent. in the same months of 1907.

Railroads are public utilities that must continue to handle business offered them no matter what happens, and so, to meet all these abnormal demands, but one course was left open to them, and that was to raise funds by issues of new stock. This, of course, amounted practically to an assessment of stockholders; as an expedient it failed because "Wall Street" had already recognized the symptoms of disease. It was too late. Money and credit attract money and credit, and confidence attracts both. There was a shocking absence of confidence in the emergency of 1907, and the railroads suffered enormously by it.

With this matter certainly Wall Street had nothing to do; it could not in fact do more than it had just done in pointing out to the country at large, through a drastic process of liquidation, the obvious withdrawal of far-sighted investors from a situation that had become tense. Nor can the railroads be censured, because the great volume of business that confronted them was not created by them, and yet had to be transported by them. The fault lay, of course, in the wholesale and reckless expansion of all lines of industry, and in the immensely increased extravagance of public and private life.

I venture the prediction that when these conditions again prevail, as they must in a great and vigorous country like ours, the Stock Exchange will still be found sounding its warnings, but it will not do to hope that those who learned the bitter lesson of 1907 will profit by that experience, because the condition of *mental* disturbance which is a part of every panic cannot be regulated by the will, nor kept within bounds by the statute law. The one lesson we have learned from the predicament of the railroads in 1907 is that there is a tendency toward disturbance in large accessions either of business or of capital. "At intervals," says Walter Bagehot, "the blind capital of a country is particularly large and craving; it seeks for some one to devour it, and there is 'plethora'; it finds some one, and there is 'speculation'; it is devoured, and there is 'panic.'"*

Summarized briefly, I have attempted to show in the foregoing pages that the Stock Exchange for many months prior to the panic had been steadily liquidating and contracting, and had served notice on the country at large that the time had come to put a stop to the prevalent over-expansion. It has been demonstrated that instead of heeding these warnings the general business of the country, as evidenced by the increases in loans and commercial discounts and by an over-speculation in real estate and in public and private extravagances, continued to expand up to the very eve of the panic, and was stopped then and there only by sheer lack of capital. Nothing can be of greater importance in any consideration of the 1907 crisis than that its overshadowing cause was the attempt to do too much business on too little capital, and compared with this all other aspects of that situation are of minor importance.

I have shown that an antiquated currency

* "Collected Works," Vol II, p. 2.

system played a conspicuous part in the crisis, through contributory negligence on the part of our law-makers. The part played by the President has been cited as a third, though somewhat negligible, factor in sowing the seed of distrust, and also the trying position in which the great common carriers of the country found themselves after the seeds of distrust had been sown. These were the four causes of the panic of 1907.*

How well the Stock Exchange did its work in that great emergency is a matter of record. It did not close its doors; there were no failures; no relaxation of the protection afforded the public; no departure from the high standard of morality which is ever its goal. In one week, ending October 25th, 5,166,560 shares passed through its

* Senator Burton "Crises and Depressions," pp. 51, 52, enumerates the important indicia of crisis-producing conditions as follows:

(*a*) An increase in prices of commodities and later of real estate.

(*b*) Increased activity of established enterprises and the formation of many new ones, especially those which provide for increased production and improved methods, all requiring the change of circulating to fixed capital.

(*c*) An active demand for loans at higher rates of interest.

(*d*) The general employment of labor at increasing or well-sustained wages.

(*e*) Increasing extravagance in private and public expenditure.

(*f*) The development of a mania for speculation, attended by dishonest methods in business and the gullibility of investors.

(*g*) A great expansion of discounts and loans and a resulting rise in the rate of interest; also a material increase in wages, attended by frequent strikes and by difficulty in obtaining a sufficient number of laborers to meet the demand.

Not one of these indications of trouble was lacking in the period preceding the panic of 1907.

hands, representing, with the transactions in bonds, a par valuation exceeding $483,000,000.

Now, in the very nature of things, a financial panic is the inability of many debtors to meet their obligations, plus the fear that many others may be in the same plight. At such a time men hasten to sell for cash that for which there is the readiest market. Thus they sell securities because securities are immediately convertible; thus they turn to the Stock Exchange, because that is what Stock Exchanges are for. Hence it follows that in a crisis such as that of 1907 the ruinous decline manifests itself more sharply, and is felt more keenly, on the Stock Exchange than on the Cotton Exchange or the Produce Exchange. Men turn to it for first aid to the injured, and the greater the casualty list, the more marked is the disturbance of values. That this is not well understood by the public often unfortunately leads to suggestions of improper methods where none exist.

Finally, where do we stand? Orthodox economists like Wells talk of over-production as a cause of panics; currency experts bewail a lack of circulating media; theorists of the school of Jevons are driven to seek in sun-spots the potent force of all our harvests; Levi and Mill dwell upon the periodicity of panics and would fix their appearance by schedules of time; politicians and thinkers-in-embryo point the finger at Wall Street, and yet, with all that has been written, thirteen great crises at home and abroad within the last century show that we have not begun to get at these disturbances. Drought has been a cause of mischief, yet we have learned to irrigate and to conserve; epidemics have smitten us, yet we have mastered sanitation; floods have ruined whole territories, yet we have built dikes and levees. But every now and then, when business seems to be at its best, when merchants are dividing large profits, and when labor is best rewarded, a panic occurs and the whole structure collapses.

To say that Wall Street or Lombard Street or any group of men anywhere can bring such conditions to pass is to deny all the facts of experience. Depressions may come from any of a hundred causes, but panics originate in the mind; they are manias. Walter Bagehot gave up trying to prescribe for them because he realized that sudden frenzy is not an ailment to be foreseen and prevented. "But one thing is certain," he said, "that at particular times a great many stupid people have a great deal of stupid money;" to which he adds, "our scheme is not to allow any man to have a hundred pounds who cannot prove to the Lord Chancellor that he knows what to do with a hundred pounds." When thousands of people ignore all the warnings of experience, as they always will do; when with a blind misdirection of energy they sink borrowed capital in quagmires at fancy prices, as they always have done; and when, shorn of their all, they are simultaneously seized with a mania to denounce others for the consequences of their own folly, as they always must do, one cannot avoid the thought that perhaps Bagehot's humorous solution is the best that has been devised.*

---

* The student who wishes to inquire at length into the subject of panics, crises, and depressions will find useful aids in the authorities already quoted, and in the following additional works:

A. Allard, La Crise Agricole et manufacturiere devant la Conference monetaire de Bruxelles; Brussels, 1893.

A. Baring (Lord Ashburton), The Financial and Commercial Crises Considered; London, Murray, 1847.

C. W. Smith, Commercial gambling, the principal cause of depression in agriculture and trade; London, Low, 1893.

C. Wooley, Phases of Panics; a brief historical review; London, Good, 1897.

C. Juglar, A brief history of panics and their periodical occurrences in the United States; New York, Putnam, 1893.

E. Goodby & W. Watt, The present depression in trade, its causes and remedies.

Henry Wood, The Political Economy of Natural Law, Boston, Lee & Sheppard, 1894.

H. M. Hyndman, Commercial Crises of the Nineteenth Century; London, Swan Sonnenschein & Co., 1892.

H. Denis, La Dépression Économique et Sociale et l'histoire des prix; Brussels, 1895.

J. Eadie, Panics in the money market, etc.; New York, 1893.

Michael G. Mulhall, History of Prices Since 1850; London, Longmans, Green & Co., 1885.

R. Browning, The Currency considered with a view to the effectual prevention of panics; London, 1869.

The Pears prize essays. London, Chatto, 1885.

W. W. Lloyd, Panics and their panaceas; London, Harrison, 1869.

W. H. Crocker, The cause of hard times; Boston, Little, Brown & Co., 1896.

CHAPTER VII

A BRIEF HISTORY OF LEGISLATIVE ATTEMPTS TO RESTRAIN OR SUPPRESS SPECULATION

CHAPTER VII

A BRIEF HISTORY OF LEGISLATIVE ATTEMPTS TO RESTRAIN OR SUPPRESS SPECULATION

In the Middle Ages the notion prevailed that there was a just and equitable price for everything, and that any person who tried to obtain more than this price was a sinner. Trade for gain was anathema; the man who bought the principal commodities of that time, such as corn or herrings, with a view to selling them at a profit, was guilty of "craft and sublety" — as the old English statutes read — that infallibly cost him his goods and brought him to the pillory. Thus in the year 1311 one Thomas Lespicer of Portsmouth was caught red-handed in London with six pots of Nantes lampreys stored in a fishmonger's cellar in the hope of a rising market. The law required that when he arrived in London from Portsmouth with his lampreys he should proceed to the open market under the wall of St. Margaret's Church in Bridge Street, and stand there four days selling at current prices to any one who cared to buy. His failure to do so, and his wickedness in attempting to "bull" the lamprey market by hiding them in the fishmonger's cellar, resulted in the arrest of himself and the fishmonger, and their trial and punishment at the hands of the Mayor and Alderman.

Professor W. T. Ashley, who cites this incident in his "Introduction to English Economic History and Theory" (London 1892), also gives another instance in which our modern theories of natural rights and freedom of contract seem to be in hopeless conflict. John-at-Wood, a baker, was arrested in 1364 charged with the profane practice of "bulling" wheat. "Whereas one Robert de Cawode," the indictment reads, "had two quarters of wheat for sale in common market on the pavement within Newgate; he, the said John, cunningly and by secret words whispering in his ear, fraudulently withdrew Cawode out of the common market, and they went together into the Church of the Friars Minor, and there John bought the two quarters at 15½d per bushel, being 2½d over the common selling price at that time in the market, to the great loss and deceit of the common people, and to the increase of the dearness of wheat." At-Wood denied this heinous offence and "put himself on the country," whereupon a jury was empanelled, which gave a verdict that At-Wood had not only thus bought the grain, but that he had afterward returned to the market and boasted of his crime, and "this he said and did to increase the dearness of wheat." Accordingly he was sentenced to be put in the pillory for three hours, and one of the sheriffs was directed to see the sentence executed and proclamation made of the cause of the punishment.

So far as I am aware the Statutes of Henry III and Edward I, under which these culprits were punished, constitute the earliest official attempts to repress speculation by law. After the Revolution, the Bank of England having been organized and bank shares created, a speculative outburst occurred that led to the enactment of fresh legislation entitled "An act to restrain the numbers and ill practices of brokers and stock-jobbers,"* but this law lapsed or was repealed ten years later. In 1707 a law was passed licensing brokers and making it unlawful for unlicensed brokers to do business,† and in 1708 City rules were established for brokers, obliging them to give bonds for the proper performance of their duties. In 1711, 1713, and 1719, laws were enacted similar to the Act of 1707.

Then came the speculative schemes of 1720, of which the most famous or infamous was the

* (8 and 9 Will, III, Ch. 32.)
† (6 Anne, Ch. 16.)

South Sea Company, designed to make fortunes for its shareholders in the slave-trade and in whale fishing. It was followed by many other projects almost fantastic in their wildness to each of which the public subscribed liberally. Where all the money came from that kept this disastrous speculative mania alive is something one would like to know. There seems to have been no limit to it. South Sea shares stood at 120 in April of 1720; in July they had reached 1020, and, after that, the collapse. The company became a "bubble," and a burst one at that — and a great popular outcry followed. It resulted, in 1734, in the passage of Sir John Barnard's "Act to Prevent the Infamous Practice of Stock-Jobbing," the preamble reciting:

> "Whereas, great inconveniences have arisen, and do daily arise, by the wicked, pernicious, and destructive practice of stock-jobbing, whereby many of His Majesty's good subjects have been and are diverted from pursuing and exercising their lawful trades and vocations to the utter ruin of themselves and their families, to the great discouragement of industry, and to the manifest detriment of trade and commerce."

This act forbade bargains for puts and calls, and also "the evil practice of compounding or making up differences"; but its principal provision was the prohibition of short selling under penalty of £100 for each transaction. There was, of course, an appeal to the courts, which held that the statute did not apply to foreign stocks nor to shares in companies, but only to English public stocks, a decision that effectually put an end to the usefulness of the law. It remained on the statute books, however, and it was occasionally resorted to by persons who sought to evade the fulfillment of their speculative contracts — a class of persons known to-day as "welchers."

Finally, in 1860, the law was repealed altogether, the repeal act reciting that Sir John Barnard's Act "imposed unnecessary restrictions on the making of contracts for sale, and transfer of public stocks and securities." Thus the first serious attempt to regulate speculation in securities by law, and specifically to prohibit short selling, came to be recognized as a failure by the frank admission of government. In 1867 the so-called Leeman Act became law, prohibiting all sales of bank stock unless the numbers of the certificates sold were specified — an attempt to prevent short selling of bank stock. Even this law was subsequently repealed, and England, to-day, has no law on the statute books restricting speculation.

As the London Stock Exchange grew in influence and importance, reflecting England's development as the world's banker, popular attack and criticism continued to assail it. It may be frankly admitted that the legitimate functions of the institution had been abused by foolish or unscrupulous persons, just as every important branch of business and politics has been misused, the world over, since civilization began. The question therefore arose whether these occasional sharp practices proved the Exchange to be an excrescence on the body politic, or whether, on the other hand, its importance in the mechanism of modern business merely required improvements and reforms. In this situation, which occurred in 1877, and which caused considerable agitation on the part of both parties to the controversy, a royal commission was appointed "to inquire into the origin, objects, present constitution, customs, and usages of the London Stock Exchange." The Exchange and its critics thus reached the parting of the ways. A year was spent by the commission in examining witnesses and conducting investigations along special lines, and in 1878 its report, with the evidence, was published in a Parliamentary Blue Book.

The report absolutely upheld the purposes and functions of the Stock Exchange and the legitimacy of speculation in securities, and it went further in pointing out the danger of attempting to force any form of external control on the institution. The evils of that form of Stock Exchange speculation which closely approaches mere gambling were plainly stated, and the report suggested that the Exchange authorities restrain such practice in so far as was possible.

As the conclusions of the royal commission are of very great importance, marking as they do the first serious official study in modern times of the Stock Exchange theory, I quote from the Blue Book in the hope that Stock Exchange critics of to-day may understand how these conclusions were reached. "In the main," reads the report, "the existence of the Stock Exchange and the coercive action of the rules which it enforces upon the transaction of business and upon the conduct of its members has been salutary to the interests of the public. We wish to express our conviction that any external control which might be introduced by such a change should be exercised with a sparing hand. The existing body of rules and regulations have been formed with much care, and are the result of the long experience and vigilant attention of a body of persons intimately acquainted with the needs and exigencies of the community for whom they have legislated. Any attempt to reduce this rule to the limits of the ordinary laws of the land, or to abolish all checks and safeguards not to be found in that law, would, in our opinion, be detrimental to the honest and efficient control of business."

In 1909 similar criticism in New York having led to the appointment of the Hughes Commission to inquire "what changes, if any, are advisable in the laws of the State bearing upon speculation in securities and commodities, or relating to the protection of investors, or with regard to the instrumentalities and organizations used in dealings in securities and commodities, which are the subject of speculation," the commission reported to the Governor, after six months of laborious investigation, in these words:

"Speculation in some form is a necessary incident of productive operation. When carried on in connection with either commodities or securities it tends to steady their prices. Where speculation is free, fluctuations in prices, otherwise violent and disastrous, ordinarily become gradual and comparatively harmless. For the merchant or manufacturer speculation performs a service which has the effect of insurance. The most fruitful policy will be found in measures which will lessen speculation by persons not qualified to engage in it. In carrying out such a policy exchanges can accomplish more than legislation. We are unable to see how a State could distinguish by law between proper and improper transactions, since the forms and the mechanisms used are identical. Rigid statutes directed against the latter would seriously interfere with the former. Purchasing securities on margin is as legitimate a transaction as the purchase of any property in which part payment is deferred. We, therefore, see no reason whatsoever for recommending the radical change suggested that margin trading be prohibited."

Here are two reports at an interval of thirty-one years, made by independent investigators of high character, concerning the two foremost Stock Exchanges in the world. Both of these reports recommend changes and improvements, and each is firmly of opinion that the changes recommended are such as can be carried out by the Stock Exchanges themselves without the assistance or interference of the legislature.

As the London Stock Exchange is a voluntary association similar to that in New York, it was inevitable that the question of incorporation should have been brought before the royal commission of 1877, and that the question as to whether the public interest would be promoted by such incorporation should be given careful attention. As a result of these deliberations, a majority of the commission recommended that the London Stock Exchange should voluntarily apply for a royal charter or act of incorporation, but the reasons upon which this recommendation were based had to do with the temporary or shifting character of the membership, which gave very little assurance to the public of the permanence and stability of the rules, since members of the

London Stock Exchange are only elected for one year. It need scarcely be added that such an argument would not apply to the New York Stock Exchange.

Now it so happened that, despite this opinion by the royal commission, the London Exchange was not compelled to incorporate, and remains to-day a purely voluntary association or club. The reason for this lies, in large measure, in the very intelligent minority opinions filed with the Board's report by those of its members who dissented from the recommendation. As this is a matter of interest to members and friends of the New York Stock Exchange, I give herewith the substance of these dissenting opinions, calling the reader's attention to the fact that the Hughes Commission of 1909 rejected similar proposals regarding the New York Stock Exchange.* The Hon. Edward Stanhope, M. P., said, regarding the proposed application for a charter:

"Supposing such an application to be made, and Parliament to be prepared to incorporate the Stock Exchange on the terms which are embodied in the report, the consequence would be that rules so established would be stereotyped, and could only be altered, even in the minutest details, with the approval of a department of the State. In my opinion this requirement would be either mischievous or nugatory. To attempt to regulate the manner in which business is

* See appendix.

conducted in the great money market of England is going far beyond the province of the State, nor is any government department in any way qualified to undertake it. The report, indeed, recommends that external control should be exercised with a sparing hand. But experience seems to show that the first commercial crisis, or the discovery of any gigantic fraud, would cause a pressure for further restrictions which the department entrusted with these duties could not possibly withstand. If incorporation is to be anything more than a theory, it seems to me that it must either be imposed compulsory upon the Stock Exchange, or it must be offered to them on terms which will make it worth their while to accept it. The first alternative I reject, for the reason given by the select committee on foreign loans, that it would destroy that freedom which is the life and soul of the institution. If, however, any voluntary scheme commends itself to the opinion of the Stock Exchange, its primary condition should be to reserve to that body absolute liberty in the transaction of their ordinary business (as to which we are all of opinion that, speaking generally, no just fault can reasonably be found), and also the power of adapting their rules, with the utmost ease and freedom, to the varying wants of the time."

Mr. S. R. Scott of the dissenting minority was even more emphatic in his objections to incorporation. He said:

"In fixing my name to this report, I desire to make the reservations following: 1. With regard to incorporation, I object to recommend it for the following reasons: Hitherto, the Stock Exchange has been carried on with great success as a voluntary association, and has had a vigorous growth. It has not enjoyed a single legal privilege, yet it has thriven and the public have neglected more than one effort to establish an open market to resort to it for business, and to give it exclusive confidence. This royal commission has been sitting more than twelve months, yet no important or reliable evidence has been volunteered of a character adverse to the general practices or conduct of business on the Stock Exchange. If proof be required that the internal legislation and administration of the Stock Exchange enforce a higher standard of morality than the law can reach or enacts for the regulation of other trades, such proof is to be found in the fact that recently the committee of the Stock Exchange were assailed at law by a member whom they expelled on a charge of dishonorable conduct, the lawsuit being based on the ground that the action of the committee was not justified in law. The trial lasted seven days and proved abortive, the distinction between the standard enforced by the committee and the statutory provisions of the law not being appreciated by the special jury promiscuously selected from various trades, although quite intelligible to the judge. In maintaining this high standard the committee are compelled to go beyond the common law, binding their members to the observance of their rules and practices, even though not enforceable in a court of law. If, however, they should submit to incorporation, their rules would have to be assimilated to the law, and their freedom of action would be curtailed — results which might tend to cripple them in sustaining the standard alluded to, and operate in many ways as a hindrance to that rapidity of action which is an absolute necessity in critical times. Further, incorporation implies, in some sort, monopoly, and it remains to be proved that the public would gain by any restriction of the freedom of trade, even in stocks and shares. I adhere to the opinion expressed in 1875 by the Committee on Foreign Loans, on page 47 of their report, as follows: 'That such a body (the Stock Exchange) can be hardly interfered with by Parliament without losing that freedom of self-government which is the only life and soul of business.'"

As I have outlined elsewhere in this volume the cogent objections to incorporation of the New York Stock Exchange, it only remains to say here that the great argument against such a step consists in the Governing Committee's absolute power of summary discipline over the members, a power that greatly exceeds the authority of the common law, and one that protects the patrons of the Exchange to an extent that would not be possible if, under incorporation, members could invoke their constitutional prerogatives.* Said the governors in reply to a question of the Hughes Commission: "Appeals to the courts have been rare, considering the number of cases in which such power of discipline has been exercised, but we may well cite as substantiating in an extraordinary degree the fairness and right-mindedness with which members have been held to their obligations, the fact that, although in a number of instances appeals have been made to the courts for reinstatement by members who have been expelled or suspended for infraction of the rules, or for conduct which, although it might not be in violation of any express rule or regulation, or in violation of any law or legal obligation, the committee have held to be inconsistent with the maintenance and exercise of those standards of

* See p. 140.

honorable dealing which it is the function of the Exchange to inculcate and maintain; nevertheless, in the last twenty-eight years there has not been a single instance of the judgment of the Governing Committee being reversed by the courts."

The distinction between the expulsion of a member of such a voluntary unincorporated association and the expulsion or removal of a member of a corporation is very important. The moment the body receives a charter a different set of principles comes into play as regulating the relations between the member and the body.*

Germany dealt with a similar situation in very different fashion. In the autumn of 1891 there were disastrous failures of certain German banking houses, resulting from criminal misuse of bank deposits and from an undue participation in speculative transactions by the general public. The outcry that followed was no new thing in Germany, for as early as 1888 conditions that had arisen in the Berlin market and the Hamburg coffee market had led to petitions to the Reichstag

---

* For a legal opinion concerning the rights of plaintiffs arising from memberships in a *corporation* as contrasted with those arising from memberships in a *voluntarily unincorporated association* the reader is referred to White vs. Brownell (2 Daly at p. 337), opinion at Special Term by Justice Van Vorst; and the same case at General Term, opinion by Justice Daly. The courts of New York State have on a number of occasions expressed their approval of the manner in which the Stock Exchange has discharged its functions under this form of organization. The reader's attention is called to Belton vs. Hatch, 109, New York, 597, Court of Appeals.

demanding remedies for speculative evils. The cumulative effect of these difficulties was such that, as related by Doctor Loeb, bills directed against speculation on the Exchanges were introduced in November, 1891. "As early as February 16, 1892," according to this authority, "the Chancellor of the Empire appointed a commission of inquiry of twenty-eight members, most of them lawyers, but with representation also of landed proprietors, economists, and merchants. The chairman was the President of the Directorate of the Reichbank, Doctor Koch. The commission began its inquiries in April, 1892, held 93 sessions, and summoned 115 witnesses, of whom the great majority were persons engaged in the transactions which it was proposed to regulate. The commission also made inquiries as to the state of legislation and trade usages in the several states of the Empire and in foreign countries.

"The commission presented a majority report on November 11, 1893, recommending certain statutory and administrative changes. The principles on which these recommendations rested was that, in view of the importance of the interests which were represented at the Exchanges, modifications should be made with caution, and the existing complicated trade usages and methods should not be disregarded; while, on the other hand, there was no occasion for regarding with mistrust, still less with hostility, interference in the free working of industrial forces."*

Up to this point, it will be observed, the German investigators followed precisely the same lines as the English Commission of 1877 and the Hughes Commission of 1909. Mistakes are recognized, but modifications are to be made "with caution." But it so happened that the recommendations in this respect were not followed. German politics at that time were in a state of turmoil in consequence of the Agrarian agitation, and in the various phases of political expediency that attended the uproar, first the government and then the Reichstag insisted upon more and more stringent enactments concerning legislation against the Exchange, until finally a hostile law was enacted quite out of line with the original recommendations of the committee of inquiry. In other words, the politicians ignored the labors of the committee and took matters into their own hands. The three important provisions of this law were these:

(1) All exchange dealings for future delivery in grain and flour were forbidden.

(2) All exchange dealings for "the account" in the shares of mining and industrial companies forbidden.

* "The German Exchange Act of 1896," by Dr. Ernst Loeb, in the *Quarterly Journal of Economics*, July, 1897.

(3) An "Exchange Register" was established in which was to be entered the name of every person who wished to engage in exchange transactions for future delivery. Contracts made by two persons entered in the register were declared binding and exempt from the defence of wager.

The immediate effect of this law on the German grain market was disastrous. Futures were not suppressed. The grain trade was simply forced by the law to give up the modern machinery that experience had developed, and go back to antiquated forms of dealing. "It was like taking machinery out of a mill," says Frank Fayant, "and putting manufacture back to hand labor." As to trading in securities "for the account," here, too, the law failed utterly. Even the government — at that time most unfriendly to the Exchanges — admitted in its official reports that the law had "proved injurious to the public," and that "the dangers of speculation have increased." We have high authority for a detailed examination of the disaster attending this costly experiment in the remarks of Professor Emery, who tells us not merely *how* the German law failed, but *why:*

(1) Fluctuations in prices have been increased rather than diminished. The corrective influence of the bear side of the market having been restricted, the tendency to an inflated bull movement was increased in times of prosperity. This in turn made the danger of radical collapse all the greater in

proportion as the bull movement was abnormal. The greater funds needed to carry stocks on a cash basis further increased the danger when collapse was threatened. The result was an increased incentive to reckless speculation and manipulation. Says the report of 1907, "The dangers of speculation have been increased, the power of the market to resist one-sided movements has been weakened, and the possibilities of misusing inside information have been enlarged."

(2) The money market has been increasingly demoralized through the greater fluctuations in demand for funds to carry speculative cash accounts. The New York method is held in abhorrence by German financiers, who attribute to it, in large part, the wild fluctuations in New York call rates, the frequent "money panics" and the tendency to reckless "jobbery." In proportion as the new Berlin methods approached the cash delivery system of New York, these evils have appeared there.

(3) The business of the great banks has been increased at the expense of their smaller rivals. The prohibition of trading for the account made it difficult for the latter to carry out customer's orders because the new methods required large supplies of both cash and securities. Furthermore, an increasing share of the business of the large banks came to be settled by offsets among their customers, and the actual exchange transactions became a proportionally small part of the total transfers.

(4) This has a twofold effect. Business within the banks is done on the basis of exchange prices, but these became more fluctuating and subject to manipulation as the quantity of exchange dealings were diminished and were concentrated in a few hands. The advantages of a broad open market were lost. The object of the act had been to lessen the speculative influence over industrial undertakings. Its effect was to increase it.

(5) Finally, the effect of interference, increased cost, and

legal uncertainty was to drive business to foreign exchanges and diminish the power of the Berlin Exchange in the field of international finance. The number of agencies of foreign houses increased four or five fold and much German capital flowed into other centres, especially London, for investment or speculation. This in turn weakened the power of the Berlin money market, so that even the Reichbank has at times felt its serious effects.*

Concerning the "Exchange Register" (which the government has now abolished as a complete failure) and the effort to keep the public out of the speculative markets, Professor Emery says:

In one sense the fate of the famous exchange register is laughable, but in a deeper sense it is genuinely sad, for the object was a worthy one and the new scheme was adopted with high hopes. Its failure was inevitable, since it did not remove the temptation to speculate. The men who felt this temptation most, and whose position least warranted their yielding to it, were of course the very last men to have themselves registered. In fact the whole public revolted. The number of registrations never reached four hundred, which number would not begin to cover the banking and brokerage concerns. The number of "Outsiders" registered never reached forty. Even the conservative banks had to choose between giving up all such business and dealing with non-registered parties.

(1) The uncertainties of the new situation were most likely to exclude the cautious and well-to-do from participation in the market. The reckless gambler of small means was less likely to be disturbed in his practices.

(2) The act aimed to establish legal certainty by means

* "Ten Years Regulation of the Stock Exchange in Germany," by Henry Crosby Emery in the *Yale Review*, May, 1908.

of registration. It proved a direct incentive to fraud. The customer was not legally liable on his contracts; therefore, every reckless and dishonest little plunger, who could get a broker to trust him, could take a "flyer" with everything to gain and nothing to lose. Cases increased rapidly in the courts and the worst element of the public was active to the relative exclusion of the better. Instances even occurred where a man would play both sides of the market at the offices of two different brokers and simply refuse to settle on the losing contract.

(3) As affecting this phase of the question, references should be made again to the transfer of business to foreign exchanges. Morally and socially it is as bad for the German public to speculate in cheap mining stocks on the London Exchange as to do so at home. The flow of German funds into the market for South African securities would indicate a further way in which the purposes of the act were defeated.

(4) Finally, the question must be faced of the effect of eliminating the public from the speculative market even if it could be accomplished. It is supposed sometimes that such a result would be all benefit and no injury. On the contrary, the real and important function of speculation in the field of business can only be performed by a broad and open market. Though no one would defend individual cases of recklessness or fail to lament the disaster and crime sometimes engendered, the fact remains that a "purely professional market" is not the kind of market which best fulfills the service of speculation. A broad market with the participation of an intelligent and responsible public is necessary. A narrow professional market is less serviceable to legitimate investment and trade and much more susceptible of manipulation.*

It is not surprising that such a law, enacted to meet political clamor, in defiance of the recom-

* *Ibid.*

mendations of the committee, and in the face of all the economic experiences of the century, should have proved a fiasco in a double sense. Not only did it fail to accomplish its purpose, but, as we have seen, it brought about a new chain of evils vastly more distressing to German commercial development than all the evils that gave it birth. The report of the Deutsche Bank for 1900 said: "The prices of all industrial securities have fallen. This decline has been felt all the more as, by reason of the ill-conceived Bourse Law, it struck the public with full force without being softened through covering purchases of speculative interests." Four years later the same bank reported: "A serious political surprise would cause the worst panic, because there are no longer any dealers to take up the securities which, at such times, are thrown upon the market by the speculating public." In 1905 the bank again forcibly urged the revision of the law in these words:

"In our last report we referred to the great danger which may be brought about through delaying the revision of the Bourse Laws, and we are now pointing to it again because we consider it our duty to impress again and again a wider circle of the public with the economic value of the Stock Exchange and its important relation to our financial preparedness in times of war."

Again, the following year the bank kept pounding away on the same theme: "If it had still been necessary to furnish proof of the regrettable fact that the German Bourses are no longer able to accomplish their task — equally important to the welfare of the people as to the standing of the Empire — the trend of events during the past financial year in general, and the result of the last German Government issues in particular, would have furnished that proof."

Meanwhile, other leading financial institutions took up the same cry. Thus the Dresdner Bank in its report in 1899 said: "The danger which lies in the ban put on speculation, especially in the prohibition of trading for future delivery in mining and industrial securities, will become manifest to the public, if, with a change of economic conditions, the unavoidable selling force cannot be met by dealers willing and able to buy. It will then be too late to recognize the harmful effects of the Bourse Law." In 1902 the Disconto-Gesellschaft reports: "The unfortunate Bourse Laws continue to be a grave obstacle to business activity." And again in 1903: "The Bourse will not be able to resume its important economic functions until the restrictions upon trading for future delivery have been removed."*

The lesson to be learned from the failure of the German Bourse Law of 1896, and from the frank recognition of that failure as evidenced by the repeal of 1908, cannot be overestimated in its importance. It is inconceivable that law-makers of to-day may ignore such a warning. I have quoted freely from Professor Emery of Yale University in pointing out the deplorable results of that legislation because his study of the subject has made him the foremost authority. The remonstrances of the German banks and business men have also been cited because they were on the spot; they saw and felt the prostration of German business that followed swiftly on the heels of this law; they were a unit in pronouncing it a wretched failure. In the appendix to this work will be found the report of the Hughes Commission in which the ten experts on that board unanimously reported "the evil consequences" of Germany's experiment, its "grotesque" operation in practice, and its utter failure.

It is a simple matter for the querulous and discontented element of a community to reason along the lines of least resistance and demand the

* "The German Bourse Law," by G. Plochmann, *North American Review*, May, 1908.

enactment of laws to right every fancied wrong. But the patient study of such matters, the nice balancing of probabilities, the penetrating investigation of similar experiments elsewhere and the analysis of their bearing on the larger affairs affected by them — all this requires critical judgment of a high order. When such an issue is evolved laymen stand aside for a while, until the evidence of experts has been submitted to minds competent to decide in accordance with evidence.

Applying this principle to the ever-present menace of legislation in America directed against the Stock Exchange, we find each witness testifying to the fact that the German law of 1896, far from benefiting the public, injured it immeasurably. It put a premium on reckless speculation and offensive manipulation; it demoralized the money market; it choked the small banks and made virtual monopolies of the large ones; just in proportion as it stifled speculation it put an end to industrial undertakings that depend for their success upon the spirit of adventure and risk; it drove money and credit out of Germany and into London and Paris; it removed from the Berlin market the support of the bears, thus exposing the whole investment structure to violent collapse. The layman must consider this and the men who make our laws must look before they leap.

Speculators in the region of criticism, whether of theology or economics, who find themselves face to face with a fact too stubborn to fit in with their opinions or conclusions, have but two courses open to them: either to reconsider in the light of testimony the conclusions they have reached, or to denounce and discredit the inconvenient witness. In this instance the inconvenient witness cannot be denounced; his name is legion. Every merchant in Germany will tell you the Bourse Law was a sad mistake and will deplore its enactment. Nor can such witnesses be discredited; therefore the advocate who believes that in legislation lies the remedy for what he conceives to be the evils of speculation must perforce choose the other horn of the dilemma; he must reconsider.

It is a gratifying fact that in America, where law-makers are prone to enact a hodge-podge of laws on every conceivable subject, there has been no such serious mistake made by the Federal Government as that which occurred in Germany. In 1812, five years before the New York Stock Exchange was organized, an act was passed by the New York State Legislature entitled "An act to regulate sales at public auction and to prevent stock-jobbing," its essential purpose being the prevention of short selling — the bête-noir of all the early amateurs in economics. This was the only anti-speculation act ever placed on the New York Statute books. The act read:

> That all contracts, written or verbal, hereafter to be made, for the sale or transfer, and all wagers concerning the prices, present or future, of any certificate or evidence of debt due by or from the United States or any separate State, or any share or shares of stock of any bank, or any share or shares of stock of any company, established or to be established by any law of the United States, or any individual State, shall be, and such contracts are hereby declared to be, absolutely void, and both parties are hereby discharged from the lien and obligation of such contract or wager; unless the party contracting to sell and transfer the same shall at the time of making such contract be in actual possession of the certificate or other evidence of such debt or debts, share or shares, or to be otherwise entitled in his own right, or duly authorized or empowered by some person so entitled to transfer said certificate, evidence, debt or debts, share or shares so to be contracted for. And the party or parties who may have paid any premium, differences or sums of money in pursuance of any contract, hereby declared to be void, shall and may recover all such sums of money, together with damages and costs, by action on the case, in assumpsit for money had and received for the use of the plaintiff to be brought in any court of record.*

The effect of this law was precisely the same as that which followed the enactment of Sir John

*"An act to regulate sales at public auction and to prevent stock-jobbing," New York State Legislature, 1812.

Barnard's Law of 1734 in England; it did not prevent short selling, it accomplished no useful purpose, and it merely served to enable unscrupulous speculators to "welch" on their contracts. In 1858 it was repealed, and short selling, having demonstrated its usefulness in many ways, was thenceforth declared to be legal in a statute which read as follows:

> No contract, written or verbal, hereafter made for the purchase, sale, transfer, or delivery of any certificate or other evidence of debt due by or from the United States, or any separate State, or of any share or interest in the stock of any bank, or of any company incorporated under the laws of the United States, or of any individual State, shall be void or voidable for want of consideration, or because of the non-payment of any consideration, or because the vendor, at the time of making such contract, is not the owner or possessor of the certificate or certificates, or other evidence of such debt, share or interest.*

The United States Government's attempt to regulate or restrict speculation is confined to a single instance, the Gold Speculation Act of 1864, a law which enjoyed a brief existence of but fifteen days.† In 1864 there were large issues of paper currency that drove gold out of circulation and caused it to be bought and sold as any other commodity. Thus a large supply of gold fell

* "An act to regulate sales at public auction and to prevent stock-jobbing," New York State Legislature, 1858, repealing act of 1812.

† "Statutes at Large," Ch. 127 and Ch. 209, repealing Ch. 127.

into the hands of speculators, and as its price rose more than 100 per cent., the public jumped to the conclusion that this portentous increase was due to the operations of speculators, and that the rise could be stopped by prohibiting such practices, hence all gold speculation was forbidden by statute. As a fallacy this was monumental. Professor Hadley tells the story in this way:

> The effect was precisely the opposite of what had been anticipated. Every man who was engaged in foreign trade had to provide security for being able to make gold payments in the immediate future, if called upon to do so. Being prevented from dealing with speculators, he now had to accumulate a reserve of his own. This caused an increased demand for gold at a time when it was unusually difficult to maintain an adequate supply. Under two weeks' operation of the act the price of a hundred gold dollars rose from about two hundred paper dollars to very nearly three hundred. So obvious was its evil effect that it was hurriedly repealed as a means of preventing further commercial disasters.
>
> Again, in the early part of 1866, there was a rise in the price of gold, which was attributed by public opinion to the speculators. Their machinations were defeated, not by legislation, but by the issue to the market of a part of the gold lying in the Treasury of the United States. For the moment the price of gold fell and people rejoiced that the plans of the speculators had been defeated. But a short time later, when the war between Prussia and Austria caused a demand for gold in Europe, there were large exports of the metal, and its price arose by natural causes. The United States was obliged to buy back, at a decided loss, a part of the gold which the Treasury had so unwisely issued.

It turned out in the end that the operations of the speculators in anticipating the wants of the future would have prevented a loss to the country, and that the attempt of the Treasury to defeat those operations was attended with expense both to the government and to the mercantile community.*

Ex-Governor Horace White deals with the gold speculation of the '60's as follows:

During seventeen years the business of the country was regulated by the quotations of the Gold Exchange. The export trade of the country necessitated the selling of gold in advance of its delivery. A buyer of wheat or cotton for export would make his purchase according to the current price of gold, but he would not get his returns from abroad in some weeks. If the price of gold should fall meanwhile, he would be a loser. So, he would sell at once the gold he expected to receive later. . . . Black Friday and its evil consequences were due to the existence of a bad currency and a fluctuating standard of value. The Gold Room was at that time a necessity. Business could not be carried on without it, but it offered temptations and facilities for gambling which could not be resisted.†

In the various States of the Union, where law-making goes on all the time with surprising zeal, there is, of course, a bewildering array of crazy-quilt laws on the statute books dealing with speculation, but these are relatively unimportant. Some of the States, Wisconsin, Louisiana, California, Montana, North Dakota, and South Dakota,

* "Economics," by Arthur T. Hadley, New York, 1896.

† "Money and Banking," by Horace White, New York, 1895.

have laws similar to those of New York State, legalizing short sales of commodities and securities. Other States prohibit dealing in futures, short sales, corners, forestalling and speculation in general, and two States actually license bucket-shops*.

It by no means follows because of the failure of the German Bourse Law of 1896 and of all similar earlier attempts to regulate or restrict speculation, that the issue has become moribund and that nothing more will be heard of it. On the contrary, just as each one of these abortive attempts at legislation, and each of the Government Commissions we have described grew out of excess in speculation and consequent losses to the public, so, no doubt, future extravagance in the world of speculative undertakings will be attended by similar outcries and similar results. There were debates in Congress for three years over the Hatch Anti-Option Bill, and while this measure failed of enactment into law, something akin to it will no doubt come up again one day when the public is in the mood.

It is probably true that in such event the lessons taught by earlier legislative experiments, and particularly by the German fiasco, will have their

* In the appendix to his work, "Some Thoughts on Speculation," New York, 1909, Mr. Frank Fayant gives a summary of the laws of all the States, pp. 57–58. I am greatly indebted to this pamphlet for many authorities quoted in this chapter.

effect in checking hasty legislation; in any event it would seem impossible that the teachings of all the economists — scientific contributions to literature that to-day comprise a large library — can be ignored in any future discussion of this subject. Meantime, accepting as our major premise the enduring presence of speculation as a fixed and immutable characteristic of human nature the world over — there remains the plain warning to Stock Exchanges and their governors that fences must be mended as gaps occur, and that the control of the business in the interest of the public must be the loyal motive of all these institutions. It will not suffice to whitewash indefensible conditions, nor to hide from public scrutiny any detail of a business which that public is asked to support. Conversely, it may be pertinent to say that in the effort to remedy some of the evils of speculation the private citizen has his responsibilities as well as the stockbroker.

Looking forward toward the great questions of the future having to do with State regulation of industry and commerce of which the Stock Exchange is a part, the student finds no solution so satisfactory as the doctrine of *laissez faire*, assuming always that those in control of the business under scrutiny shall do their full duty.

Under this policy England has risen to unexampled commercial supremacy, while America, because serious mistakes have been made, finds its advocates of State regulation growing daily in number, with consequent danger to all its delicate commercial machinery. These tendencies, and the theories that lie behind them, have no place in our discussion. We may, however, turn with profit to the recent utterances of the world's foremost economists in our effort to study the probable effect of State regulation of the Stock Exchange in the light of the experiences cited in this chapter.

"The world has outgrown the time-worn conception of the citizens as the children of an all-wise and benevolent government. It has been realized that governments are not always benevolent and never all-wise, and that with the growth of capital and competition better results can be secured by the repeal of the complicated and often contradictory provisions which throttle production and check initiative. It was this that the French manufacturers meant when they told Colbert *laissez nous faire* and thus introduced a celebrated phrase. It has been found requisite, however, in recent times to modify both the theory and practice of *laissez faire* in order to safeguard the interests of various classes of society. The complex requirements of modern life have necessitated a governmental regulation of many business enterprises in behalf of the producers, of consumers, of investors, or of the general public. Interference is justified only as leading to a surer and greater general liberty."*

* "Principles of Economics," by Edwin R. A. Seligman (New York, 1905).

"It is true that many of the largest fortunes are made by speculation rather than by truly constructive work; and much of this speculation is associated with anti-social strategy, and even with evil manipulation of the sources from which ordinary investors derive their guidance. A remedy is not easy, and may never be perfect. Hasty attempts to control speculation by simple enactments have invariably proved either futile or mischievous; but this is one of those matters in which the rapidly increasing forces of economic studies may be expected to render great service to the world in the course of this century."*

"The old Corn Laws in restraint of dealing and speculation were in many ways analagous to the laws against lending money at interest or usury. Just as it took centuries of thought and of experimental legislation and practice to separate legitimate interest from unjust usury, so it took centuries to get rid of the odium attached to the trade of a corn dealer. It was not until the ninteeenth century that the restraints on speculation were abandoned."†

"All legislation against the speculative market is liable to prove disastrous. The trade in futures is, when carried on properly, a blessing to both the producer and the consumer."‡

"The great danger of all governmental interference is that it might go to injurious extremeties, as in the case of the German Bourse Law of 1896. The importance and delicacy of the mechanism of speculation in modern commercial life is a thing understood by few outside of the ranks of professional economists. Even the average broker probably,

* "Principles of Economics," Ch. "Progress in Relation to Standards of Life," by Alfred Marshall (London, 1890).

† "History of the English Corn Laws," by J. Shield Nicholson (London, 1904).

‡ "Economics," by Frank W. Blackmar (New York, 1907).

while he could give some minor reasons why the Stock Exchange is one of the essential factors of modern life, could hardly give a clear-cut exposition of its economic functions. This being the case, there is a certain class of hasty meddlers who would seek to check all dealings on stocks on margins, and all contracts for future delivery of products on the ground that they represent gambling contracts."*

"Speculation in securities is bound up in the closest way with the whole matter of the investment of capital and the accumulating of the necessary means for carrying out great industrial enterprises. Just in so far as the stock market has a speculative clientele, it becomes an open and broad market and facilitates the disposal of great issues of stocks and bonds which are necessary for the carrying out of the industrial undertakings of the present age.

"The limitation of this broad market must invariably prove a hindrance in the financing of the most legitimate enterprises, and any interference with the freedom of speculation must inevitably lessen openness of the market, If we attempt to secure the benefits while restricting the evils of speculation, through discriminating against certain kinds of transactions, we find it impossible to really discriminate in any way according to the form of the transaction, while, inevitably, by restricting the forms of commerce and of commercial methods, we put a severe handicap upon entirely legitimate enterprise. There is only one way in which speculation can be stopped altogether, and that is by giving up the system of private property and adopting the socialistic state.

"It will be seen then that speculation is not a product of stock and produce exchanges. Speculation existed long before them, and it was only when speculation from natural causes became more and more important that men engaged

* "The London *Statist*, discussing the State Investigation of the New York Stock Exchange, 1909.

chiefly in speculative trade, formed organizations in order to adopt a general system of rules for the conduct of such business. The real cause then of the modern exchange in modern speculation is to be found, so far as commodities are concerned, in the marvelous improvements in the methods of transportation and communication which have made the market for staple commodities a world market, in which prices are determined by the conditions of supply and demand of many different sections separated by thousands of miles. So far as speculation in stocks is concerned this has been the inevitable result of the enormous multiplication of securities, due to the extension of corporate methods to business, which in itself is the result of huge modern enterprises demanding contributions of capital from a large number of small investors. The material progress of the last half century would have been impossible without such investment. Such investment would have been impossible without the multiplication of such securities of varying values, and the multiplication of such securities inevitably brings about speculation.

"Speculation even on the part of the public, with all its evils, has a very important beneficial effect. Unless the public speculates to some extent the market will not only be very restricted but will be in consequence much more open to manipulation. The bigger and broader the market the less chances there are for rigging prices. It may seem a very high price to pay for the open market that the speculative spirit should continue on the part of the public, but it would be a mistake to suppose that speculation can be confined to a few great operators and still offer the benefits which the present market gives.

"From a study of the effects of speculation and the effects of all suggested methods of controlling it, the conclusion is almost irresistible that legitimate and illegitimate transactions are so closely bound together, and the whole business of speculation is so closely connected with the interests of actual commerce, that any interference with the delicate machinery by the blundering fingers of the law will diminish the beneficial elements of speculation without effectively diminishing its evils."*

---

* *Journal of Accountancy*, "Should speculation be regulated by law?" by Henry Crosby Emery (April, 1908).

THE FLOOR

View from the Visitors' Gallery. In the centre are the sixteen trading posts. The four smaller posts are telegraph desks, whence quotations are conveyed to the tickers. On the right is the Chairman's Rostrum. The booths in the back-ground contain the private-line telephones to the offices of members. The indicator boards on both walls display members' numbers, by which they are called to their telephones.

CHAPTER VIII

THE DAY ON 'CHANGE, WITH SUGGESTIONS FOR BEGINNERS

CHAPTER VIII

THE DAY ON 'CHANGE, WITH SUGGESTIONS FOR BEGINNERS

THE stockbroker's praises are never sung; if he has good qualities, one seldom hears of them. Doctor Parker once defined the Stock Exchange as the "bottomless pit": Doctor Johnson said a broker was "a low wretch"; politicians vie one with another in painting him a parasite and a social excrescence. Impatient idealists who would take a short cut to perfection assert that he is of no real economic value, and would enact laws to restrain him. In the novels and on the stage he becomes sleek, cunning, convivial, and slippery, while there is ever about him a rank smell of money and a Machiavellian sublety that enables him to get something for nothing. Without understanding him and without comprehending his devious ways, we feel somehow that he lacks what Lord Morley calls "original moral impetus," and that in some mysterious way there is a stratagem lurking in all his actions. When he enters the stage or the story we say:

> "By the pricking of my thumbs,
> Something wicked this way comes."

Members of the Stock Exchange are more or less familiar with Baron Munchausen and Mother Goose — for if rumor be credited both these characters live in Wall Street — so they accept with good humor the epic touch of playwright and novelist who thus take poetic liberties with them and their profession. But the iron enters into their souls when you term them non-producers and parasites, and long into the night they will debate it with heat, bringing down the lath and plaster on their detractors with the heavy artillery of all the orthodox economists, and painting in gloomy colors the picture of a commercial world without its great Exchanges.

At such times they become very earnest, and the listener, who perhaps never thought of it before, comes away at least partially persuaded that society as it is constituted to-day will have to undergo a very decided transformation before it can get along without the machinery of which these maligned persons are so important a part. It has stood the test of time; it has come to stay; its fundamental idea, economy and utility in trade, began with the Agora of ancient Greece and the Forum of Rome. If there is something apocryphal, then, in the tradition that derides the profession, here at least is evidence of its early origin, its growth, and its power of endurance. In any case, membership in the Stock Exchange is to-day the ambition of good citizens everywhere, and affords to many a father a solution of the question at once difficult and important, "What shall we do with our sons?"

There are arguments against such a career, of course, just as there are against all roads that lead anywhere this side Utopia, but nevertheless, a man with capital, average intelligence, and good health, daily contributing by his labor to the silent forces that ebb and flow within these walls, can do well on 'Change without sacrificing anything that makes for self-respect and without diminishing in any degree his value as a useful member of the community. Moreover, he is free from things sedentary and is brought into daily contact with men and affairs that broaden and instruct him. He becomes a thinking and observing person, one whose mind never becomes atrophied for want of material on which to feed. He must be equipped with patience and philosophy to enable him to endure, without losing his nerve, the long periods of dulness that are a sorry part of the business, but he will not complain of wasted days if he learns to know that waste time, like waste material, may be converted into valuable by-products; that just as manufacturers are vigilant in turning their scrap-heaps into commercial utilities, so, in his daily economy the Stock Exchange member may, if he has the right stuff in him, turn the ashes, slag, and refuse of the hour into things of practical value. Once he has learned to do this, the novitiate has surmounted the most serious obstacle in his profession.

His days on "the floor," as it is commonly termed, will bring him in contact with many different types. He will find here all that is finest in human character, and many withering things that are most fatal to it; these he may find anywhere, because there will always be men who carry all sail and no ballast, "men who cannot believe life real until they make it fantastic." But the Stock Exchange is a great leveler; infallibly its swift analysis of character will search him out, weigh him and measure him, and place him just where he deserves to be. Nowhere else among business men does this silent and sure appraisal of worth find a more perfect result. It has nothing to do with the size of one's purse nor the blue in one's veins; it takes no account of what a man has been nor of what his ancestors were. Commercial honor is what counts, and within these four walls it is raised to a high plane and maintained with reverence. They live a touch-and-go life, with quick changes and nerves all in action, but they make no mistakes when they analyze character in their great crucible.

Those brutal aphorisms, "money talks," "might makes right," "whatever is, is right," and all similar phrases, become meaningless in the matter-of-fact subordination of externals that one witnesses daily on 'Change, where life is stripped of all save elementals. It is character that "talks" here, not money; if might makes right, it is the might of decency and not of brute force or "pull"; whatever is, is "right" only so far as it conforms to the code of gentlemen and exalts the square deal. Unless a candidate understands this in its fullest sense, and is determined to make it his goal, he had better avoid the Stock Exchange. Conversely, we find in this critical atmosphere another reason why honorable men are ambitious to become members, for it is something inspiriting to have won the discriminating approval of a critical assembly abounding in experience and guided by good traditions.

The New York Stock Exchange is an association and not an incorporated body. It resembles a club in its organization, and hence through its governing board it exercises a control over its members that could not be maintained by differently constituted authority. From the moment a man signs that Ark of the Covenant, the constitution, and thereby becomes a member, he places himself, his partners, his customers, his employees, his books and all his business affairs unreservedly in the hands of the Board of Governors. This body, which is composed of members of the Exchange, is chosen in classes of ten, by the full Board at an annual election. It consists of forty members, divided into eleven standing committees, of some of which the President, Vice-President, and Treasurer are also members.

It has been urged in times past, by those who have not understood the peculiar powers of this Governing Board, that the Stock Exchange should incorporate in the manner provided by law, and thus place its affairs within the control of the State authorities, so that if mistakes occur and wrongdoing becomes evident offenders may be dealt with by the legal authority vested in the Courts. But the essential point altogether missed in this suggestion lies in the fact that the absolute power vested in the Board of Governors, by the existing plan, gives the Stock Exchange authorities vastly greater control over its members than any law on the statute books could possibly give. The Hughes Commission, which went thoroughly into the affairs of the Stock Exchange in 1909, recognized this fact, and its report emphasized the point that if changes were necessary they should come from within the Exchange itself, because of the broad control vested in it by its constitution.*

The manner in which the Board of Governors handles offences as they occur, and the way punishment is meted out, would not have a constitutional leg to stand on if, as an incorporated body, offenders could invoke their legal privileges. Under its present organization, for example, the Board may, if it sees fit, intercept and cut off a member's telephone connection; it may dictate with whom he may or may not do business, and in its wisdom it may determine how, when, and where that business shall be conducted. If it were an incorporated body and each offender could resort to the courts in instances such as I have cited, what would become of its rules, and how could the Exchange authorities maintain its absolute determination to protect the public at all hazards? Under the existing system, which true friends of the Exchange and of the public may well wish to see maintained, the governors are enabled to find the direct way and the commonsense way, without being blocked by a jungle of legal technicality. They are not to be delayed

---

* The London Stock Exchange is also an unincorporated body. See pp. 231 *et seq* for the report of the royal commission bearing on this matter.

or restricted by alibis, by pleas of immunity, or by States' evidence, nor are they to be interfered with by the rain of legal writs through which an accused man, in the courts, may twist and double and block and delay the punishment for his sins, if sins there be.

Wonderment is often expressed by men in other lines of business at the severity of the punishment sometimes inflicted by the governors in this autocratic control. To expel or even to suspend a member, and thus bring upon him great pecuniary loss as well as disgrace, all because of an offence which might go unpunished in other professions, naturally seems to an outsider to be unnecessarily severe. The answer to this is, of course, that the governors, recognizing their great duty, accept as a public trust the power and the ability to maintain it. No matter whose head is hit, the rules will always be vigorously enforced because they are designed to protect the public — a public, I am sorry to say, that has not always tried to understand what the Exchange stands for. That is why no statute of limitations can interfere to protect any one of its members from the penalties that attend a departure from the straight line of business morality. A rigid enforcement *from within* is the only efficient way, and no one who knows the governors and their arduous labors on behalf of the principle for which the Exchange stands can ever doubt it. The members themselves, no matter who is punished, are a unit, and an enthusiastic unit, in upholding the disciplinary action of the governors every time.

The best course for a young man to pursue who wishes to become a member is first to spend a year or more as clerk in a well-regulated broker's office. The business is by no means intricate, and there are details with which he should familiarize himself. If in future years his partners are absent, he can then go over his firm's books and acquaint himself, as he should, with all its affairs. A dishonest partner could ruin him, or, what is worse, disgrace him, for the governors recognize no distinctions as between partners, nor is ignorance accepted as an excuse. Office partners who are not members of the Exchange do not always understand the rules, nor the rigorous spirit in which they are enforced, and just as the Board member is held accountable for his partners, so he must pay the penalty for their misconduct.

This means that a member must choose his partners carefully, must familiarize himself with what they are doing, and must know how to read every entry on the firm's books. Then, too, it is immensely satisfactory to one who has been on the floor all day and more or less out of touch with his office details to learn of his own knowledge each day, before he goes home, just where the firm stands. He looks over the customers' accounts, the loans, and the nature and amount of the firm's unemployed resources, including its balances at the banks. Such a man sleeps well, and reduces to a minimum the anxieties that, at critical times, make of this a nerve-racking occupation. It is all simple enough, and in the modern methods of office economy in bookkeeping he can do it without loss of time. Above all other considerations, such a man knows his business thoroughly from top to bottom, and he should not think of investing his capital on any other basis.

Perhaps a word will not be amiss regarding partnership agreements. A Stock Exchange commission business is one that should be conducted like any other business — that is to say, reserves should be laid aside and surplus balances created for the inevitable rainy day. That this is not done by all brokerage houses in the way it should be done is due to the curious habit that has grown with the years, whereby stockbrokers spend their money, uptown and down, with a lavish hand. Too many men of the younger generation thus give hostages to fortune in their private extravagances by "drawing down" their credit balances as fast as they accrue. "Easy come, easy go," seems to be the guiding principle, and when hard times come, as come they must, debit balances are created that soon eat into capital account.

No hard and fast rule can be laid down to meet conditions like these, but the best method I have seen, and the one most wisely designed to avoid mishaps for beginners, consists in a partnership agreement by which each member of the firm may draw a monthly sum, worked out to meet his normal requirements, *and no more.* All that remains is then turned into capital account, where it draws interest, becomes a producer, and grows by what it feeds on. I have in mind a firm of young men who some years ago resorted to this method of compulsory saving, with such success that, despite the vicissitudes of the passing years, the members comprising it are now all wealthy, attributing their good fortune wholly to this wise and provident copartnership agreement.

New York Stock Exchange memberships are obtained in only one way. Having assured himself that he can meet the requirements of the Committee on Admissions, and having provided himself with two sponsors, the candidate enters into negotiations with the secretary of the Exchange for the purchase of a "seat," as it is termed. As there are only 1100 members, and as the membership is always full, he must either purchase the seat of a deceased member, or make a bid sufficiently high to attract a seller. He may, of course, subject to approval by the committee, inherit a seat or acquire it by private transfer, but the customary process is to buy openly through the secretary, a salaried officer of the Exchange, whose authority in matters of infinite detail is such as to make him a mighty power in executive affairs. Thereupon he pays over the purchase price, together with an initiation fee of $2000, and presents himself and his sponsors before the Committee on Admissions.

This committee first calls his proposer, and then his seconder, and they are subjected to a careful inquiry as to how long they have known the candidate, and whether in a business or social way; his qualifications for membership, his health, his character and reputation, and his previous business experiences are all subjected to a microscopic scrutiny. His sponsors are also asked if in the ordinary course of business they would accept his check for $20,000.* If the answers

* The question put to sureties on the London Stock Exchange is, "Would you take this man's checque for £3000 in the ordinary way of business?" to which an unprepared sponsor once replied, "Well, I should not pick it out."

A similar question by the governors of the New York Stock Exchange once met with the reply, "Yes, but I would have it certified as quickly as possible."

to these questions prove satisfactory, the candidate himself is summoned and put through a similar examination. As his name has been publicly posted on the bulletin board for two weeks, anything detrimental concerning him will probably have been communicated to the authorities before he is examined, but if not, provided he proves satisfactory and the particular department of Stock Exchange work which he proposes to undertake meets with the approval of his inquisitors, and provided also his partners are not objectionable, he is elected to membership after he signs his name to that *magnum opus*, the constitution.

The price paid for memberships in recent years has varied widely with the condition of the times and the state of the stock market. In the halcyon days of December, 1905, and the opening months of 1906, there were several transfers at $95,000, the high-water mark. Following the panic of 1907 seats declined in December of that year to $51,000 and rose again in 1909 to $94,000. The only dues are $100 annually, together with $10 voluntarily paid by members to the heirs of each of their deceased colleagues, but this amount is, under the regulations of the Exchange, limited to $150 annually, the balance, if more than fifteen members die in any one year, being paid out of reserve funds. The sum of $10,000 which thus accrues to the heirs of deceased members is, of course, much cheaper than any other form of insurance. The Exchange is enabled to maintain it by the $10 contribution as described, and the general fund is kept intact because the 1100 members actually contribute $11,000, of which the extra $1000 is set aside as a reserve, which is prudently invested.

If we accept the fallacious argument that a thing is worth just what one can get for it, there can be no argument as to the value of Stock Exchange memberships, but that is not the way to approach the subject. It may be said with certainty that no matter how much has been paid in the past, or how much may conceivably be paid in the future, a purchaser who devotes to his business the same time and labor that he would devote to any other business in which a similar capital was invested will always be able to earn a good return. Those awful periods of stagnation will appear now and then, and accidents in the shape of losses will occur and return again to plague him, but, nevertheless, the hard worker will find no cause for complaint when he sums up, let us say, a five-year average. This is demonstrated by the fact that it is only on rare occasions a Stock Exchange member changes his vocation, which is another way of saying that memberships are held at high prices because holders are prosperous and will not sell.

In considering the value of Stock Exchange memberships it is important to include the "unearned increment" that goes with them. Despite all that may be said against it by members themselves, who in dull times denounce their calling with cynical extravagance, membership carries with it certain undefined advantages. It is a centre of the financial world in America; the business is one that quickens enterprise and encourages adventure; it undeniably gives a man a certain standing and character among his fellows; he is always abreast of the times, his hours are not long, he acquires habits of deduction, analysis, and observation that sharpen his wits and give zest to life; he is surrounded at all times by a great storehouse of wit, wisdom, and experience, and from the very nature of his business he is often brought into contact with important news of which he can take advantage and which may lead to highly profitable opportunities for investment or speculation. He would be less than human if he did not avail himself of such opportunities, and the business would lose much of its enjoyment; indeed "the tranquillity of dispassionate prudence" of which Goldsmith speaks may easily be carried too far on 'Change.

When a newly elected member makes his appearance on the floor he is taken to the rostrum by one of his sponsors, who introduces him to the Chairman. That formality concluded, he is greeted by shouts of "New Tennessee," and is instantly surrounded by a howling mob of young members bent on initiating him. The origin of this war-cry, "New Tennessee," is an enigma one would like to solve, but it is lost in obscurity. Even the board-room antiquarians have no clue. One of the members tells me that his grandfather, who was a member of the old Exchange that stood at the corner of Wall and William streets in the early 1830's, often told him that the phrase was in use then, just as it is to-day. Its early origin, at least, is thus established, and one's curiosity concerning it is proportionately increased. However it originated, it remains the popular slogan, and when a shrill-voiced member in any part of the room cries out above the din, "New Tennessee," there a crowd of the boisterous younger element gathers to welcome a new member.*

To-day, thanks to the prudence of the Com-

* A similar cry, "Fourteen hundred," was long used for the same purpose on the London Stock Exchange. For a time there were but 1399 members, and each stranger who appeared was thought to be number 1400. Hence, the words came to be applied to all new members, long after the membership exceeded that figure.

mittee of Arrangements (which has charge of the board-room discipline), the hazing of new members is confined to harmless pranks, but up to a year ago the process was a severe one. Newspapers rolled into clubs were used to beat the novitiate over the head; he was pelted with everything within reach; his collar and tie were torn off, and after a hundred strong young men had thus jostled and mauled and pounded him all over the room, he was a sorry sight. It began to be felt, after a peculiarly severe hazing of this sort, that something might happen one day to bring reproach upon the Exchange and sorrow to the members themselves, so the committee wisely put a stop to the practice.

When the new member settles down to serious work he will find open to him several different methods of doing a brokerage business, and in this respect the New York Exchange differs widely from those abroad. In London, for example, there are but two classes, jobbers and brokers, to only one of which a member may belong. Until very recently the distinctions between the two classes were but vaguely defined, and even now frequent undercurrents of resentment are aroused between them because of the alleged encroachments of one class upon the domain of the other. In Paris, where the seventy

Agents de Change enjoy an absolute monopoly by government authority, there is very decided opposition by the less fortunate members of the fraternity, and there are many who predict that the friction and dissatisfaction which monopolies arouse in this day and age will sooner or later bring about a reformation of the French system.

Here there are no such distinctions, and no friction. A member may be any one of several different kinds of brokers, or he may be all of them at once, if his arms and legs will stand the strain, and if his financial resources will enable him to meet the losses arising from mistakes. These mistakes are a sorry part of the business, and they are bound to occur every now and then, no matter how careful a man may be, but I have observed that they come about most frequently in the case of men who try to do too much.

A man may, if he chooses, become a partner in a commission house, and confine his time to the execution of orders for his firm's customers. For these services his firm receives and is compelled to collect, by the rules, a commission of one eighth of 1 per cent.—that is to say, $12.50 per hundred shares. Or he may be a "specialist," and establish his headquarters at some one spot in the room, and do nothing but execute orders entrusted to him by his fellow-members in the one stock or group of stocks situated at that particular spot. For his services in these transactions he receives a commission of two dollars per hundred shares, to which is added $1.13 if he is required to "clear" the trade — that is, to receive or deliver the stock. The latter is called "three-and-a-shilling business," or "clearance business."

The vocation of the specialist is one that causes frequent comment and ill-merited abuse. It has been charged that he sometimes exercises arbitrary power in executing his orders, and complaint is heard that the price at which he deals is not always a fair price. My observation is that four times out of five the fault lies, not with the specialist, but with the broker who gives him the order. The latter has been trying to do too much, he has held the order in his hand whilst engaged elsewhere in the hope of saving the commission for himself, and then, when he has "missed his market," turns the order over to the specialist and shifts the responsibility to his shoulders. This is scarcely fair, and it simply should not happen. The customer protests at the delay and at the price; he is told the specialist is responsible, and straightway another voice joins the chorus that holds the specialist in abhorrence.

Like the chairman of the House Committee of

a club, the specialist is made to bear everybody's burdens; he is the target for all the criticism that any one chooses to hurl at him. And yet he is one of the most useful and indispensable features of the Exchange machinery. Without him there would be no market whatever in very many securities; like the London jobber, he is constantly on the spot, ready to take chances by creating at his personal risk a market where none may have existed. If it be urged that the specialist should not speculate, but should confine himself solely to executing the orders on his books, it may be answered that in such a case he would often be useless, for in many instances the orders on his books are insufficient in volume to establish a close market or anything approaching it. By reason of his speculations a market is created; without them it may not exist. He speculates, therefore, for the same reason that jobbers in the London market speculate, and dealers in wheat, cotton, and wool. Like them, he must have goods on hand to supply the demand, and in the purchase of these goods (securities) he speculates, legitimately, on the hope or belief that buyers will appear.

If the new member chooses, he may become what is known as a "two-dollar broker," with a roving commission, executing orders for members in any part of the room at $2 per hundred shares. The "two-dollar man," as he is termed, is a hard worker above his fellows. He labors for a minimum wage; he must work every day or forego his revenues, for he cannot delegate his orders to any one else and receive a commission for these vicarious services. He takes big risks, because he has many orders from many different houses; the least inattention means loss. I have known one of these two-dollar men to lose $10,000 on a mistake on a 500-share order from which his commission was but $10. He is supposed to be a mine of information concerning floor gossip; his value to the houses that employ him lies quite as much in his ability as a newsgatherer as in his skill as a broker. He is on the jump every minute. The one redeeming feature of his business is that he has no office responsibilities, and none of the burdensome — and sometimes painful — duties that attend the stockbroker's relations to his clients.

There are perhaps fifty "odd-lot" brokers on the floor, and a member may, if he pleases, take up this branch of the business. It has to do with the buying and selling of fractional lots of securities, on which no commission is charged because the peculiar nature of this business enables the broker to trade against his commitments as they arise, and thus obtain compensation for his services in the resultant profit. In a small way the odd-lot broker, like the specialist, resembles the London jobber. One of the houses that confines its operations to this "odd-lot" business has nine partners, seven of whom are members of the Exchange; another has seven partners with six board-members. The fact that two such houses should have a million dollars invested in memberships, to say nothing of the large sums employed as capital, speaks eloquently for the volume of business they are called upon to handle.

This business, which includes fractional lots of securities from one to a hundred shares, is one of the most important on the floor, since it represents, very largely, the purchases and sales of an army of small investors all over the world. To such customers, very properly, the Stock Exchange gives the best it has, safeguarding their interests with quite as much care as it bestows on the greatest of market operators. The handling of all the odd-lot orders that accumulate in a busy day, the skill required in the office-machinery, the vigilance of the floor expert, and the foresight necessary to conduct the trading operations of the firm make this a most fascinating business.

Another field to which a member may turn is that which has to do with transactions in bonds.

The "bond-crowd," as it is called, makes its headquarters on a platform under the east gallery. There are about fifty of these "bond-men," and the compensation paid them for their service is the same as that paid on stocks, ten thousand dollars in bonds being reckoned equivalent to 100 shares. As there are twice as many bonds as stocks listed on the Exchange, one would think a larger number of brokers than this little coterie would be required to handle the transactions, but, despite this disparity in the relative size of the lists, it so happens that very many of the listed bond issues are rarely dealt in, and hence there is no surplus business. Moreover, brokers from all parts of the room are constantly executing their own bond orders without having recourse to the assistance of brokers who make this department a specialty.

Still another opportunity presents itself in the business of arbitraging. The arbitrageurs stick closely to the rail along the south wall, where there are pneumatic tubes connecting with the cable offices downstairs. Their business is one that calls for the utmost speed, since it involves taking advantage of fractional differences that arise from time to time in the prices of stocks that are listed on foreign Bourses as well as on the New York Stock Exchange. Thus Canadian

Pacific may sell at 270 in London and at the same time at 269½ in New York, and as an excellent cable service keeps pace with these fractional differences, the arbitrageur may buy in New York and sell in London and receive a confirmation, all within three minutes.*

Because of its complexity and its risks, arbitraging is not a business that appeals to beginners on the floor. One must have reliable colleagues on the foreign Exchanges who are constantly watchful and alert, and who are moreover possessed of sufficient capital to finance large transactions. In addition, there are labyrinthine difficulties to surmount in the way of commissions, interest charges, insurance of securities in transit, fluctuations in the money markets abroad and at home, cable tolls, letters of confirmation, rates of foreign exchange, settlement days, contangoes, and many other matters. Unless a man has had a long experience in the difficult art of arbitraging, he had better shun it or prepare for trouble.

Finally, in determining what branch of the Stock Exchange business he will undertake, a member must consider that numerous and shifty

* The celerity and accuracy of the cable service between New York and foreign centres, as perfected in arbitraging, has no parallel elsewhere. Twenty minutes are often required to complete a cable transaction between the London Stock Exchange and the Paris Bourse, and so it frequently happens, where speed is required, that messages between those two centres are cabled by way of New York.

contingent known as "floor traders." These gentlemen afford an interesting study. They do not accept orders; each man is in business for himself. They entertain no illusions, and they recognize no alliances with each other. Each one follows his own inclinations, and does not permit himself to be moved by tips, or rumors, or gossip, or sentiment. He scoffs brazenly at all forms of "inside information." His power of observation is keen, and his habit of analysis and deduction is wonderfully developed. In the surging crowd around an active stock he sees things with microscopic eye, and acts with surprising promptness; once his conclusions are reached, speed and agility are relied upon to do the rest. Age cannot wither, nor custom stale, his infinite variety. He is a bull one minute, and a bear the next. He is intent, resourceful, suspicious, vigilant, and ubiquitous. He asks no quarter, and gives none. Now he is sphinx-like, deaf, inscrutable and impenetrable; now exploding with the frenzy of battle. You may stand and chat with him, and he may seem to listen to you. In reality he does not hear you at all. His roving eye is elsewhere, his mind is intent on other things. In the middle of a sentence he may leave you abruptly and go tearing from crowd to crowd like a thing possessed, the incarnation of energy.

Visitors in the gallery who look down upon the scene on the floor in active markets, when all the Stock Exchange elements just described are striving at their utmost, come away in wonderment. The scene is one they do not understand. Such tumult is foreign to anything in their experience, and in their failure to recognize the economic forces at work in the animated panorama before their eyes they are prone to form superficial and erroneous opinions. The disorderly nature of the work seems to impress the visitor forcibly, yet the Stock Exchange is perfectly orderly; transactions involving millions come and go without the slightest friction. Nothing could work more smoothly.

It does not occur to the uninstructed spectator that mighty forces are here at work in establishing values; that the object of the Stock Exchange is to safeguard investors; that it is the one unobstructed channel through which capital may flow from sources where it is least needed into those where it may be most beneficially employed. The casual onlooker often gives no thought to the high standard of commercial honor that is maintained here; he does not realize that his own affairs, whatever they may be, would face a serious situation were this very important part of the modern mechanism of business to suffer interruption. And so it sometimes happens, in his hazy and nebulous impressions of the Stock Exchange as gathered from the visitors' gallery, that this man's mind is fertile ground for the seed which may be sowed there by every genteel humbug, demagogue, or quack whom he chances to meet.

It may be admitted freely that the facilities afforded by Stock Exchanges, like all other great public utilities, are sometimes foolishly or dishonestly abused, but by no stretch of the imagination can such abuses attain to the mischief done by those who would deceive people into the belief that the Stock Exchange, because it deals with large affairs in a large way, has some improper quality about it. Many minds, many hands, and many hours of patient labor have been bestowed on the making of the chronometer which is a vital part of a great ship; yet a child may "put it out of business," and destroy the ship's company.

That these observations apply to the New York Stock Exchange need not be elaborated when we consider that one third of our nation's wealth is represented by its securities; that there are two million owners of them; and that, through the widespread publicity of Stock Exchange quotations the world over, all these owners are given gratis the epitomized judgment of experts as to the value of those securities each day and their prospective value in the future.*

The Stock Exchange is open for business from 10 A.M., to 3 P.M., and on Saturdays from 10 to 12 noon. The broker reaches his office between 9 and 9:30 A.M., looks over his correspondence, makes a mental note of the general status of the firm's affairs, glances at the morning's news that is rapidly reeling off the ticker, reads the prices cabled over from the London Stock Exchange which has been in session four hours, and thus in a general way acquaints himself with what may be expected at the opening of the New York market. The two-dollar broker and the specialist do not concern themselves greatly with such matters, and frequently they go directly to the floor without stopping at their offices.

By 9:45 A.M. the Board is beginning to present a scene of animation. Of the 1100 members not more than 600 are in attendance, and often not more than 400; indeed, there are members who have never once entered the room. But the attendance is increased by the presence of some 230 pages in uniform, wearing five-year service stripes, of which the sleeve of the superin-

---

* Consult "The World's Wealth in Negotiable Securities," by Charles A. Conant, *Atlantic Monthly*, (July, 1908).

tendent is adorned with eight; 30 telegraph operators, whose business it is to hurry from place to place gathering quotations as they occur, and sending them out over the ticker, and by 550 telephone clerks who occupy the long booths on the west wall, where private lines connect members with their offices.

These clerks are not permitted to go on the floor. Their employers, who rent the telephones from the Exchange, pay $50 annually to the institution as a fee for each clerk. As their duties are extremely important, involving the transmission by 'phone of orders and reports that often run into millions, it will be seen that this small army of private line operators is of necessity highly trained. An instant's relaxation or inattention, or a failure to transmit promptly and correctly the verbal messages entrusted to them, may conceivably lead to confusion and losses of great importance.

At each of the sixteen posts in the room, from twenty to forty stocks are situated, and another group covers the north wall. Once a position is assigned to any security by the committee in charge, it is seldom moved elsewhere, and thus, although there are nearly six hundred different issues of securities, the broker soon learns the location of each one and turns automatically in that direction when an order reaches him. At each of the posts, and along the north wall, the specialists in these various groups of stocks are at work before the opening of the market, entering the day's orders in their books, some with the rapid energy that betokens an active opening, others with an indifference that spells dulness in their particular line.

At Post 4, in the northeast corner, there is also an ante-market gathering, for this is the spot where stocks and money are borrowed and loaned. This "loan crowd," as it is called, was formerly the gathering to which one turned to gauge the market position of the bear party, since the borrowing of stocks by "shorts," as done here, furnished an index of the strength or weakness of that interesting element. But of late it has lost its ancient prestige as a guide in such matters, because in order to hide the information sought, borrowing of stocks on a large scale is now done privately. This "crowd" has been the scene of some tremendous excitement, as in the Northern Pacific corner of May 9, 1901, when the price soared to $1000 per share and the shorts were trapped, and on that day in October, 1907, when money, after loaning at 125 per cent., was not to be had, for a time, at any price, although brokers with the best collateral would have paid

200 or 300 per cent. for accommodation, and ruin stared every one in the face.

As the hour of ten draws near, activities increase. On the south wall the arbitrageurs are busy deciphering their code messages and distributing orders, many hundred telephone bells are ringing in the long booths where clerks are hastily writing their messages; crowds of visitors gather in the gallery, while beneath it the bond-brokers prepare for their labors; indicator boards on the north and south walls, like great kaleidoscopes, display and hide their number with the same electric suddenness that seems to characterize everything and everybody — then bang! the gong rings, the chairman's gavel falls, and another day begins. Yesterday is embalmed with the Pharaohs; they never speak here of what *has* happened, but only of what *will* happen — and this is a new day.

Naturally, certain securities are more active than others, and here there are the largest crowds. As the limits surrounding the trading-posts are but vaguely defined, one crowd will sometimes get mixed up with another, whereupon confusion results, and good-natured if earnest appeals are heard to "get out," and "get over." Into one of these struggling masses a broker with an order or a trader with an inspiration literally hurls himself; each sound in the jargon of voices, which means only Bedlam and Babel to the visitor, is to him perfectly understood. He may be pushed this way and that, or tossed aside, or hidden altogether by bigger men who surround him, yet he has no difficulty in determining the price and in doing what he came there to do; all this with surprising celerity and accuracy. The business done, he hastens to his telephone, makes his report, and is ready for the next order. The manner in which some of these transactions take place between brokers has long been a subject of praise. A word, or a nod, or an upraised finger, or a tap on the arm, and hundreds of thousands of dollars change hands without a scrap of writing or a witness. A magazine writer thus describes it:

> One pastime of the American public is the manly sport of throwing mud. A shovelful of scandalous mud — a clean white target, and many a reputable and disreputable citizen is having the time of his life. We bespatter our philanthropists, our statesmen, merchants, lawyers, and divines. We vilify our art, our architecture (I take a hand in that sometimes myself), our literature, or anything else about which some one has spoken a good word.
>
> One of the time-honored institutions of our land — one which has never ceased to be the centre of abuse — is the New York Stock Exchange. Here conspiracies are organized for robbing the poor and grinding the rich; so despicable and damnable that Society is appalled. Here plots are hatched which will eventually destroy the nation, and here the Gold Barons defraud the innocent and the unwary, by

stock issues based solely on hot air and diluted water. Here Senators are made, Congressmen debauched, and judges instructed — even plans consummated for the seduction and capture of the Supreme Court. All this is true — absolutely true — you have only to read the daily papers to be convinced of it.

There is one thing, however, which you will not find in the daily papers. It is not sufficiently interesting to the average reader who needs his hourly thrill; and this one thing is the unimpeachable, clear, limpid honesty of its members.

When you buy a house even if both parties sign, the agreement is worthless unless you put up one American dollar and get the other fellow's receipt for it in writing. If you buy a horse or a cow, or anything else of value, the same precaution is necessary. So too if you sign a will. Your own word is not good enough. You must get two others to sign with you before the Surrogate is satisfied.

None of this in the Stock Exchange. A wink, or two fingers held up, is enough. Often in the thick of the fight when the floor of the Exchange is a howling mob, when frenzied brokers shout themselves hoarse and stocks are going up and down by leaps and bounds, and ruin or fortune is measured by minutes, the lifting of a man's hand over the heads of the crowd is all that binds the bargain.

What may have happened in the half hour's interim, before the buyer and seller can compare and confirm, makes no difference in the bargain. It may be ruin — possibly is — to one or the other, but there is no crawling — no equivocation — no saying you didn't understand, or "I was waving to the man behind you." Just this plain, straight, unvarnished truth, "Yes, that's right — send it in."

If it be ruin, the loser empties out on the table everything he has in his pockets; everything he has in his bank; all his houses, lots, and securities — often his wife's jewels, and pays 30, 40, or 70 per cent., as the case may be.

> What he has saved from the wreck are his integrity and his good name. In this salvage lies the respect with which his fellows hold him.
>
> Every hand is now held out. He has stood the test, he has made good. Let him have swerved by a hair's breadth and his career in the Street would have been ended.*

Of course mistakes and misunderstandings do sometimes occur, and these are the banes of the broker's life. He will lose $500 with equanimity on a personal venture, but he will howl in distress over a loss of $25 on a mistake, and apply to himself a lurid mosaic of epithets because of it. The one merely shows bad judgment and is one of the little amenities; the other he feels is stupidity. At such times the stockbroker adopts Talleyrand's bold hyperbole when he heard of the death of the Duc d' Enghien, "It is worse than a crime; it is a blunder."

When a "mix-up" occurs in a crowd, as when four or five men make claim to having supplied a bid simultaneously, everybody produces a coin and "matches" on the instant. It is a case of "odd man wins," and no time to lose. The market may be active and differences of seconds may spell losses of thousands. In less time than it takes to tell it, everything is adjusted and forgotten. But sometimes a mistake occurs

* Hopkinson Smith, in the *World's Work* (August, 1912).

which is not discovered by either party until after the market has closed. A man may think he sold 500 shares, for example, whereas the buyer has only 400 on his book. In a case of this sort, the discrepancy is covered "at the market" next morning and the loss or profit is divided. Differences between members are seldom irreconcilable, and when they assume serious proportions any third man will act as arbiter and speedily settle them. It is a significant fact that the Committee of Governors selected to arbitrate disputes is rarely called upon. Rarely, too, is there acrimony or hard feeling. The use of epithets is forbidden; to call a man a liar means prompt suspension. And so they live on raw nerves, with incidents occurring daily that add to the strain, yet ever with good-humored acquiescence toward whatever fortune deals out to them, and with generous camaraderie one to another.

As the day advances on 'Change, news and gossip and rumors of all kinds pour in, and to these the active broker must devote a large part of his time. It is astonishing to what extent the public, or that part of it that lingers in brokerage offices, calls for news from the floor. The demand is insatiable. "What do you see over there?" "Who is buying Steel?" "Who is selling Union?" "What's the news in Copper?"

"What do you think of the market?" These are the messages that come over the wires all day long, not merely from the New York offices, but from Montreal, Boston, Chicago, St. Louis, and many other points. And no matter how busy the floor broker may be, time must be found, somehow, to reply to every question as best he may, for at the other end of the line there is a customer waiting to hear from him.

Just why this customer yearns for news from the floor has always been a mystery to me. What does he expect to learn? What value attaches to a list of names of brokers who buy or sell Steel, when everybody knows that really important principals in these matters invariably hide their hands? All the significant news of the day is printed on the news tickers and reaches the customer's eye before the broker or the floor knows anything about it, yet never an hour passes but he is importuned to "say something" about what is happening on 'Change, although half the time nothing whatever is happening. The climax of this sort of thing is reached when the floor man is asked to predict the future course of the market, a request that reaches him a dozen times a day. Now, in the name of common sense, what does he know about whether the market is going up or down? How can a man who is swimming with the current tell how fast he is going? If he were a seer who could foretell such things he would have all the money in Wall Street, in which case he wouldn't remain a broker very long.

Just watch him; he is as busy as a man can be; his hands are full of orders, his head is occupied with many anxieties, his eye is on the indicator board, or scanning the room; arms and legs are working as fast as nature will permit; he must concentrate at all times. His ears ring with the strife of the room; all sorts of rumors, many of them ridiculous, are hastily whispered to him; "boos" and groans from the bears, shrieks and yells from the bulls — this is the sort of thing he hears all the day long. How can he form an opinion when thus distracted? He stands too close to the picture; he lacks perspective. What such a man thinks of the market isn't worth anything; indeed, he does not "think" at all except about executing his orders, and heaven knows that is enough to engross him.

Answering all the questions that come to him over the wires is the hardest task, and the most distasteful thing the floor man is called on to do. He knows that he doesn't know anything; from his point of view no information is better than misinformation. He feels with Josh Billings, "It's a mitey site better not 2 no so mutch than 2 no so mutch that ain't so," but nevertheless he must continue to express views and theories and opinions and predictions, whether he likes it or not. Some of his oracular utterances are illuminating. "Market is going down," he replies, "because there are more sellers than buyers." Inexorable logic.

There was old Y ——, who used to talk to his customers sitting near his office window, which faced Battery Park. He was a shifty professor of finance who never was known to hold the same opinion of the stock market two days running. "This market," he said one day, "is going away up, crops are good, money is easy, railroads are rolling in wealth, and — look over there" — pointing to a line of immigrants walking through the park from the landing place — "the brawn and sinew of old Europe coming over here to develop our resources." The very next day the market had what is called a "healthy reaction." Quite unmindful of his consoling prophecies of yesterday, old Y —— looked at the tape and said, "This market is going away down. Crops are poor, money is tight, railroads are in a bad way, and — look over there" — pointing to another procession of immigrants — "the scum of Europe coming over here to rob our American laborers."

If that portion of the public which buys and sells stocks often has its little joke at the expense of brokers, so also brokers in their turn frequently have cause to laugh at their clients. "Cheer up," was the message sent over the wire by a hopeful broker to a despondent client; "cheer up, the market can only go two ways." "Yes," was the reply, "but it has so damn many ways of going those two ways." During the rubber boom of 1910 on the London Stock Exchange, a broker wired to a client in Ireland, "Rise in bank rate considered likely," to which he received a prompt reply, "Buy me five hundred." A telegram came over a private line one day last summer from a customer in Montreal. It was a deadly dull period, when, owing to the indifference of the public, stockbrokers were not making expenses. "What are you chaps doing over there?" said the telegram. "Why don't you start something?" to which the floor member replied, "Read St. Luke 7:32."* This must have been the same member who, when customers were few and far between, hastily 'phoned his office partner, "Put all our customers into copper," to which his partner replied with grim resignation, "He won't be down to-day."

* "They are like unto children sitting in the market-place and calling one to another, and saying, 'We have piped unto you, and ye have not danced; we have mourned to you, and ye have not wept.'"

When the gong rings at three, the day's work on 'Change is at an end, and the shouting and the tumult dies. It is then 8 P. M. in London, and there in the Street hard by the Exchange, even at that ungodly hour, brokers and jobbers in the "Yankee" market are still at work in all kinds of weather. "The American market," says the (London) *Quarterly Review*, "continues, as a rule, to deal up to 8 P. M. (5 P. M. on Saturdays), when the cable offices on this side close down. Up to that time wires are coming in continually from New York with orders and prices; and a man would be ill advised to undertake jobbing in the American market unless he has a splendid constitution and lives within easy reach of town. Every year the Yankee market levies a death-tax upon its members through the medium of pneumonia and other complaints brought on by long exposure in the Street after official hours; and very little is done to provide these late dealers with adequate accommodations or shelter."*

Before leaving the Board after the official close, the broker will stop for a moment at the loan crowd to borrow or lend his stocks, after which he spends a half hour or so in his office, going over the events of the day with his partners and customers, and familiarizing himself with the day's

* July, 1912, p. 94.

doings. The specialists, floor traders, and two-dollar men, many of whom have no partners and no office staff, will go directly home, loitering perhaps for a late luncheon, or something stronger, at the club upstairs, or at a famous café across New Street. When times are brisk it is not an uncommon thing for partners to remain at their offices until a late hour, and clerks are often on duty until the small hours of the morning, spending what is left of the night at a nearby hotel in order to save time.

Holidays are not numerous on the Stock Exchange, being limited to the days set apart by law, and to very rare occasions in dull times when by petition of a majority of the members a Saturday half holiday is granted by the governors. It is felt, very properly, that special holidays should be granted but rarely, because the intimate relationship of the banks to brokerage houses is such that whenever the banks are doing business large borrowers should always be prepared to meet calls that may be made upon them. On the London Exchange, what with bank holidays and the festival seasons of the Church of England, the stockbroker has many more holidays than his American colleague.

Life on the Stock Exchange is by no means unpleasant. It is not the idle pastime that many writers picture it, with easy hours and long intervals for luncheon, nor is it the depressing and nerve-destroying centre that many of the members would have us believe. One may certainly linger over the midday meal for hours — for that matter one may absent one's self altogether — and conversely, one may worry and fret over the day's vexations until life becomes unpleasant for him and for every one near him. But by far the larger number find their work as congenial as earning the daily bread may be, and vastly more diverting than many of the sedentary occupations in other lines of business. Elsewhere I have said that the long periods of dulness on the floor constitute the most serious obstacle the broker has to meet. Accustomed to physical activity and with a mind inured to occupation, he chafes under a stagnation that is foreign to his habits and desires, until worry — the disease of the age — claims him for its own. Almost every broker's wife knows what I mean. It becomes a habit with such a man; unconsciously he grows "bearish" on his business, on himself, and on his associates, and at such times he is an awful bore.

The essential thing for a man to bear in mind who finds himself growing into this mood is that nature abhors a vacuum. His mind is empty because there is nothing to do; he must therefore *find* something to do — some mental occupation that will banish from his mind the worries that beset him. In order to do this many members of the Exchange carry some light reading in their pockets for use in an idle hour; at the spot where the National Lead Company's securities are dealt in the specialists maintain a compact circulating library of all the magazines and periodicals; others spend idle moments pouring over a pocket chess-board; the Reading Railway post has a constantly increasing collection of all kinds of puzzles, riddles, problems — anything to keep the mind active on the principle of *similia similibus curantur.*

The newcomer on the Stock Exchange will do well to fortify himself in some such way, for it may be accepted as gospel truth that the paralyzing effect of worry in this peculiar environment will inevitably lead to hasty actions, mistakes, and errors of judgment, unless the victim learns early in the game how to arm himself against these misfortunes. One word more: When the day's work is done, the young member must learn Doctor Saleeby's great lesson, that a round of the links, or a set at tennis, or any other form of out-door diversions so dear to the youngster's heart, will not of themselves suffice to banish cares.

He has now become a thinking animal; he lives by his wits, and he suffers from the worries incidental to brain work coupled with responsibility. I have just said that nature abhors a vacuum — in his case this especially applies to his mind. Care and worry are not driven away merely because he has made his "round" in 80 strokes — they must be pushed out by something else, something more than mere play or sport *per se*. What he requires is a new *mental* interest, not merely to serve as a counter-irritant for the worries of to-day, but as an investment for all the years that are before him. He must have a "hobby" of some sort, no matter what, so long as it is a mental occupation which he does for the love of it — books, pictures, music, postage stamps — anything will do the trick so long as it occupies the mind and is done *for fun*. We old timers have only to look about us on the Board to see who the really happy men are, the men who are never nuisances. They are the men whose minds are not content with doing nothing.*

In the matter of creature comforts, members of the New York Stock Exchange have provided themselves with everything that gentlemen require. Their beautiful building, an architectural masterpiece and one of the city's ornaments, has often been described; here it is sufficient to

* "Worry, the Disease of the Age," by C. W. Saleeby, M. D., F. A. Stokes Co. (New York, 1907).

say that nothing is lacking in the way of conveniences necessary to the physical ease of the members. Barbers, valets, messengers, and attendants of every description are on duty; a well-equipped hospital room is ready for emergencies; showers and needle-baths, smoking-rooms, lounges, writing-rooms, reading-rooms, coffee-rooms, and a spacious luncheon club, contribute their share to the refreshment of the outer and inner man. The luncheon club, which occupies the whole upper floor, is the last word in culinary perfection. In the lounging-rooms adjoining are all the magazines and periodicals, and the walls are covered with a collection of rare prints of old New York, together with mounted trophies of the hunt presented by sportsmen members. In other days before the Exchange built its present structure the club was housed in modest quarters across New Street and a few non-members of the Exchange were admitted to membership, but now its facilities are taxed to meet the demand, and membership is restricted to the Stock Exchange, although guests are admitted at all hours.

The atmosphere in the city is often trying in the summer months because of the excessive humidity, and extraordinary measures were resorted to in the construction of the building to minimize this unpleasantness on the crowded floor, where the presence of a large number of men in a greater or less degree of physical animation but adds to the general discomfort. To meet this condition an air-cooling plant was provided — the first and the foremost example of its kind in existence, both in point of magnitude and in the exacting demands involved. By means of this remarkable triumph of mechanical skill, outer air at a temperature of say 90° is taken into the basement, eighteen hundred pounds of water (humidity) are squeezed out of it per hour, it is purified and cleansed through many walls of cheesecloth, the temperature is refrigerated down to 60°, and then, after again raising it to a point at which no dangerous results may affect a member passing in and out of the room, it is finally supplied to the great floor and again exhausted by methods that obviate drafts or dangerous currents of any kind. Aside from the members and attendants, the only person having access to the floor is the chief engineer who controls this remarkable air-cooling plant. A wizard in a way, it is curious to watch him threading in and out of the busy crowds, tasting and feeling the air which, under the black art of his necromancy, turns intolerable conditions into others quite delightful.

The history of the New York Stock Exchange has been written many times, and need be but briefly referred to here. Something approaching an organization was effected May 17, 1792, when, under a tree which stood opposite what is now 60 Wall Street, twenty-four "Brokers for the Purchase and Sale of Public Stocks" signed an agreement to charge not less than a commission of $\frac{1}{4}$ per cent. It was a day of small things; the national debt was but $17,993,000; there was but one bank in the town. Through the fragmentary data that has survived, we learn that occasional meetings of the brokers were held during the next twenty-five years at the old Tontine Coffee House, at Wall and Water streets. In 1817 the formal organization was effected and the meeting-place fixed at the Merchants' Exchange, later the site of the Custom House, and now the property of the National City Bank. In 1853 the Stock Exchange moved to Beaver Street and in 1865 to its present situation. The "Open Board of Brokers," a rival organization, was absorbed in 1869, and ten years later the "Gold Board" also joined forces with the parent body.

The development of the New York Stock Exchange in its early days was but a record of the country's growth, and this in turn depended upon speculation. It was, indeed, speculation such as the world had never witnessed. How our western borders were extended as the railroads pushed onward; how trade was stimulated throughout christendom by the discovery of gold in California; how the national debt expanded at the time of the Civil War; and how, after the war, construction went ahead at tremendous pace — all these served to fan the flames of adventure and enterprise, which are the bases of speculation. The panics of 1837, 1857, and 1873, severe enough to give pause to another and less vigorous nation, seem in the retrospect to have been but starting points for a fresh development of the national spirit — a spirit which owes to speculation the extension of frontiers, the bridging of waters, the unlocking of mountains, and the transportation of wealth. In this splendid work of conquering a continent the Stock Exchange has kept pace with the march of industry. It has supplied the one great central market for the expression of the country's progress as measured by the country's securities, and it will continue to do so as long as an evergreen faith in America exists among its people.

The Stock Exchange is often defined as the nerve-centre of the world, and, just as every happening of importance finds an instant effect on the market, so members instinctively apply to current events habits of close analysis and nice discrimination. A failure at Amsterdam may result in liquidation in Atchisons, long a favorite of Dutch investors; prolonged drought in the Argentine may increase our foreign shipments of grain; a great engineering project, like the Assouan Dam, may lead to handsome contracts for American steel-makers; any fluctuation in rates of foreign exchange must be watched carefully to see if exports or imports of gold are impending; if a rich man dies possessed of large amounts of certain securities, sellers must be critically observed for evidences of liquidation by the heirs; speeches in Congress or in Parliament, or the unguarded utterances of statesmen, must be weighed and measured for their effect on the public mind; a great fire may lead to selling of investments by insurance companies; a revolution in Mexico may imperil American investments there; if there are political disturbances in the Balkans, the continental Bourses may be frightened; every move of the great foreign banks must then be watched closely, for the bankers to-day are the war-lords of creation, and so every event of importance the world over makes its impression on the Stock Exchange barometer.

What is going on in the Transvaal or in Alaska, the latest outbreak in China, the areas of barometric pressure in the grain country, the ravages of the boll-weevil, the market in pig iron, the latest labor difficulty, the tendencies of Socialism, the cost of living, the outgivings of our law-makers — a knowledge of all these and many similar matters is a necessary part of the stockbroker's trade, and serves to keep his mental activities considerably above the dull level of mediocrity. Naturally this sort of occupation gives a zest to life, and makes impossible the sedentary dry-rot which the impatient broker sometimes thinks is upon him. At any rate no Sherman Law can be invoked to prevent him from learning all there is to know about men and affairs; and just as he becomes trained in habits of inquiry, and proficient in using facts as stepping-stones to conclusions, so he becomes a valuable and useful member of the community.

Critics in what may be termed the impressionist school — accustomed to a free, instantaneous, and often meaningless handling of their subject — are prone to condemn the Exchange because the action of the market when large reforms in business are impending seems to imply hostility to those reforms on the part of members. This may be typical modern impressionism, but it is all wrong. If the market declines when, for example, a large corporation finds itself at odds with the law, the downward tendency of the securities affected is the result of natural laws with which stockbrokers have nothing to do. They are but agents. Ten thousand owners of securities throughout the land may simultaneously become alarmed and sell — a familiar psychologic phenomenon which depresses prices — but to say that this result expresses the hostility of the Stock Exchange to the enforcement of the Anti-Trust Law is nothing less than an evidence of critical strabismus.

The men for whom I presume to speak, far from being hostile or indifferent to the call of revitalized business morality, are quite as deeply imbued with the potent spirit of business reform as are the men who make the country's laws. Careful, well-considered legislation that broadens and deepens the channels of American development, that provides adequate supervision and such publicity as will guard against selfish perversion, is welcomed with gratitude by the Stock Exchange. Any thinking man ought to see at a glance that the very object of the Exchange's existence is benefited by such laws, and prospers with their enforcement. The Cordage Trust, the Salt Trust, the Bicycle combination and the Hocking Coal episode are still bitter memories on 'Change; any law that will prevent a recurrence of these and kindred calamities is a law that strengthens the hands of every member and gives him fresh courage.

It would be difficult to find anywhere a more intelligent and interesting group of men than the members of the New York Stock Exchange. Some of them are men of peculiar personal charm, others are distinguished for especial ability in various ways, others are men with hobbies, nearly every one knows something that is worth knowing, and, what is better, talks of what he knows in the manner of culture. Given an idle hour with a wish to learn, and every dip of the net into the intellectual waters of this gathering brings up some new and delightful specimen to amuse and instruct.

The dean of the Stock Exchange, for example, who has been an active member for fifty-five years, and who is now eighty, spends several months of each year in exploring all the little nooks and crannies of the globe, remote and inaccessible places that are *terra incognita* to your casual tourist. He is a mine of information; to know him means, in a way, a liberal education. If you are fortunate enough to have an hour's chat with him (for when at work on the floor he is quite as active as any other youngster), you will find yourself in contact with a traveler of rare charm and culture, who will take you into strange lands of which the mere existence is but a faint recollection of your schoolboy studies.

He will tell you, with all his delightfully fresh and buoyant enthusiasm, of Agra and its Pearl Mosque, and of the surpassing beauty of the world's architectural masterpiece — the Taj Mahal — with its marbles, its mosaics, and its lapis-lazuli. He will take you into Thibet, the Forbidden Land, through the jungles of the faraway Celebes, into the least-known corners of the Straits Settlements, and to the lonely isle of Robinson Crusoe. On his vacation next year he is going to the Falkland Islands, somewhere down Patagonia way, and the year after a letter may come from him sent out from the headwaters of the Yukon, or ferried down the Congo from Stanley Falls. Wherever his fancy roams, there this adventurer goes; no thought of sickness or danger or difficulty is permitted to interfere with his delightful hobby.

Naturally, in the cosmopolitan atmosphere of the Stock Exchange tastes are catholic and run to wide extremes. One of the members is a student of Russian literature in all its phases; he can tell you of its folklore, its peasantism, its liberal thought and its ethical ideals of society; Dostoyevski is his hobby and Melshin the poet. Beside him stands a man who has mastered the culinary art; the joy of his life is to prepare with his own hands, for the palates of his fastidious guests, dainty dishes and wonderful sauces that make an invitation to his table something worth having. One of the members is an animated concordance of Shelley, whom he studies with almost fanatical zeal; another is a disciple of Heine, whom he adores. There stands a man who went into the heart of Africa as no white man had ever done — through Somaliland into Abyssinia, thence to Lake Rudolph to hunt elephants, south to Victoria Nyanza, and finally, after hunting all the wild game of the district, on foot to the West Coast.

Near by is a traveler fresh from Mukden, the scene of the world's greatest battle; he can tell you, too, some curious and little-known details of the awful engagement at 203-Metre Hill. Our Civil War has its survivors in a dozen Board members of to-day. One of them was shot twice at Shiloh and lived to fight the Sioux; another was a captain under Burnside at Antietam, charged the bridge at the head of all that was left of his company, and was rewarded for conspicuous gallantry; another was shot through the lungs at the second battle of Bull Run and lived through the carnage at Gettysburg; another was thrice wounded at Gettysburg and again in the Wilderness.

Here are some who charged up Kettle Hill and

San Juan Hill in Cuba, and there are men who served in the navy throughout that war. Officers of high rank in the National Guard and the Naval Reserve, members of important public bodies, such as the Municipal Art Commission, the Palisades Commission, the Public School Board and the various hospital boards; mayors and other officers of suburban communities, sheriffs and deputy-sheriffs, presidents of clubs, wardens and vestrymen of churches, men beloved for their philanthropies, Oxford men, Cambridge men, Heidelberg men, graduates of all the American universities — with these and very many more like them, one is brought into intimate daily contact.

There is a legion of collectors, and these are always interesting people. One of them "goes in" for old silver, of which he has gathered a valuable display; many others collect prints, etchings, or paintings; another takes pardonable pride in his Elizabethan early editions, particularly his First Folio; another has published a standard work on the portraits of Lincoln, of which he possesses nine original negatives and many rare copies of negatives; others devote leisure hours to collecting porcelains and ceramics of all kinds, postage-stamps, coins, rugs, and tapestries. You will find here men of bucolic tastes, with hobbies in farms and extensive country estates, where one grows rare orchids and another breeds highly prized cattle, or sheep, or horses, or dogs, or poultry.

As you pause in the day's work to listen to these interesting people talking of their pet diversions, you see why it is that hobbies are so necessary to the modern mind, and particularly to the worried mind of the Stock Exchange man. You see that the man who has nothing to divert him in leisure hours is becoming a really rare type, whereas the man of curious, busy, and active brain, who must have a hobby to be happy, is becoming more and more common. In this very marked tendency among the members of the Exchange there has been a great improvement within the last decade, and one, as I have said, that not only serves to banish the cares of to-day, but promises to become a valuable investment for the years that lie ahead.

There are some talented musicians on the floor, men who are not only proficient themselves, but who by their liberal support of all forms of music do much to encourage and maintain New York's supremacy as a musical centre. Grand opera, the Philharmonic Society, the symphony orchestras, the choral organizations, and the army of virtuosi from abroad who have earned applause and money on these shores — all are accorded cordial support by Stock Exchange members. One of them gives rein to his altruistic tendencies by providing free concerts once a week for the submerged tenth in a crowded foreign quarter of the East Side.

In the realm of amateur sport and sportsmanship the Exchange has many enthusiastic devotees. There are several tennis champions, one of them holding a title in singles for seven years, and another a title in doubles for five years. Famous university oarsmen, football and baseball players, American golf champions, expert yachtsmen and commodores of fleets, four-in-hand drivers, polo players, horse-show judges, breeders and owners of famous stables, racquet, court-tennis, and squash champions, deep-sea fishermen and disciples of the placid Izaak, who lure their game from cowslip banks; hunters in every quarter of the world, motor-boat racers, swimmers, men of muscle and mind, men of brain and brawn, these are types that keep ever in mind the *joie de vivre*, the blue sky above, and all the stimulating enthusiasms of youth.

There is little need to speak of the New York Stock Exchange's charities and benefactions, because these are well known. Scarcely a day passes that some one of the members does not ask of his fellows a contribution, however small, for a worthy charity with which he or the ladies of his family have come in contact, and invariably the mite is freely given, although there may not be time to spare to hear the story. The private and unostentatious benefactions of members go on at all times, and cannot be discussed here.

When the *Titanic* went down, a fund of $25,000 was raised in a day, and a committee of members of the Exchange was on the pier when the survivors arrived to do what could be done. The Mississippi floods met with a similar response; indeed, every great calamity that spells suffering and sorrow and need finds an instant expression of sympathy and practical assistance from the floor. In times of national gravity, such as an outbreak of war, the Exchange will alway be heard from with its volunteers and its funds for equipping a regiment; hospitals, churches, and all worthy charities well know that appeals are responded to with a zeal that is alike nonsectarian and generous.

Never in my experience on the floor have I heard a complaint from a deserving employee of the Stock Exchange. Salaries are wisely increased with length of service, pensions are given by the governors to aged servants; hospitals, medical treatment, nurses, and sanitariums are provided for the sick, and funds are supplied to families of deceased employees. A spirit of helpfulness, sympathy, and generosity is in the very air of the Stock Exchange, an absolutely fine spirit that takes pride, too, in caring for its own members who have been unfortunate.

Finally, let it be said that the Stock Exchange man is human. He knows the "rub of the green," he suffers as all men suffer, but he does not complain, nor solicit odds. All he asks is fair play; a little patient study of what the Exchange stands for; a little better understanding of its usefulness in our commercial life; a little recognition of each man's effort to uphold a high standard of business honor; a little of the cordial support which he himself, with stout optimism, extends to every worthy thing.

CHAPTER IX

THE LONDON STOCK EXCHANGE, AND COMPARISONS WITH ITS NEW YORK PROTOTYPE

CHAPTER IX

THE LONDON STOCK EXCHANGE, AND COMPARISONS WITH ITS NEW YORK PROTOTYPE

THERE were Exchanges in London in the sixteenth century. Merchants from Lombardy had given their name to a street, and had flourished so well that they had branched out in the business of money-changing — that is, of exchanging worn, abrased and clipped coins, foreign and domestic, for those of standard weight and fineness. As trade increased and the first faint signs of progress in the matter of wealth began to develop, it was seen that this business of exchanging money was sufficiently important to warrant royal recognition; accordingly there was created the office of Royal Exchanger, and the person entrusted with this office was given the privilege of exchanging coins in the manner described. Smaller offices for the purpose were farmed out in other English towns, and each place where the business was carried on thus came to be known as "The Exchange," a name that was ultimately applied to any covered place where merchants met to buy and sell commodities.

After the money-changers came the money-lenders — Jews, more Lombards, and finally the Guild of Goldsmiths. The last named, having long practised the business of money-lending, finally became money-borrowers, issuing receipts for these borrowings known as Goldsmiths' Notes — the earliest form of English bank-notes — and the first step in the convenient process of translating capital, and debt, and credit, into bits of interest-bearing paper.* This was the state of English finance until 1694, when the Bank of England was founded, and stocks and shares came into being since the bank was a joint-stock affair. That the invention of stock certificates was a popular one, and that the authorities and the public seized upon it as a convenient means of directing capital into new and hitherto untried forms of enterprise is seen by the rapidity with which fresh undertakings were put forth. In 1698 the New East India Company loaned its

* The English Exchequer has left a permanent impression on the language no less than on the world's finance. Such words as "cheque," "tally," and "stocks," in the sense of securities, possess an interesting history easy to trace. If one lent money to the Bank of England down to so comparatively recent a period as one hundred years ago, tallies for the amount were cut on willow sticks just as they were cut at the Exchequer in the time of the Crusades; the bank kept the "foil," and the lender the "stock" — the earliest "bank-stock" on record. Very recently a bag of Exchequer tallies was found in a chapel of Westminster Abbey.

capital to the government; by 1711 there was a funded debt of £11,750,000 in the shape of bank stock, East India stock, and annuities. There was also the famous South Sea Company, to be followed ten years later by a reorganization of the company with its first subscription of a million in £100 stock at £300, and a second and third subscription of larger magnitude, each accompanied by prodigious promises, and each snapped up with avidity by a public saturated with the new and hazardous pastime of speculation.

"All distinction of party, religion, sex, character, and circumstance," writes Smollett, the historian of the time, "were swallowed up in this universal concern. Exchange Alley was filled with a strange concourse of statesmen and clergymen, churchmen and dissenters, Whigs and Tories, physicians, lawyers, tradesmen, and even with multitudes of females. All other professions and employments were utterly neglected; and the people's attention wholly engrossed by this and other chimerical schemes, which were known by the denomination of bubbles. New companies started up every day, under the countenance of the prime nobility. The Prince of Wales was constituted governor of the Welsh Copper Company; the Duke of Chandos appeared at the head of the York Buildings Company; the Duke of Bridgewater formed a third, for building houses in London and Westminster. About a hundred such schemes were projected and put in execution, to the ruin of many thousands. The sums proposed to be raised by these expedients amounted to three hundred millions sterling, which exceeded the value of all the lands in England. The nation was so intoxicated with the spirit of adventure that people became a prey to the grossest delusion. An obscure projector pretending to have formed a very advantageous scheme, which, however, he did not explain, published proposals for a subscription in which he promised that in one month the particulars of his project should be disclosed. In the meantime he declared that every person paying two guineas should be entitled to a subscription for £100, which would produce that sum yearly. In the forenoon this adventurer received a thousand of these subscriptions; and in the evening set out for another kingdom."

No sooner were there bits of paper to deal in than jobbers or brokers sprang up to handle them, and by natural gregarious processes these dealers gathered in one spot. Thus competition was stimulated and active markets created. The rotunda of the bank and the Royal Exchange were their first haunts, indeed until Archbishop Laud drove them out they were to be found bargaining on the wide floors of St. Paul's Cathedral. As the business expanded they took to the neighboring streets and coffee houses, and so Change Alley, Jonathan's Coffee House, Cornhill, Lombard Street and Sweeting's Alley became their familiar retreats. Old Jonathan's burned down in 1748 and New Jonathan's in Threadneedle Street succeeded it. Here, in July, 1773, "the brokers and others at New Jonathan's came to a resolution that, instead of its being called New Jonathan's, it should be called 'The Stock Exchange,' which is to be wrote over the door." Thus while business in the public funds was still conducted on a large scale at the bank, and dealings in foreign securities still centred at the Royal Exchange, London may be said to have had a Stock Exchange in the modern sense from that day in 1773 when the name was "wrote over the door" at New Jonathan's.*

We have authority for the early history of the London Stock Exchange in a report made in 1877 by the officials of the institution to the Royal Commission. From this report it appears that

* The first Stock Exchange book was published in 1761 — "Every Man His Own Broker, or a Guide to Exchange Alley," by J. Mortimer. Mortimer, Mr. Hirst tells us, had been British Consul in Holland, and had seen the workings of the Amsterdam Bourse and the arbitrage business between London and Amsterdam, which was considerable in the middle of the eighteenth century. The book shows that many phases of speculation were already in vogue before the Stock Exchange was formally organized.

the Stock Exchange at New Jonathan's in 1773 "afforded a ready market for the operations of the bankers, merchants, and capitalists connected with the floating of the numerous loans raised at that period for the service of the State." The members or frequenters paid a subscription of sixpence to defray expenses, drew up rules, and placed its control in the hands of a "Committee for General Purposes." The functions of this committee were then, as now, "judicial as regards the settlement of disputed bargains, and administrative as regards rules for the general conduct of business and for the liquidation of defaulter's accounts." The earliest minutes on record are dated December, 1798.

War loans and a national debt increasing by leaps and bounds, with consequent activity in consols, was the principal source of business in those early days, and as these increased, so also the savings of the public and a new national spirit led to a steady growth in the business of dealing in securities. The dim receding voice of those early days still echoes in Capel Court through the medium of two holidays — May 1st and November 1st. More than a century ago these days marked the closing of the Bank of England's books for the transfer of consols, and as consols were the only things then traded in, there was nothing for stockbrokers to do on those occasions; hence they took a holiday. And they still close the Exchange on these days — an eloquent instance of the Englishman's adherence to tradition.

By 1801 there was not room enough in the old building, and, moreover, the report says: "It became apparent that the indiscriminate admission of the public was calculated to expose the dealers to the loss of valuable property." Accordingly a group of Stock Exchange men acquired a site in Capel Court, close to the bank, raised a capital of £20,000 in four hundred shares of £50 each, and in May, 1801, laid the foundation of what has become through numerous additions the London Stock Exchange of to-day. The building was opened in March, 1802, with a list of five hundred subscribers, and the deed of settlement (March 27, 1802), vested the management in a committee of thirty members, chosen annually by ballot, with nine trustees and managers, separate from the committee, to have charge of the treasury and represent the proprietors. Although the rules and regulations have been amended and enlarged from time to time to meet new conditions, the constitution of the London Stock Exchange remains substantially unaltered.

As it stands to-day, there are nine managers

who represent the shareholders or proprietors, and thirty committeemen, who look after the administration of the Exchange and the well-being of the members. The managers are elected in threes for terms of five years by the votes of the shareholders. They fix the admission fees, appoint almost all the officials, and look after the building and the property in general, while the thirty committeemen enforce the rules and regulations, adjudicate differences, and regulate the admission of securities. They are elected every year by the members, and they choose from their number a chairman and vice-chairman. In March of each year, before retiring from office, the committee elects all the old Stock Exchange members who wish to be re-elected, membership on the London Exchange being granted for one year only. Any member may object to the re-election of any other member, but this is a very unusual incident.

"The great principle upon which the committee acts," says Mr. Francis W. Hirst, "and to which most of its regulations are directed, is the inviolability of contracts. It has power to suspend or expel any member for violating its rules, or for non-compliance with its decisions, or for dishonorable conduct. A member of the London Stock Exchange is prohibited from advertising or from sending circulars to any but his own clients. He is also forbidden to belong to any other Stock Exchange, or 'bucket-shop,' or other competing institution. New members are now compelled to become proprietors by acquiring at least one Stock Exchange share, paying a heavy entrance fee and an annual subscription of forty guineas. Yet the precautions against impecuniosity are inadequate. Defaults are far too common."*

In such a dual form of control as that of these managers and committeemen it is obvious that causes of friction must of necessity arise from time to time, and that jarring and discord are inevitable. The owners or proprietors are, of course, a minority of the members, and their decisions on matters that come before them are necessarily biased in favor of a course that will increase the dividends on their shares. Naturally they would favor a practically unlimited membership, since the dividends are largely acquired from this source.

The plan of compelling each new member to become a shareholder or proprietor was devised

---

* "The (London) Stock Exchange," Francis W. Hirst, London, Williams and Norgate, 1910. The attention of the reader is invited to this book. As a short study of investment and speculation in England it is exceedingly instructive, doubly so in that it comes from the pen of the editor of the *Economist*.

to meet this difficulty, and in a measure it has succeeded. "Within the course of the next half century," says the *Quarterly Review*, "it is pretty certain that the Stock Exchange, as a company, will belong to the members, of whom each will have a stake in the enterprise; and that happy consummation, when it arrives, will put an end to a good many minor problems which still harass the House in its workings, and possibly check those bolder plans for reform which are advocated by many of the members."* The difficulties arising from these causes had their origin, as we have seen, as far back as the year 1801, when the new building was erected. As only the wealthier members of the association had provided the capital for the Capel Court structure, in order to protect their investment, they demanded control of its financial affairs; thus the Stock Exchange thenceforth consisted of two distinct bodies, proprietors and subscribers.

While there is but one way by which a man may become a member of the New York Stock Exchange, in the London Exchange there are various ways. The most direct way, and the easiest but most expensive way, is to pay an entrance fee of 500 guineas, and find three members who will stand surety for four years for the

* The *Quarterly Review*, July, 1912.

sum of £500 each, this £500 being forfeited to the estate if the member is "hammered" — i. e., if he fails during the period. The candidate must in addition buy three Stock Exchange shares, the price of which at present is about £190 each.* He must also purchase from a retiring member a nomination, which can be bought at present for £40, although they have sold as high as £700. Candidates who wish to join the Exchange under easier conditions may have their entrance fees reduced to 250 guineas if they have served for four years in the Stock Exchange as a clerk; and for these candidates concessions are also made in respect to sureties, of which they need provide but two, and to shares, of which they are required to buy but one instead of three. The committee is also empowered to elect each year a few candidates without nomination.

This is a rather curious practice which requires a word of explanation. In England, as elsewhere, there is a latent objection to monopolies of all forms, and the foresighted governors of the Exchange, with an eye to the possibility of difficulties that might be raised against their institution at some time in the future on the ground of monopoly, hit upon this expedient as a precautionary measure. Should such objection be raised,

* There are 20,000 shares (£13 paid) and £416,700 debentures outstanding.

the governors have only to admit a few more members without nomination. The door is thus thrown open; and there is no *de facto* monopoly. It is very simple and very ingenious.

In all these cases the annual subscription, or dues, is the same. These, which were originally 10 guineas, then 20 and 30, are now 40 for all new members, while old members pay, of course, the subscription prevailing at the time of their election. As a condition precedent to election, a candidate must present himself before the committee with his sureties, and each of them must give satisfactory answers to the questions put to him.

From this it will be seen that a man who wants to become a member of the London Stock Exchange without first serving an apprenticeship of four years as clerk must pay for his entrance fee 500 guineas, his shares £570, his nomination £40, and his annual dues 40 guineas, or a total of about £1150, of which £570, the price of his shares, yields him a return in Stock Exchange dividends. These shares are, of course, excellent investments, and the managers may be relied upon to see to it that their value is not impaired. During the first seventy-five years of its existence Stock Exchange shares paid an average dividend of 20 per cent.; for the last completed year the dividend was 100 per cent. No one person may hold more than 200 shares, and holders must be members of the Exchange in all cases except those where representatives of proprietors acquired their shares before December 31, 1875. When a proprietor dies, his shares must be sold to a member within twelve months. The membership is not limited, strictly speaking, and whereas in 1802 there were 500 members, in 1845 there were 800, in 1877, 2000, and in 1910, 5019.

I say the membership is not limited, but when the time arrives, as it probably will within this generation, that the 20,000 shares are divided at the ratio of three shares for each member, 6666 members will then own all the shares and the membership will be full. Hence there is, in a way, a limit to the total membership.

One important respect in which the London Stock Exchange differs from all others — American, Continental, or Provincial — is the division of its members into two classes, jobbers and brokers, a division that appears to be as old as the Exchange itself. As to which of these classes it is better to belong there are differences of opinion, but the wise men in the business seem to be a unit in recommending a few years' experience as a broker to be followed by the business of the jobber. The broker, under the London system, deals with the outside public and acts merely as agent between the public and the jobber, with whom he trades on the floor of the Exchange. The jobber, on his part, is not allowed to deal with the public at all, but must confine his activities to the brokers and to his fellow jobbers. "Thus the broker," as Mr. Hirst puts it, "feeds the jobber much as the solicitor feeds the barrister," or, continuing the metaphor, we may say that like the barrister the jobber gets the *cause célèbre* and all the great prizes, and like the solicitor the broker hunts up the business and must be content with small returns. The broker works for his commission; the jobber for what he can get out of the trade in the way of a profit.

The system in vogue in the New York Stock Exchange would seem to possess many advantages over this curious division of functions between the two classes. Here, as every one knows, brokers are not restricted in their operations; the field is alike open to all members, and the market is not limited by placing it in the hands of any one man or any group of men. On the London Exchange the attempt to define strict dividing lines between brokers and jobbers has not been successful; for years there has been a strong undercurrent of resentment between them because of acts which each regards as encroachments by the other upon its especial domain.

The quarrel reached an acute stage in the paralysis that hit the Stock Exchange after the South African war; there were too many members and too little business. Brokers took it upon themselves to make prices and to deal directly with other brokers and with outsiders, disregarding the jobbers altogether; and jobbers in turn sought in self-defence to establish connections of their own, outside the Stock Exchange, and with non-members. Both parties have violated the spirit, if not the letter of the Stock Exchange rules, and even at the present time, when much stricter rules have been passed defining the limitations of each division, the same unfortunate feeling of resentment is heard daily. Violations of the rule, however technical, are bound to create friction, and friction among the members of a Stock Exchange is not a good thing for the members nor for the business. Fortunately, there is nothing of that sort in the New York Exchange.

In active securities where there are very many transactions, Mr. Hirst is disposed to think that the separate existence of jobbers makes for a free market and close prices the very essence of an Exchange's functions. This may be true, since the jobber is a host in himself, specialist, speculator, trader and jobber — all in one. Where there is a free market, the presence of such a participant undoubtedly adds to it, as any one knows who has dealt with him in lots of from 5,000 to 10,000 shares, at a difference of only a sixteenth. Such a market is a close market *in excelsis*. But in the New York Stock Exchange the same result is obtained far more openly and above-board by the presence in all active securities of a host of such jobbers — brokers, traders, specialists, and speculators — each actively bidding and offering by voice and gesture, and without collusion, and each thereby contributing to the making of the freest possible market and the closest possible price. In New York no middleman stands between the public and the market.

It is a fact recognized by all economists that the larger the number of dealers and the freer the competitive bidding, the more accurate the resultant price and the nearer its approach to true value; hence it would seem to follow that in this highly desirable attainment the New York system is superior to that of London. The same comment applies to the market for inactive securities. In London, notwithstanding the quotations printed in the Official List, the public has no assurance that jobbers can be found to deal at those prices, or at prices approaching them. "And when there is a slump in the market and a rush of selling orders with no support," as Mr. Hirst candidly admits, "as happened in rubber shares in the months of June and July, 1910, the jobbers are apt to be away at lunch all day, and the brokers have to report to their clients that they simply cannot find a purchaser."*

Such things do not happen in the New York Exchange, for when there is a slump in any group of shares, instantly there gathers a number of individuals who are there for the very purpose of making a market. It may be a "soft" market, with wide fluctuations, but it is a market for all that, and the timely absence at an all-day luncheon of any one man or any group of men cannot possibly affect it. There have been occasions on the New York Stock Exchange, no doubt, where a broker with a "hurry" order in a very inactive security has not found a market awaiting him, but there are various ways by which he may seek the desired market and ultimately he is sure to find it. In any case such an incident is the exception that proves the rule that a free market, affording all the advantages which excellent markets possess, is nowhere to be found more easily and more quickly than on the floor of the New York Stock Exchange. "American securities," says the Paris correspondent of the *Journal*

---

* It should be said, in fairness to the London jobber, that the incident here mentioned by Mr. Hirst is a rare exception.

of Commerce in his cabled despatches of October 23, 1912 — referring to the Balkan crisis in that city — "may with complete conservatism be regarded as having received a splendid advertisement in the French market by reason of their recent remarkable instantaneous conversion into cash."

In the course of many years of active experience as broker, trader, and speculator, I do not now recall an instance in which I was unable to find a market on the New York Exchange for any security, however inactive, which I wished to buy or sell. If the specialist in this particular stock cannot satisfy me with his quotation, there are always room traders to whom I may submit my offer; there are also arbitrageurs, wire houses, and banking houses interested in this particular security. Somewhere among all these agencies the New York broker must inevitably find or create a market. But I fancy he would have a sorry time of it were he restricted, under the rules, to dealing with a jobber who "is apt to be away at lunch all day," when trouble comes and risks are involved.

Such a system, it would seem, is all very well for the jobber, but quite unfair to the outsider and to the conscientious broker who is striving all the while to protect the interests of the public and maintain the welfare of the Exchange. Indeed, as it works out in London, the broker has all the worst of it in many ways. Even though the jobber "runs a book," as the phrase is, his work is done at 4 P.M. — when the market closes — and if he is not doing a large business he may then follow his inclinations. Unless his business involves dealing in South Africans or Americans, his work is substantially completed with the official closing of the Exchange. But the broker, on the other hand, enjoys no such freedom. After the closing he must go to his office — for in the nature of things he must have one — and there he will find correspondence awaiting him, orders to be executed in the "Street markets," and telephone messages to send to his customers. The mere fact that a London broker must use the London telephone is in itself a curse, for nowhere under the canopy is there a telephone service so dreadful and so exasperating.

Even in the ebb-tide of a dwindling summer business the London broker, who cannot begin his day's correspondence until four, finds it difficult to leave his office until an hour long after his American colleague has played his eighteen holes or dressed for dinner. Aside from the horrors of the telephone service, this is due in a measure to the fact that they have no ticker in

London and the mechanical efficiency with which this machine faithfully records all over America each fluctuation of the market, finds no counterpart in England. The broker in London has therefore to perform, in a measure, the work of the ticker in New York. Perhaps I should not say they have no tickers in London. In point of fact there is such an instrument, identical with our own, which four or five times a day, at stated intervals, reels off with mechanical monotony a list of quotations in certain active securities — the same group every day. They are limited in number, almost nobody looks at them, and many really enterprising houses do not install them at all.

Worst of all, the London broker until very recently was not properly paid for his work; he was not protected by a rigorous commission law, as we are in the New York Exchange. In New York a broker charges $\frac{1}{8}$ per cent. commission on the par value of every hundred shares in which he deals for a non-member, each way, and the rules of the Exchange compel him to collect it in all cases. The slightest departure from this rule, however technical it may be, is severely punished, and no statute of limitations or other expedient will save him from the consequences of it. Thus all the brokers are insured an equal footing; competition for business is prevented, and the public which the Exchange seeks to serve is assured of equally fair dealing in every quarter. So rigorously is this rule enforced that the large and important branch of the Exchange's business which has to do with joint-account trading between New York and foreign centres has recently been seriously restricted because, in the judgment of the governors, it involved an infraction of this important commission law.

On May 22nd of this year (1912) the London Stock Exchange put into effect an official scale of commissions, which was designed to remedy the unfortunate conditions that had prevailed, and this scale is now enforced. It provides for a charge of ⅛ per cent. on British government securities, Indian government stocks and foreign government bonds; ¼ per cent. on certain other special cases, ⅛ in railroad ordinary and deferred ordinary stocks at prices of £50 or under, and a sliding scale on shares transferable by deed, ranging from commissions of 1½d. per share to 2s. 6d. per share. On American shares the commission to be charged is 6d. per share on a price of $25 or under, 9d. on prices from $25 to $50, 1s. on prices from $50 to $100, 1s. 6d. on prices from $100 to $150; and 2s. on prices over $200.

In many other transactions the commission to be charged is left to the discretion of the broker who may, if he is doing a large business with a client in high-priced and low-priced shares on which the official scale of commission varies, arrange to charge $\frac{1}{8}$ on all transactions, regardless of the rules. Whatever the London broker may lose in the quality of his commissions as compared with the New York broker appears, however, to be compensated by their quantity. A firm of jobbers of my acquaintance once handled in a single day 262,000 shares of "Americans" alone, and when it is borne in mind that this was but one of perhaps 150 firms doing a similar business, an idea may be gained as to how London brokers and jobbers contrive to keep the wolf from the door.

The system of settlements twice a month as employed in London is another method quite different from that employed in New York, and one, too, that seems to suffer by comparison with our system. On the New York Stock Exchange everything is settled on the day following the transaction. Each broker and each customer knows just where he stands, and every trade is settled in full when the next day ends. Tell an English broker that on a single day our Clearing-House settled and balanced transactions in more than 3,000,000 shares of an approximate value of 50,000,000 sterling and he gasps. He says that such a thing would be impossible in London, and he is right, it would be impossible indeed. Clearings in London vastly exceed ours, but they do not occur daily; indeed our system would not do at all in a centre that transacts, as London does, a large international business in which transfers must be sent hourly to Egypt and India and to all quarters of the globe. Daily clearings in such circumstances would be very troublesome and vexatious.

The New York system, however, makes failures and defaults commendably rare, while the London system, by postponing the day of reckoning, actually invites over-extensions in speculation leading to failures that could not possibly occur here. To make this point clear to the layman it may be said concisely that the man who settles daily is in a safer position both toward himself and his creditors than is the man who postpones his settlement. The daily settlement protects the public, as well, by putting limits on speculative commitments. These matters are self-evident.

A gentleman who was for many years identified with a London firm of jobbers, and who is now a member of the New York Stock Exchange and, therefore, quite familiar with the different methods employed in these Exchanges, tells me that the London system of brokers and jobbers, commission laws, and fortnightly settlements, is the best possible system for the London Exchange, while the very different methods employed in New York seem to him to be the best that can be devised for the New York Exchange. This may be true, since conditions governing the two markets are widely different. In New York the whole system is cash; in London, credit. Here brokers may accept business with considerable freedom, knowing that but a single day elapses before the reckoning; in London brokers exercise greater caution because they must trust their clients until settlement day.

Another point of difference between the methods of the two Exchanges lies in the phlegmatic deliberation of the Englishman. Here in New York there is a slap-dash, touch-and-go system that is greatly facilitated by the use of the telephone and the private telegraph lines; a single commission house has 10,000 miles of leased lines. In London, where telephones and private lines are but sparingly used by brokers and clients, a broker often finds on his desk in the morning three or four hundred letters and telegrams. The care and attention required to handle an enormous lot of orders given in this deliberate manner is something with which New York stockbrokers are quite unfamiliar; indeed it may be doubted if they could meet such an emergency with their present facilities.

Publicity, as we are learning in the New York Stock Exchange, is a prime requisite of the business, and the advantages that thus accrue through the use of the ticker and the published summary of each transaction in the day's work cannot be overestimated in its importance to the public and to the banks. In London, where a jobber may buy or sell large quantities of securities, the business is done quietly. Outside of the active participants in a transaction, nobody is permitted to know anything about it. There is no ticker service worthy of the name, nor is there a list of transactions published at the end of the day.

This, it seems obvious, would not do at all in America. We have here not only the ticker-tape, which prints an almost instantaneous report of prices all over the country, together with the volume of business done at those prices, but there are similar reports of the day's business printed in all the morning and evening papers — one of the last-named going so far as to reproduce on its financial page a copy of the day's tape from beginning to end. All the newspapers, moreover, print opening, high, low, and closing prices, together with the bid and offered price of each security at the market's close.

In the course of the two days in which these lines are written, for example, 257,000 shares of Reading Railroad stock have changed hands within a range of $1\frac{3}{8}$ per cent. The public is enabled, through the medium of the news-ticker, to learn who the buyers and sellers were that engaged in these transactions; the tape shows the specific volume of business done at each fraction, the various news agencies contain all the information and gossip that throws any light on the matter, and the financial columns of the morning and evening newspapers comment freely for the public benefit.

The total amount of information that is thus laid before the public is as complete and as instructive as could be desired, and yet in London and on the Continent such information is never published, although the two leading financial newspapers in London, because of the immense field covered, actually publish a mass of miscellaneous news and gossip that exceeds any similar American effort. They make it pay, too; dividends declared by these newspapers are altogether unapproached by the American financial press. The essential information lacking, however, is the number of shares dealt in, and at what prices; even if they had a thoroughly good ticker system I doubt if this information could be recorded, because the volume of business done is too great. It is encouraging in this connection to note that so eminent an economist as M. Leroy-Beaulieu frankly concedes our superiority in these matters over the practice of the foreign Exchanges and urges their immediate adoption abroad.*

The second serious objection that may fairly be lodged against the London system applies, as I have said, to the increased inducements offered to foolhardy and reckless speculation by the plan of deferred settlements. Whether members of the various Stock Exchanges in the world's capitals like it or not, they must recognize the fact that there are evils in speculation just as there are benefits, and that these evils are becoming a subject of increasing comment. The recent attempt to repress speculation in Germany and the conditions which led to the appointment of the Hughes Committee in New York are signs of an aroused public sentiment that cannot be ignored.

With these examples before them, members of Exchanges everywhere must realize that if it lies within their power to discountenance and

* *L'Economiste Francais*, Paris, October 5, 1912.

discourage foolhardy ventures into speculation by persons ill-equipped to undertake them it is their plain duty to do so. The London Stock Exchange's system of fortnightly settlements clearly does not aim at this highly desirable object as well as the method of daily settlements employed in New York, for it requires no student to see that by postponing the settlement risks will be incurred that would be impossible if a reckoning were called for each day. Moreover, the fact that there are ten failures on the London Stock Exchange to one in New York furnishes ample proof that the precautionary restriction imposed by daily settlements is quite as important to the welfare of brokers as it is to the protection of the public.

As a matter of fact, failures of brokerage houses are peculiarly abhorrent to every one concerned. In the Paris Bourse a broker must give security at $50,000, and his bankruptcy in all cases is considered a fraudulent one, rendering him liable to arrest. The French *Agents de Change* enjoy an absolute government monopoly, and naturally in the circumstances they are held to the strictest accountability; but aside from that a tendency is plainly discernible nowadays in all large financial centres to demand of stockbrokers on the Exchange a rigid adherence to such business methods as will prevent bankruptcies of dealers to whom the public entrusts its money.

The danger of the London fortnightly settlement system lies not in the deferred delivery of securities, but in the fortnightly settlement of "differences." A London broker may be actually bankrupt, yet if he is desperate or unscrupulous, knowing that his differences will not have to be settled for a fortnight, he may plunge into speculative risks fraught with the utmost danger. If the market goes his way he is saved; if it goes against him, he is still no more than bankrupt. But in his fall, as a result of this dishonest venture, he may conceivably ruin many others, and a chain of disasters may follow his excesses. It should be said in this connection that London jobbers and brokers keep a sharp watch on each other; it is extraordinary how quickly the news gets about if this man or that is over-extended. Again, either broker or jobber may discriminate in his dealings, taking care to avoid those against whom there is a suspicion.

Notwithstanding the points of merit in the New York system, at some time in the future when local Stock Exchange business has expanded to proportions approaching those of the London Exchange, modifications must be made. If banks and brokerage houses are given a week or ten days to settle transactions, everybody will have a tolerably clear idea of what money will be required, and lenders will be enabled to make provision. London passed through the 1907 panic, under this arrangement, with a maximum rate of 7 per cent., while we in New York would have been glad to pay 200 per cent., and this, despite our deplorable currency system, could not have occurred had there been ample time for the banks to make preparations.

From these observations it may be suggested that perhaps the time will come when the governors of the New York Stock Exchange may find it necessary to put in force a combination of daily settlement of differences, such as we have at present, with a periodical delivery of stock such as they have in London. Transactions for cash need not be affected by this arrangement, nor would the public lose any of the protection it now enjoys. In any case, if such a plan resulted in minimizing those violent fluctuations in our call-money market which have so long afflicted us, it would prove a permanent blessing.

As there is no currency system anywhere in the civilized world so crude and inadequate as that of the United States, it is unnecessary to say that London jobbers and brokers experience none of the difficulties with money markets that occur periodically on this side. The carry-over on the other side of the water is frequently a matter involving immense sums of money, but rates fluctuate normally and are in large measures governed by automatic processes both simple and sane. Perhaps the less said about similar conditions here the better. The spectacle presented by strong and solvent houses ransacking the street for funds secured by prime collateral and bidding 25, 50, and even 100 per cent. for accommodation — something that has occurred within the last decade and may conceivably occur again — is one upon which the candid American observer does not care to dwell; such a man may well look with longing and envy to London, where capital, credit, and currency are so firmly established that the Bank of England dominates and controls all the money markets and gold movements of the world, lending freely at home and abroad whenever funds are needed, and acting as a civilizing force in supplying with British funds the commercial needs of all new countries.

In this connection we may point out the method of borrowing from the banks the funds required to carry speculative commitments in London. It was formerly the practice for the banks to lend large sums to brokers, who employed the money inside the house in carrying over the accounts of their clients. This class of business is still large, but nowadays clients are not always satisfied to borrow through brokers, and not infrequently they go direct to the banks and borrow from them. This has the effect of disguising the real character of the business. To all appearances the securities have been bought and paid for, and the trade seems to be an investment, but the client has, as a matter of fact, "pawned" the security with a bank.

This practice is inconvenient in a way, because where the jobbers in important markets formerly compared notes at each settlement and were thus enabled to form a pretty good idea of the condition of the speculative account, it is less easy to do so nowadays, when so many clients carry on their own borrowing. A similar tendency on the part of the public is noticeable in New York, although, of course, the daily settlement on this side obviates the necessity for arriving at conclusions in advance as to the requirements of funds.

A word should be said about the methods of London stockbrokers in carrying stocks for their customers, because this also is quite different from the practice in New York. Here the strongest houses rarely loan stocks, unless attracted by unusual rates of interest; in London it is the common practice of even the best houses to carry-over, or as we term it, loan, a great part of the commitments entered into during the account. One reason for this is that in London customers buy their stocks outright more frequently than is done here. Scalping small profits is not practised on anything like the New York scale. Most of the stocks dealt in do not pass from hand to hand like American stocks, but must have a transfer form with the name and address of the buyer and seller attached to the certificate. There is also a government stamp-tax of ½ per cent. on the money involved, which tax must be paid by the buyer when the stock is transferred to him. When the buyer sells this stock he may not have immediate use for the proceeds, and so, instead of delivering the stock standing in his name, he instructs his broker to borrow it from account to account, thus receiving interest on his money. The tax is a heavy one — figured in American money it amounts to $50 per hundred shares at par — and the Englishman very naturally resorts to methods such as these to recoup at least a part of it.

Again, from the stockbroker's point of view, if he buys securities on margin for a customer, he (the broker) must either carry them with the jobber or with another broker, or he will have to pay the government tax himself. Naturally he hastens to loan them, because, should the client sell the securities in the course of the next account when they would have to be delivered, the broker would lose the tax. He avoids this loss by instructing a jobber to contango or carry-over the securities until the following account day. On the other hand, if the broker is certain that his client has purchased his securities for a long pull on a margin basis, he will often pay for the stock himself, transfer it to his own name, and willingly submit to the government tax, knowing that he can recover the outlay from the handsome rate of interest charged the client.

Another vital point of difference between the London and the New York Stock Exchange lies in the nature and volume of the business done. Americans are prone to think of their foremost Exchange as one which, in the volume and extent of its transactions, compares favorably with the great Bourses of the world; they like to think of New York as the financial centre of the universe, and they paint rosy pictures of America as a great creditor nation. But they err in each of these ambitious dreams. The New York Stock Exchange, with all its magnitude, cannot compare with its London prototype; New York is by no means the financial centre of the world, and America is not a creditor, but a debtor nation.

Perhaps in time America's relationship to England and to the rest of the world may change in these matters — certainly its increase in per capita wealth and real property is such as to justify the hope — but at present the day when we may speak of American financial supremacy seems a long way off. We have not yet forgotten, for example, the panic of 1907, and our helpless situation as revealed by our demand for gold, nor are we likely soon to forget the funds that were then promptly supplied us by London without any dangerous depletion of the Bank of England's reserve. So smoothly, so automatically are these large affairs conducted by the Bank that the outflow of gold to New York found a prompt response in the inflow from twenty-four countries, including the Colonies. Within six weeks after the American drain began, the bank's stock of bullion actually exceeded its original store. Small wonder that Englishmen are proud of their bank; and that London should have become the world's centre for the investment of capital and the diffusion of credit.

The New York Stock Exchange business differs radically from that of all other great Exchanges in the one respect that its dealings are practically confined to home corporations, whereas the Bourses in Paris and Berlin, and more particularly the Stock Exchange in London, embrace in their daily lists securities representing many different countries all over the world. Here we have Canadian Pacific Railway shares, and various Mexican Railway securities, together with some issues of Japanese and German bonds, London Underground Railway bonds, and a few others. But these, with the exception of Canadians, are dealt in sparingly and with a rather nominal market. Our list of securities is composed almost entirely of home rails and industrials companies, representing, to be sure, an enormous total of capital investment and signifying the tremendous growth of a comparatively new country backed by the energies of a thrifty and enterprising people, but compared with the London Stock Exchange's Daily Official List ours is meagre in the extreme.

The London Daily List covers sixteen pages as large as our daily newspapers, each page printed closely in small type, and containing the names, amounts, interest dates, rates of dividend, and occasional quotations of approximately 4700 different listed securities. This long list, moreover, contains the names only of the securities that have received an official settlement and an official quotation as well. There are certainly as many more securities dealt in that have not received an official quotation and hence are not permitted to appear in the List, so that the total number of different securities represented on the London Exchange in one or both of these ways probably exceeds 9000, half of them occupying a position somewhat similar to the Unlisted Department which once had a place on the New York Stock Exchange, but which is now abolished.

It is the largest and most varied list of securities in the world. The price of a single copy is six-pence; it is published by the trustees and managers, under the authority of the committee. Not the least interesting feature of the List is its continued expansion in the last half-century. Up to the year 1867 one page sufficed, then four till 1889, eight till 1900, twelve till 1902, and sixteen thereafter, this expansion closely following the nominal value of the securities quoted, which were £5,480,000,000 in 1885 and £10,200,000,000 in 1909. The latter figure is about equal to the combined nominal capital value of the securities quoted on the Paris Bourse and the New York Stock Exchange. In 1907 the total number of bonds then listed on the New York Stock Exchange was 1100, and the total number of stocks

502, these together representing a total par value of $21,079,620,430. In 1912 this total amounted to 1,028 bonds and 555 stocks, with an aggregate par value of $26,243,291,803.

The London List is conveniently divided into thirty-eight different classes, among them British Funds, Corporation and County Stocks of the United Kingdom, Public Boards, Colonial and Provincial Government Securities, Indian and Colonial and Provincial Government Securities, Indian and Colonial Corporation Stocks, Foreign Corporation Stocks and Bonds, Ordinary Shares and Stocks of English Railways, Railways leased at fixed rentals, Railway Debenture Stocks and Guaranteed Stocks and Shares, together with preference shares, Indian Railways, Indian Native Raj and Zemindary loans, Railways in British possessions, American Railroad Stocks and Bonds, Securities of Foreign Railways, Banks and Discount Companies, Breweries and Distilleries, Canals and Docks, Miscellaneous Commercial and Industrial Companies, Electric Lighting and Power Companies, Financial, Land, and Investment Companies, Financial Trusts, Gas Companies, Insurance Companies, Iron, Coal, and Steel Companies, Mines, Nitrates, Shipping, Tea, Coffee and Rubber, Telegraphs and Telephones, Tramways and Omnibus, and Water Works. Of these the Commercial and Industrial Companies List is by far the largest, covering three pages.

A cursory glance over this really formidable Official List brings forcibly to mind London's supreme position as banker, broker, and clearing house for the wide world, while it emphasizes the constantly increasing overflow of British capital into channels that make for enterprise and development even in the most remote quarters of the globe. Here we find set forth Ceylon, Fiji, Tasmania, and Cape of Good Hope debentures; Stocks of Saskatchewan, Antigua, Johannesburg and the Straits Settlements; Harbor Board Mortgages of Oamaru and Wanganui; Rangoon Sterling Loans; Municipal Stocks of Pernambuco; Budapest, St. Louis, Tokio, Lima and Aarhus; Ecuador salt bonds and bonds of the Grand Duchy of Finland; securities of the Greek Piraeus Larissa Railway, Honduras 10 per cent. loans, loans of Liberia, Persia and Siam, and certificates of the Venezuela Diplomatic Debt. There are securities of the Ionian Bank, the Natal Bank and the Bank of Abyssinia. The Terra del Fuego Development Company is represented, and likewise Amazon Telegraphs, Malacca Rubbers, Singapore Electrics, Rangoon Tramways, Montevideo Water Works, and Sao Paulo Match Factories. Soda and newspapers, theatres and sawmills, hotels and clothiers, sponges and molasses, soaps and cereals, these are some of the items that catch the eye as one glances over the List. What would be found there if all the securities admitted to the House were published in the List may be left to conjecture; and what will this eloquent array of enterprise in figures look like a century hence, if the List continues its present rate of growth?

As Great Britain is a country where there is never any difficulty about raising capital for the creation or extension of any business which offers a reasonable probability of large profits, it is natural that new countries where capital is scarce and credit scarcer should turn to London. Thus governments, municipalities, company promoters and manufacturers from all over the world are constantly making application for funds with which to supply their needs. Greek railways, Abyssinian banks, Ceylon tea and Malay rubbers hasten to register themselves at the world's centre of capital and offer their shares to a public whose taste for all kinds of world-wide industrial and commercial ventures seems never likely to be satiated, since the really good and profitable home enterprises are seldom open to public subscription. The insiders in those bonanzas naturally keep their treasures to themselves and their friends, unless after a time the concern is turned into a limited liability company with good-will as a conspicuous asset and over-capitalization as the dominating motive; then, as elsewhere, the market is invited to assist. But that is another story.

What is of especial interest to a Wall Street man who looks over the enormous list of London's Stock Exchange securities is the function and method of the Listing Committee that has to pass on all these concerns before admitting them to the House. In New York the Stock Exchange's "Committee on Stock List" insists that the applicant company must be able to show at least one year's earnings — a most important condition. In London somewhat different conditions prevail. The committee looks into the bona fides of an applicant company and makes inquiries concerning the people behind it, but it does not require that it shall have done business for at least a year and show a year's earnings, because if that were insisted upon as a condition precedent, the banks would not finance it, nor the public support it. They have no "curb market" in London where a new company may pass through a seasoning or preparatory period while awaiting admission to the Stock Exchange, and as a settlement day with Stock Exchange authority is rigorously insisted upon by those who provide the funds, it follows that companies must be admitted at least to "official settlement" privileges as soon as they are organized.

One point upon which the London Exchange authorities lay great weight in the admission of new securities, consists in obtaining assurances that a sufficient number of shares has been allotted to the public before admission is granted. This is a thoroughly wise precaution, designed to prevent corners and, as far as possible, improper manipulation. Another very interesting, and I may say, a very wise precautionary measure of the London method of listing, is the prohibition placed upon vendor's shares — a plan that might well be adopted in New York. In London, for example, a vendor — i. e., a seller of the property — who receives shares in consideration of the sale, cannot have his shares listed until six months have elapsed after shares of the company have been offered to the public. The protection afforded the public by this plan is obvious, and requires no further comment.*

* Rule 150 reads as follows: "The committee will not fix a special settling day for bargains in shares or securities issued to the vendors, credited as full or partly paid, until six months after the date fixed for the special settlement in the shares or securities of the same class subscribed for by the public, but this does not necessarily apply to reorganizations or amalgamations of existing companies, or to cases where no public shares are issued for cash." — Rules and Regulations of the Stock Exchange. London, June 3, 1911, pp. 64–5.

If the London share certificates required, as in New York, only a simple endorsement for transfer, much of the annoyance and confusion that sometimes takes place would be avoided. The market for mining shares, for example, had until 1888 only a very small place in the London Stock Exchange, but the discovery of gold in the Witwatersrand changed all that, and by 1894 the number of brokers engaged in handling mining shares actually exceeded those in any other department. It was found necessary to provide a special day — one day before the regular settlement commenced — for carrying over bargains in mines, but owing to the fact that mining shares, like nearly all securities in London, were "registered" and not "to bearer," the clearing house was taxed beyond its powers by the immense volume of work thrown upon it, and once or twice it broke down completely.

An extraordinary number of small investors bought fractional shares; the offices of the companies were not prepared for the rush and could not handle the large carry-over, hence for a time the "Kaffir Circus," as the speculative mania of the day was called, promised to embarrass seriously the whole Exchange machinery. All this could have been avoided by making the shares "to bearer." Yet the London authorities feel — and not without reason when we consider the volume of their business and the remoteness of their clientele in many instances — that bearer certificates are not safe, and that what is lost in the time spent in transferring certificates is amply compensated in the resultant security against fraud and forgery.

It is interesting to note in connection with the enormous business done on the London Exchange — a business which makes New York's high totals seem insignificant — on what a vast scale London's exports of capital are conducted. This may properly be noticed here, since these capital exports have great economic significance and bear close relationship to the transactions on the Stock Exchange; indeed were it not for the work done by the Exchange in providing markets and settlements and all the details of the security business, it is fair to say there could be no such public issues of capital. In 1910, for example, new capital expenditures amounted to the extraordinary figure of £267,439,000, of which £60,296,500 was expended in the United Kingdom, £92,378,100 in the various British possessions, and £114,764,500 in foreign countries. Of the grand total £49,974,-000 went into foreign railways, £10,096,000 into Indian and Colonial railways, £35,631,600 into Colonial government loans, £18,431,000 into foreign government loans, £18,343,100 into explorations, and £19,143,800 into rubber.* The year 1910 was, of course, a year of great prosperity in England, and it was a year made famous by speculative activity in various directions, especially in rubber, so that the totals given above are larger than they had ever been before. But the point for us in America to bear in mind in considering these figures is their immense significance as showing England's complete supremacy in capital, credit, and the art of banking.

The immense number of securities dealt in, coupled with the speculative propensities of the people and the ramifications of British finance, naturally go to make that Exchange a peculiarly sensitive and vulnerable spot, and the American visitor may well wonder what would happen there if the ancient bogy of war between England and any other first-rate power should some day become a reality. War is, as every one knows, the greatest destroyer of capital. England's little Transvaal war cost $1,000,000 a day, and by the Chancellor of the Exchequer's report resulted in a total expenditure of $1,085,000,000. The war between Russia and Japan cost upward of $3,000,000 daily and $2,000,000,000 all told. What a great

* These figures are taken from Mr. Hirst's Chapter VIII on "The Creation of New Debt and Capital," pp. 212–241.

war would cost England if that country were to cross swords with one of the powers may be conjectured; what would happen in the Stock Exchange taxes the imagination.

In the month in which these lines are written the London Stock Exchange and all the continental Bourses are having their periodic scare over a war in the Balkans. British consols have fallen almost seven points from the high price of the year; French rentes seven, German 3s. six, and Russian 4s. seven.* These are very severe declines for government securities of that class, and if they can fall abruptly over difficulties in the Balkans, what would happen were these countries themselves involved in war with foemen of their own class? Russian consolidated 4s. fell eleven points and Japanese 5s. twelve in the first month of the Manchurian war, and in our war with Spain, Spanish 4s. fell from 61 to 29¾. If such things can happen to government securities, what would happen to all the 9000 odd industrial and kindred securities dealt in on the London Exchange should England take up the sword with, let us say, Germany? We are not left to conjecture on this point, for in the week that has just witnessed

* It should be said that at least a part of the decline in these securities had taken place before the Balkan scare became a reality. A foreknowledge of what was impending may have influenced the earlier decline; certainly the event itself accentuated and hastened it.

the Balkan scare there have been some really tremendous slumps in securities — collapses out of proportion, it would seem at this distance, to the magnitude of the political issues threatened.

In Paris, for example, there has just been witnessed a two-day break of 185 points in Sosnoviche Collieries, a one-day break of 165 points in Bakou Naphtha, a decline within a few hours of 115 points in Russian Naphtha and overwhelming breaks of from 50 to 150 francs in Paris Light and Transport shares, Rio Tintos, and Electrics. No such demoralization has been seen in any foreign financial market within twenty-five years. This slump was no doubt due in large part to a top-heavy speculative position and to consequent financial congestion, but it was the Balkan war-cloud that caused the real difficulty none the less, and it supplies an outsider with an idea of what may happen in a real emergency.

Foreigners are prone to speak of Yankee speculation as foolhardy and reckless, as no doubt it is at times, but never in American history has there been a panic with anything like the severe declines, in so brief a period, as those just recorded. For that matter, we in America have never experienced a boom in any sense commensurate with London's rubber boom of 1909–10, nor a collapse as sudden and as thoroughly deserved as that which followed it. Again, London's Kaffir Circus of 1894–5, and the furious speculation in Panama shares in Paris in the early nineties, have had no parallel in American stock markets. This is only another way of saying that the speculative mania which seizes upon nations at periodic intervals is not a matter of latitude and longitude in any sense.*

In trying to picture what would happen in the London Stock market should such a war as that which Englishmen are always discussing really occur, we must take into account not only the mass of securities that would be directly affected, but also the great burden borne by London banks and bankers in security issues all over the world. On another page we have seen that London's capital expenditures on new issues in various quarters of the globe in a single year exceeded £267,000,000; in the quarter just closed (September, 1912), these disbursements ran £25,000,000 above the previous year.

That they will continue so to increase is open to no doubt as long as England's abstention from war is assured; but if there should arise even the

* London jobbers were, in a way, instrumental in checking the furious speculation in "rubbers" toward the culmination of the boom of 1909–10. Their absolute refusal to carry rubber shares for brokers, and their concerted insistence that such shares should be paid for in full on the ensuing account day, undoubtedly put the brakes on a furious speculation, and prevented many failures.

possibility of war, it would result in an embarrassment of credit with terribly serious results, such as have never been dreamed of in the world's history. The many years of peace between the great powers, the many new countries that have been opened to commercial development, and the countless new fields of industrial endeavor that have come into being while this peace has lasted, have served to create a British credit situation huge and complicated beyond all precedent. Any serious interruption or derangement of so vast a system would find a very different situation from that which existed on the Continent in 1870. It would be appalling.

And yet, ere we go too far afield in search of the shivers, the observer must bear in mind that this great credit system of which London is the banker and clearing house, in reality knits together in its international web all the great powers, and binds them so closely together as to guarantee, in some measure, the preservation of peace. That peace hath her victories, and that the creation of wealth through industrial pursuits may serve in this way to prevent armed strife — these are, after all, encouraging indications quite as strong as treaties. To-day the bankers of London and Paris are the war lords of creation. Both these centres loan money, on early maturing bills, to all the world. Stop London's discounts through an outbreak of war, and gold would pour into that centre at the rate of $200,000,000 a month. "It might be possible to starve her population," says a recent writer, "but no combination of the Powers could bankrupt London. In the event of war Paris could bankrupt Germany in a week. No war could disturb the credit of the Bank of France; but the German Reichsbank would inevitably go down in the smash. All Germany's capital is in her own shop. She is doing a great business, and, quite properly, a great part of it on borrowed money. But if her loans were called, she must put up the shutters."*

Let us now observe the London broker at his work. The Stock Exchange, as has been described, settles nearly all of its transactions twice a month, upon officially appointed "account days," which fall about the middle and the end of every month. Smith, a broker, receives an order to buy, let us say, 500 East Rands, and goes to a jobber who makes a specialty of that department. The jobber, Jones, is a wise man and a clever trader, who knows all there is to know about supply and demand and regulation of prices to meet them, otherwise he would soon be out of business. Smith does not tell him what he pro-

* The *Wall Street Journal*, November 13, 1912.

poses to do, but asks for a price, which in normal markets Jones quotes at $3\frac{1}{2}$ to $3\frac{9}{16}$, this being the method of implying, in pounds sterling, that he is prepared to buy at 70s., or to sell at 71s. 3d. The broker will probably say that the price is too wide, whereupon Jones quotes a figure "close to close," reducing the quotation $\frac{1}{64}$ each way, at which figure the transaction is closed.* Smith enters in his book that he has bought of Jones 500 East Rands at the price stated, and Jones, that he has sold at this price to Smith. The customer is then advised of the transaction, and next day he receives his stamped contract, with details covering the cost of the shares together with brokerage and other expenses, if any, and informing him of the date of the next account day, when payment will fall due.

Beneath the main floor of the Exchange is the settling room, and here the clerks of broker and jobber check the transaction that has taken place. Two days before the account the name of the person for whom the East Rands were bought is written on a ticket — hence "ticket day" — and handed to the Stock Exchange Clearing House, which, after the manner of the Stock Exchange Clearing House in New York,

* On the New York Stock Exchange the minimum difference between prices is one eighth and splitting of this fraction is prohibited save in the case of "rights" to subscribe or similar instances.

eliminates all the intermediaries through whose hands the shares may have passed ad interim, and puts the selling broker into direct communication, by passing him the ticket, with the broker of the buyer. This done, the seller receives the ticket with the buyer's name on it, and prepares a transfer deed as the law requires.* Had the client bought the shares of an American railway instead of East Rands, the procedure following the purchase would have been somewhat different, because American shares bear a form of transfer on the back which requires the signature of the seller only, and which becomes, by reason of this fact, almost as readily negotiable as bank-notes.

In London consols can be dealt in in this way, but the customary form of conveyance of the funds, and of Indian and Colonial stocks, consists of a brief transfer on the books of the bank acting as agent for the particular issue. Thus the Bank of England keeps the books for consols and India government stocks, and sellers or their attorneys must attend personally at the bank and sign the transfer. The bank insists that every seller must be identified by a member of the Stock Exchange, whose signature must be registered there, and it places full responsibility upon

* In the settling room on ticket day stocks that are not cleared pass by ticket from broker to broker in much the same way as that provided by the Clearing House.

these members for correct identifications. This was long a sore point with the Stock Exchange, and it was fought to a finish in the courts, but the Bank won "in a walk."

The transaction just cited in the case of East Rands is based on the supposition that the original buyer proposed to "take up," or pay for his shares in full. If he is merely a speculator, hoping to sell at a profit before the settling day and pocket the difference, a somewhat different procedure is involved, especially if at the approach of settling day the hoped-for rise has not appeared. In that case he asks his broker to "carry-over," "contango," or "give on," the shares he has bought, and the broker, to whom this is an hourly occurrence, naturally has at his finger tips ample facilities for doing what is required.

Going to the jobber, he says he wants to "give on" five hundred East Rands. The jobber says he will "take them in," which means that he will lend the money until next following settlement, charging interest at, say, 5 per cent., while the broker in turn charges his client $5\frac{1}{2}$ per cent. and takes the interest difference as compensation for the service. The buyer's speculation is thus extended to the next settlement, and the statement given him shows that he has been debited with the interest upon the "making-up price," at which the transaction is arranged. The rate of interest is called the "contango," and "contango days" are the two days during the settlement when these arrangements are in effect:*

"The Stock Exchange has witnessed many periods of wild excitement and speculation, reminding one of the famous South Sea Bubble — perhaps the most remarkable "boom" on record — the story of which, however, has been so often and so vividly told by Smollett and later writers that we need only refer to it here. Just before the middle of the last century came the great railway boom. It began about 1834, and within one year more than six hundred propositions for railway lines in the United Kingdom were placed before the public, the nominal capital required being over 600,000,000 pounds sterling. Panic, of course, followed the boom; and, as an example of the rapidity with which prices moved, it may be mentioned that the Great Western Railway stock rose to 236 in 1845, and fell back to 55½ within three years, while Midland stock rose to 183 and fell to 64. After the railway boom and panic came several banking crises, of which the worst were those identified with the names of Overend, Gurney, & Co. in 1866, and of Baring Brothers in 1890. For five years after the latter, the Stock Exchange lay fallow, with business and credit worn to a shadow. Then came the famous Kaffir boom, of which it may be said

* Although an effort has been made in these pages to avoid complicated Stock Exchange technique, the contango, which is not fully understood in America, requires technical explanation. It may be defined as a double-bargain, in that it consists of a sale for cash of the stock previously bought which the broker does not wish to carry, and a repurchase for the new settlement two weeks ahead, of the same stock at the same price as the sale, plus interest agreed upon up to the date of that settlement.

that Cecil Rhodes stood out as the colossus. The madness of that boom has rarely been equaled, even in the history of the Yankee market. It makes one hot even on a cold day to think of the time when, as a clerk, one tore off coat, waistcoat, collar, and tie in order to run the faster in the settling room beneath the Stock Exchange, "passing names" (as it is technically called) in connection with that gamble. A Rugby football scrum was child's play to the continued struggles; and, after the most violent excitement had subsided, there were always fights to be settled before one went upstairs to work the whole night through.

"A period of collapse followed this episode. After various minor upheavals there came in 1910 the rubber boom, which, perhaps with the Kaffir Gamble, more nearly recalls the excitement of 1720 than any other, The rubber boom had not, indeed, the same noble backing which the South Sea Company boasted; but clergymen and ladies were prominent operators as 'bulls,' 'stags,' or both."*

The thought will no doubt occur to an American who reads these pages, whether the day will come when American banking will extend, as in England, to every quarter of the globe, and whether the New York Exchange, like its London prototype, will become a centre of the world's commercial activities. This is a far cry, of course, and the answer will not be known in our generation. But it may be said without fear of con-

---

* The methods of transacting business on the London Stock Exchange are admirably stated in condensed form in an article by Walter Landells in the *Quarterly Review*, July, 1912, pp. 88–109, and I am indebted to his article for many of the foregoing facts, and for this brief summary of London's booms and crises.

tradiction that when a great nation like ours, in which the spirit of enterprise is manifest, has reached the point where its own domain has been developed, when it has perfected a sound banking and currency system, when it has recovered its lost shipping and mastered those economic lessons that the future has in store, it may confidently be expected to push out into new lands and supply their demands for capital.

Already we have in America a world's storehouse of necessary commodities, with wealth and intelligence that increases by leaps and bounds. No nation stands a better chance of escaping the horrors of war and its ruinous losses. China remains a fertile field for commercial endeavor in the years to come, and our neighbors on the south may one day know us more intimately. The retrospective eye, surveying commercial and financial America in the sixties and contrasting it with America of to-day, sees clearly that progress has been made, and looks beyond toward progress to come. In any case civilization must advance and trade expand, and American energy must advance and expand with them. I wish I might visit Wall Street and the Stock Exchange a century hence.*

* In addition to the authorities quoted in the foregoing chapter, the atten-

tion of the reader is directed to the following works having to do with the London Stock Exchange:

Lombard Street, by Walter Bagehot, New York, Chas. Scribner's, and Sons.

Stocks and Shares, by Hartley Withers, London, Smith Elder, 1910.

Stock Exchange Law and Practice, by W. A. Bewes, London, Sweet & Maxwell, 1910.

Rise of the London Money Market, 1640–1826, by W. R. Bisschop, London, King, 1910.

The Mechanism of the City, by Ellis T. Powell, London, King, 1910.

CHAPTER X

THE PARIS BOURSE; A MONOPOLY UNDER GOVERNMENT

CHAPTER X

THE PARIS BOURSE; A MONOPOLY UNDER GOVERNMENT

"PATRIOTISM makes it a duty for us to acknowledge the fact that the Bourse represents one of the live forces of France," wrote Anatole Leroy-Beaulieu in one of the finest tributes ever paid to a Stock Exchange. "It has been for France an instrument of regeneration after defeat, and it remains for us a powerful tool in war and in peace. Let us recall the already remote years of our convalescence, after the invasion, years at once sorrowful and comforting, when with the gloom of defeat and the suffering of dismemberment, mingled the joy of feeling the revival of France. Whence came our first consolation, our first vindication before the world? Whether glorious or not, it originated on the Bourse."

The victorious Prussians were at the door in the humiliating crisis of 1870 and '71 to which the author refers, France was prostrate. Alsace and parts of Lorraine were to be ceded to the victors, together with an indemnity of five billion francs, and Paris was in control of the Reds. In that dreadful saturnalia of violence and crime which has made the name of the Commune infamous, the honor of France was threatened, and the credit of the new Republican government, especially its ability to maintain its authority and to fulfill its terms with the Prussians, seemed hopeless and cheerless indeed. How Thiers became the brains of the rehabilitation of France, with what vigor he entered upon the task that has handed down his name as the most influential political figure in French history—with what rigorous measures MacMahon suppressed the Commune — these are spectacular incidents with which every schoolboy is familiar. But the work of the Bourse in that episode — silent, unobtrusive, and lacking the sensational features of which popular histories are made, is by no means so well known, although upon its labors devolved the real upbuilding of France. Thiers never ceased to congratulate himself on the assistance it gave the country at a time when the liberation of French territory hung in the balance.

"The Paris market came out unscathed from the ruins of the war and of the Commune," continues our author, "and straight from the hardly ratified peace and quelled insurrection it threw itself into the work for France's regeneration;

because it was, indeed, for France's regeneration that the stockbrokers and merchandise brokers worked under Thiers and MacMahon. In the worst days the Bourse had the uncommon merit of showing an example of faith in France. When more than one political skeptic and discouraged thinker allowed themselves to write down upon the crumbling walls of our burned-down palaces "Finis Galliae," the Bourse kept its faith in France and her fortune, and that faith in France was spread by it all around, at home and abroad.

"Speculation was patriotic in its way; it exhibited a confidence in our resources which the discretion of many a wise man rated as foolhardy. Have we already forgotten our great loans for liberation? Without the Bourse, these colossal loans, the amount of which exceeded the dreams of financiers, would never have been subscribed for, or, if ever, it would have been only at rates much more onerous for the country. Without the Bourse, our French rentes would not have taken such rapid flight; our credit, restored even more quickly than our armies, would not have equaled that of our victors, on the very morrow of our defeat. In that regard, all that justice demanded us to say previously of the higher banking institutions may with right be repeated concerning the Bourse.

"To those who lived through that pale dawn of France's recovery — the rush of the Bourse and of capitalists to offer us the thousands of millions which we required exceeded the eagerness and boldness of speculation. But even if we were to consider it but gambling and betting for speculation, such speculation was betting for France's regeneration; it bravely placed its bet on the vanquished. Those national and foreign financiers, who have been accused of pouncing upon her like birds of prey, brought to the noble wounded their dollars and their credit, and if they reaped a profit thereby, are we to reproach them for it, when they helped us to reconstruct our armies, our fleet, and our arsenals?

"If France regained her rank among the nations of the world so quickly, the credit for it should be mainly given to the Bourse. And to its services in war, we should, if we wanted to be just, also add its services in time of peace. Without the extensiveness of the Paris market, and the stimulus given to our capitalists through speculation, how many things would have remained unaccomplished in the recklessly overdriven condition of our finances? We should have been unable to complete our railroad system, or renew our national stock of tools, or create beyond the seas a colonial empire which shall cause France to be again one of the great world powers. When the Bourse is on trial, such credentials should not be overlooked. Before condemning it in the name of morality and private interests, a patriot should give due consideration to its services rendered for the national weal; if all its defects and misdeeds be heaped up on one scale tray, then services of like importance will easily counterbalance them."*

Singing the praises of Stock Exchanges is a thankless task, and one that falls upon deaf ears. The very nature of its functions makes dull reading. It cannot hope to enlist the lively enthusiasm of the casual observer, nor has it picturesqueness to brighten the pages of history. The layman visits the great exchanges as a matter of course; the scene is animated and diverting; he sees the outward manifestations of energy and movement, but too often he misses the great silent forces at work. The eye has a fine time of it, but the intellect comes away empty. These are reasons why I have ventured to quote the foregoing passages from M. Leroy-Beaulieu. Somewhere in his earnest tribute to the work of the Paris Bourse the reader may find food for thought.

---

* Anatole Leroy-Beaulieu, La Régence de l'argent, "Revue des Deux Mondes." February 25, 1897, pp. 894 and 895.

(M. Leroy-Beaulieu is the elder brother of Paul, the French economist. In 1881 he became professor of modern history at the Ecole Libre des Sciences Politiques, and in 1887 was made a member of the Academy of Moral and Political Sciences. His fame as a publicist is established.)

The Bourse in Paris differs from all others in that its membership consists of but seventy. These *Agents de Change*, as they are called, enjoy an absolute monopoly not only to trade in government and other officially listed securities, but also to negotiate bills of exchange and similar instruments of credit. In these circumstances it is easy to see why the Bourse is an institution of enormous strength, notwithstanding the fact that, because of the deep-rooted conservatism of the French in financial matters, it stands a poor second to London in international business.

It exists by virtue of the decree of October 7, 1900, regulating the execution of article 90 of the Code du Commerce and of the law of March 28, 1885, as modified by the decree of January 29, 1898. These laws provide that *Agents de Change* of the Paris Bourse must be French citizens over twenty-five years of age, and in possession of civil and political rights; they must be nominated by official decree signed by the President of the Republic. They must have performed their military service or satisfied the law as to such service, they must produce a certificate of fitness and good character signed by the heads of several banking and commercial firms. *Agents de Change* are, in reality, officers of the government, since the seventy ministerial appointees are entrusted with the exclusive right of dealing in government securities; all such dealings, in fact, when not made directly by private individuals, must be made through *Agents de Change.*

The enjoyment by stockbrokers of a complete monopoly under government is sufficiently unique to warrant an inquiry as to the origin of such a curious privilege. The employment of stockbrokers by persons who wished to sell certificates, or other negotiable instruments of the period, was made obligatory by an edict of Louis XIV in 1705. Twenty "offices" (memberships) of brokers in Paris were then created, and these twenty were accorded a monopoly similar to that of to-day. Prior to that period there had been "offices" of exchange brokers, bank brokers, and merchandise brokers, but the King felt that these were not contributing enough to the Royal exchequer and swept them all away in the edict of 1705, when the present system had its birth. The wars and the King's extravagances had placed the exchequer in a bad way, and between 1691 and 1709, some 40,000 privileges of various kinds were sold for cash, among them the privilege under which these twenty men were to do the business of stockbroking in Paris. "Sire," said Pontchartrain, "every time Your Majesty creates an office, God creates a fool to buy it."

But the stockbrokers were not to remain in undisturbed possession of their new privileges, for, whenever the state of the Royal finances was low, the King withdrew the old offices in order to grant new ones, always for cash, to fresh buyers, and this was repeated again and again. Thus the next King Louis XV, whose personal follies, together with the schemes of the Scotchman, John Law,* brought the country to the verge of ruin, repealed in 1726 the Edict of 1705 and returned to it again in 1733. His successor, the weak and incapable Louis XVI, repeated this performance in 1785, 1786, and in 1787. In 1788, the stockbrokers having agreed to waive accumulated interest on their security deposits, were again established in their powerful monopoly. The critical financial situation that arose in the early days of the Revolution saw them again legislated out of office (June 27, 1793); the Bourse was closed, the stockbrokers arrested and their goods confiscated, because, in the imperfectly understood economics of the period, the decline in Frenchpaper currency (assignats) was attributed, *faute de mieux*, to stock-jobbing. Two years later the Bourse was opened again, and after eight days — the assignat continuing to decline, it was again closed. Meantime France went into bankruptcy.

* John Law was the inventor of "bearer" certificates.

In 1801 the modern Bourse was established and firmly fixed by the legislative work of the Consulate. The law then enacted requires that stockbrokers be appointed to their public trust by the government, which shall be guided in its choice by their moral character and their professional knowledge, and shall, besides, demand the pledging of a part of their fortune with the State as a guarantee of their good conduct and of proper expiation for their errors or failures. The law also emphasizes the principle of the freedom of commerce, expressly stating that nobody is obliged to have recourse to an intermediary, if he does not desire it. Further, the stockbrokers were subjected to several regulations with a view to prevent speculation and stock-jobbing. Thus, they were obliged to keep a journal; their books were to be marked and signed by the president of the *Tribunal de Commerce;* they could not trade nor carry on banking for their own account; no one who had been in bankruptcy was allowed to assume the duties of a stockbroker.

The law also makes the stockbroker responsible for the delivery of the securities sold and for the payment of the sums stipulated, even before either have been received by him from his clients, his security being appropriated for this pledge if need be. This responsibility was intended as a check upon transactions for future delivery, which, however, were made legal in 1885.* This law of 1801, it will be observed, provided that stockbrokers were to be *appointed by the government*, and that their commissions were subject to repeal. In 1816 they scored a great advantage by securing the enactment of a measure by which they were permitted to introduce their successors with the consent of the government. This "right of introduction," says M. Vidal, "is practically an article for sale. The stockbroker, on retiring, does not sell his office (membership), but he sells to his successor the right of introduction."

The price of this right in recent years has varied from 1,500,000 to 2,000,000 francs ($300,000 to $400,000). A candidate, proving satisfactory to the government, must in addition deposit 250,000 francs ($50,000) as a bond or security to the government, which pays interest on the deposit, and 120,000 francs ($24,000) as a fee to the *caisse commune* of the *chambre syndicale*, which means the treasury funds of the institution. The variations in the price of the "offices" or memberships have an interesting history. The first office sold was valued at 30,000 francs; about 1830 they rose to 850,000 francs; after the July

* "The History and Methods of the Paris Bourse," by E. Vidal, Senate Document No. 573, Sixty-first Congress (Second session), pp. 161–2.

Revolution they fell to 250,000 francs, and rose again to 950,000 francs before 1848. They declined at that time to 400,000 francs, and in 1857 reached 2,400,000 francs. After the war they fell to 1,400,000 francs.* In 1898, when the number of *Agents de Change* was increased from sixty to seventy under the government's reorganization, designed to meet the expansion in business, it was provided that each of the ten new members should purchase the offices from the old members at 1,372,000 francs each.

While the stockbrokers, as I shall term the *Agents de Change* henceforth, are placed by law under the disciplinary rule of the Minister of Finance, they themselves, as an association, choose by ballot a governing board (*chambre syndicale*) of eight of their members, to whom, with a chairman (*Syndic*) are entrusted the maintenance of discipline, the listing of securities, and all general matters concerning the welfare of the body.

In addition to the exclusive privileges entrusted to stockbrokers as already cited, they are constituted the sole authority for the quotations of the securities in which they deal, including quotations of metals; they alone give the necessary certificates for transfers of government securities

* "Opérations de Bourse et de Change," Courtois, 13th ed., p. 239.

on terms provided by law; they regulate processes by which lost or stolen certificates are rendered non-negotiable or restored to owners; they may be commissioned by the courts to negotiate loans, to liquidate pledged securities, and to dispose of the property of minors. Settlement days in Paris are similar to those in London, occurring twice a month. That at the end of the month lasts five days, and that in the middle of the month four days. French rentes are settled only at the end of the month.

In forming partnerships, only one person in the firm is entitled to act as stockbroker; the other partners must be simply financial partners, responsible for losses, as "special" partners are in New York, to the extent of the capital contributed. The holder of the membership must be the owner, in his own name, of at least one quarter of the sum representing the purchase price of his membership, plus the amount of the bond or security given. Stockbrokers are forbidden by law to disclose the name of any person for whom they buy or sell; for this reason all dealings are made in the broker's own names, as are also transfers. They must not, under any circumstances, carry on trading or banking operations for their own account, under penalty of expulsion. The bankruptcy of a stockbroker is prima facie a fraudulent bankruptcy, rendering him liable to arrest and other penalties, even under circumstances where an outsider would be immune.

While the impression prevails in many quarters that members of the Bourse are made responsible by law for any liabilities that may be incurred by their colleagues, such is not the case. The practice is, however, that the *chambre syndicale*, or governing body, voluntarily meets the liabilities of defaulting members from the general funds, although not compelled to do so. The nature of the monopoly which stockbrokers enjoy in Paris, and their position as officers of the French Executive government, renders this a thoroughly wise method, for, as we shall presently see, there is grave opposition to the exclusive rights entrusted to them, and it would not be good policy to fan the flames of this hostility by anything less than a mutual guarantee of solvency.

Rates of commission to be charged by stockbrokers on the Paris Bourse are fixed by the decree of the Minister of Finance (July 22, 1901). These are the minimum charges, and no stockbroker is allowed to reduce them under any circumstances. He may, however, and usually does, share them with intermediates who bring him business.

If a client gives, say, an order to buy "at the

average price" (*cours moyen*), the transaction takes place in this way: Before the opening of the session the stockbrokers and their clerks meet in a special room, where bids and offers are made "at the average price," which is as yet undetermined; it will be decided during the session. When an offer and a bid coincide, the transaction is closed; only the price is missing. When the bell rings to announce the opening of the market, the brokers and their clerks leave the special room and proceed to the public hall around the railed enclosure (*corbeille*) whereupon the day's business begins.

As orders are executed the dealer gives the price to a marker, whose entries establish the prices for the official quotation list, and, when this has been made up, those who have traded on the basis of "the average price" ascertain it by striking a mean between the high and low level. If only one price is quoted, that, of course, takes the place of the average price. If orders are given at fixed prices, or "at the market," they are executed as elsewhere. It is important to note in this connection, that the market in Paris enjoys an intimate connection with many banks and credit institutions that act as intermediates in procuring business. Orders transmitted to the Bourse by the Bank of France in 1908, for account of its clients, amounted to 98,721, involving 500,000,000 francs capital.

While, as we have seen, stockbrokers alone have the right to deal in government and other listed securities, there are very many securities dealt in, in Paris, that have not been admitted to the Official List, either because the stockbrokers did not care to adopt them or because the securities did not fulfill the very rigorous statutory conditions. These may, however, be dealt in outside the Bourse, and the law recognizes and protects such transactions. In what I have written heretofore, I have confined myself to the operations of the parquet, meaning the stockbrokers market, and so called because of the parquet floor on which they stand; we come now to the dealings on the coulisse, or curb, named from the narrow passageway, la coulisse, in which these curb brokers congregate. This market is called "the banker's market" (*marche en banque*), but for our purpose we may call these dealers curb brokers, as distinquished from the stockbrokers of the parquet.* The number of curb brokers is not limited; any one may become a

* Provincial bourses in France are divided into two classes — those with parquets, and those without them. Bourses with parquets are those at Lyons, Bordeaux, Marseilles, Nantes, Toulouse, and Lille. The Minister of Finance is in control of these parquet bourses, while the Minster of Commerce controls those that have no parquet.

coulissier if he is a French subject. He must have a capital of 100,000 francs in order to do business in the cash market for rentes, and of 500,000 francs for the settlement market. The curb is governed, as is the parquet, by two *chambres syndicale*, one for the account, and one for the cash market.

Although the French law provides that dealings in French rentes are the sole prerogative of the monopoly of stockbrokers, and fixes punishment for any intrusion into that field, the curb brokers, as a matter of fact, deal extensively and openly in rentes, and are powerful competitors of the stockbrokers. Their operations are not valid, strictly speaking, but they are tolerated by the government for the reason that the credit of the State is benefited by making the market for rentes as free and extensive as possible. This tacit recognition by the government, of the fundamental law of economics that wide and unrestricted markets are the best markets, would seem on its face to raise a point as to the wisdom of a system that perpetuates a monopoly of seventy stockbrokers. The question is not a new one; it has been agitating financial Paris for years. Monopolies of any kind are not considered beneficial in this enlightened age; monopolies that make markets and establish values and prices are peculiarly abhorrent. On this point we may quote M. Vidal, the author of a brilliant study on this subject:

"The actual financial power of the Paris stock-broker is put forward as an argument," he says, speaking of the argument in favor of continuing the monopoly, "and it is affirmed that our financial market is the first in the world. In our opinion, even granting that this is true, which is far from having been proven, the cause is confounded with the effect. When a country, owing to its geographical location, its climate, and the character of its inhabitants, possesses numerous natural riches, and even moral riches, they co-operate in increasing its wealth; when it has the advantage of certain political and economic conditions, when it enjoys a monetary and commercial organization which promotes, instead of paralyzing, human activity in most of its manifestations, then that country is rich and deserves to be rich. And it may then happen that some organization, defective in itself, and the source of manifold vexations, is nevertheless prosperous, as much on account of certain facts of adaption as because it unavoidably lies within the reach of the rays of national wealth. It reflects that wealth.

"But the Paris Bourse does not owe its prosperity to its organization. Seventy ministerial appointees entrusted with the negotiation of one hundred and thirty billions of transferable securities are powerful personalities. They would be more powerful if they were but thirty-five. They would be more powerful if there were but twenty of them, or ten, or five, or even one, if there were in the market but one autocrat, a single arbiter of securities, centralizing bids and offers, and the king of the Bourse, just as we see in America an oil king and a steel king. In such a case the soundness of a market is more seeming than real. If that system had been applied to provisions and merchandise, infinitely more necessary for consumption than rentes or shares in companies, the market for wine, bread, and meat, appropriated by a few barons, might, perhaps, be stupendously high, but in this respect experience speaks in favor of freedom of trade only.

"It seems, therefore, necessary that public and private credit should enjoy the benefit of an organization more pliable and more in harmony with the general condition of a country's commerce. Let us therefore beware of mistaking the appearance of force for force itself — a deception that should impress us no more than the sight of the effigies of iron-clad warriors, standing on rich trappings in a military museum. If our financial market were opened to all who have funds and understand the profession, it would be stronger still. If the market's favorable situation were distributed among several hundred individuals, the division of risks would render the market more stable, competition would secure for our market the desired elasticity, and, if wanted, regulation under the supervision of the Minister of Finance would create a condition halfway between unlimited freedom, which, with more or less reason, scares so many people, and monopoly, which is an old outfit, in no way suiting our customs, and disturbing the harmony of our laws without rendering the services expected from it."*

From the point of view of an American this would seem to be an unanswerable argument. If seventy men are constituted sole managers of a market for 130,000,000,000 francs of transferable securities, one of two things is sure to happen; either a public market will establish itself outside these seventy men, or the seventy will prevent the establishment of the public market. The first of these alternatives has occurred in the establishment of the coulisse; the second would have occurred if the stockbrokers could have accomplished it.

While the government took no hand in the

* "History and Methods of the Paris Bourse," by E. Vidal, published by the National Monetary Commission, Washington, 1910, pp. 262-3-4.

matter, it was recognized that the coulisse gave to the public market a breadth and activity that did great good; as a matter of fact it benefited the stockbrokers themselves in a large way, for it enabled them to obtain from the government liberties not formerly enjoyed, but practised freely by the coulissiers, such as transactions in time bargains, dealings in foreign securities, and similar concessions. This grant of a right to do business on time, or as we term it "future delivery," was a tremendous step forward, since it removed an obstacle in the way of large speculative markets that had long been abolished in other financial centres. It put a stop to the "welching" of speculators on the plea of the gambling act, it legalized short sales, and it established a distinct advance in economic progress. To that extent the stockbrokers are indebted to their neighbors on the curb.*

* The report of the Paris Chamber of Commerce, February 8, 1882, which paved the way for this reform, is interesting reading:

"An administration of justice which would permit a speculator to carry on two deals of equal importance with two different brokers, one for a rise and the other for a fall, and, while collecting from one the profit he had made to advance the plea of gambling toward the other, in order to avoid paying the loss which the operation showed — such an administration, I say, could not hold any longer; that fact alone would condemn it.

"Experience shows that the plea of gambling has never protected anybody but those of bad faith, and has only encouraged the excess of speculation, as was stated by M. Andrieux in his report presented to the Chamber in 1877, in the name of the Seventh Commission of Initiative.

"Prompted by these reasons, and, considering that the present legislation, far from preventing gambling, encourages it; considering that bad faith finds protection in the jurisprudence sanctioned; and, further considering

Meanwhile, the opposition to the monopoly of the stockbrokers continues. "At all times," says M. Vidal, "whenever there have been privileges, some men have been found to oppose them. Of course, these men are not theorists or pedants; they are simply men whom this or that privilege prevents from working freely, and who represent the manifestation of that mysterious force of things which tends toward freedom of trade. Commercial law owes its birth only to these protestations of practical men in apparent revolt against the laws, which become the unconscious shapers of future legislation. From the day when there was an *Agent de Change* there was a "coulissier." The first called the second a thief, because he encroached upon his privilege. The second hurled back the compliment, because the privilege robbed him of his natural right."*

This has a familiar American ring. In 1843 a voluminous report to the Minister of Justice by the stockbrokers asked that the coulisse be

---

that in commercial affairs, as in any other, it behooves to allow every one his full freedom, as well as to hold him responsible for his actions — I beg to suggest that an address be sent to the Minister of Commerce, confirming the letter of the Chamber of Commerce of November 25, 1877, and requesting the Government to introduce a bill in the Chambers, declaring that article 1965 of the Code civil does not apply to debts resulting from dealings for future delivery, and that articles 421 and 422 of the Code penal are repealed."

The law legalizing dealings for future delivery was enacted March 28, 1885, and formally promulgated April 8, 1885.

* Vidal, p. 217, *supra.*

destroyed. Nothing came of it, but in 1859 another attempt succeeded; the coulisse was suppressed. But the level of public credit which, it was hoped, would be raised by the suppression, actually sank. The business of the coulisse, and the market it created, disappeared with the coulisse itself. The government was very sensitive then as now in the matter of market prices for its rentes, and after the laborious process of hoisting them to 71, it was distressing to find that, coincident with the abolition of the curb market, they had fallen to 69. So, in 1861, the coulisse was permitted to reappear, and I fancy the days of its suppression are now at an end.

But the old hostility will break out again when business slackens, for the French have a saying that "horses fight when there is no more hay in the manger." The problem is a pretty one from any angle, especially from the standpoint of American stockbrokers. It would seem plain that the monopoly, as such, cannot forever continue, yet the government faces a financial power of tremendous strength — a Frankenstein which the State itself has created — "and of which," to quote M. Vidal, "it can rid itself only by indemnifying it." At the present time the 70 memberships are worth 96,000,000 francs as a grand total; meantime, the longer the problem is postponed the more valuable they will become as the size and importance of the Paris market increases.

"But the French government does not seem inclined to study the question seriously; first, because the stockbrokers would have to be indemnified; and, secondly, because the stockbrokers themselves are desirous of holding on to their present monopoly. As time passes, the securities, continually on the increase, tend to increase their profits. A financial power has been created whose existence, whose ever spreading influence, forms the subject of a serious economic problem, which some day may turn out to be an even more serious political problem."*

It is interesting to note, in passing from this subject, that a much larger business is done in the coulisse than in the parquet, due to the fact that the curb brokers are not restricted in their securities as are the stockbrokers. The market for foreign securities alone, on the curb, has made wealthy men of many of the coulissiers. They publish a special quotation list, and while they have no officially fixed commission rates, these are established by custom and in practical operation they work satisfactorily. As might be expected, the curb brokers require from their customers smaller margins than those exacted

* Ibid, p. 276.

by the stockbrokers — another reason why their business is large; again, the clients of the curb broker may attend the Bourse with him, be present and confer with him while he buys or sells for them, and in this way get into close touch with the market, a privilege not so easily enjoyed by the client of the stockbroker.

The Official Paris Bourse is open from 12 noon to 3 P. M.; the coulisse from 11:45 A. M. to 4 P. M. The Official List is published daily, and is divided into two parts, the first containing a full list of all the officially listed securities and of the dealings in them, and the second part a list of the dealings in what we used to call in New York "the unlisted department." Rates of Exchange, prices of gold and silver bullion, quotations of treasury bonds, and the rates of the Bank of France for discounts, interest, and loans, are also included. The coulisse also issues a list.

The volume of transferable securities in negotiation through the medium of the Paris stock markets was estimated by M. Alfred Neymarck in his report to the Institut International de Statistique, session of 1907, at 155,000,000,000 francs, an amount slightly in excess of the listed securities on the New York Stock Exchange. Of this total, which has been incre sed somewhat since 1907 through the admission of various Russian industrial securities, 65,000,000,000 francs were in French securities, 67,000,000,000 in foreign securities on the official (parquet) market, and 18,000,000,000 on the coulisse. Of home securities, the value of French rentes is here estimated at 24,000,000,000 francs, of bonds of the City of Paris, of treasury bonds, including those of the department and colonies, at 3,069,-000,000; insurance securities at 702,000,000; those of the Crédit Foncier at 4,447,000,000; of banks and credit companies at 3,101,000,000; of railroad and navigation companies at 24,268,000,000; of railways and tramways at 2,200,000,000; of electricity, iron mills, foundries, and coal mines, at 2,463,000,000.

Of the foreign securities in the French market, Russian securities were valued at 10,000,000,000 francs in 1907, although they are to-day considerably in excess of that sum; divers foreign government funds at 47,000,000,000 and foreign railway securities at 6,000,000,000.*

Next to London, Paris easily leads the markets of the world from the standpoint of power and resources in an international sense. It is the great market for Russian bonds and for Russian industrials, speculation in the latter having reached such volume in 1912 as to lay the French

* *Ibid*, pp. 192–3.

public open to the charge of having lost its head, something that has not occurred in France since the Panama frenzy of 1894. France also holds most of the Spanish and Portuguese (3,500,000,000 francs) debt and has large capital invested in Egypt and the Suez Canal (3,500,000,000 francs). Capital investments in Roumania and Greece, Argentine, Brazil and Mexico, Tunis and the French colonies, Austria and Hungary, Italy, China and Japan, United States and Canada, Great Britain, Belgium and Holland, Germany, Turkey, Servia and Bulgaria, and Switzerland, aggregate 16,150,000,000 francs, distributed in value in the order named.

The caution of French investors is proverbial; notwithstanding the two outbursts of imprudence that have occurred in this generation, it is difficult to induce the Frenchman to place his money in anything not a safe interest-yielding security under French laws. In no other country is investment raised to a higher plane, and speculation confined to a lower one. The political nature of the relationship between France and Russia has resulted from time time, in patriotic subscription of French funds to Russian government loans, and thence to Russian industrials of all kinds, but the latter have suffered so severely in the demoralization of the autumn of 1912 as to justify the prediction that their popularity with the French has been seriously impaired.

As to Russian government loans, the French investor is in a secure position, most of these issues having been endorsed by such powerful banks as the Bank of France, the Credit Lyonnais, the Comptoir d' Escompte, and the Société Génerale, and, indeed, it is to banks such as these and to the myriad smaller institutions throughout the country that investors of the peasantry and the middle classes are accustomed to turn for advice in financial matters. The large speculative clientele, as we know it in America, in England, and in Germany, is a decided minority in France, and those who indulge freely in speculation are canny and shrewd beyond their fellows in other lands. The foresight with which they diagnosed the events of the Boer War in 1899, and the celerity with which they disposed of their large speculative holdings of South African mining shares at top prices, is said by those who witnessed it to have been a prodigy of speculative skill.

Like all other careful observers French economists realize in a large sense that the creation of negotiable instruments and their distribution throughout all the countries of the world through the medium of the Stock Exchange is a very real cause of the wealth of nations; indeed, this point seems to be more thoroughly understood and appreciated by the mass of the French people than by the public elsewhere. When, in 1885, the government legalized transactions for future delivery and thus placed transactions in securities in the same category, under common law, with all other commercial transactions, it established a free market in France that has done wonders for the credit expansion of the Republic — an expansion likewise due, in no small measure, to the growth and development of the coulisse and to the consequent enlargement of a market that must have been restricted, of necessity, by a too rigorous strengthening of the stockbroker's monopoly. In a word, the government, by France, of credit in its higher forms, clearly recognizes that as states, railways, and industrial enterprises have need to resort to credit through issues of securities, a wide market in constant contact with sources of wealth is required, and that nothing should be done by the government to interfere with the ebb and flow of these essential forces.

"The creating and successive issuing of this mass of securities," to quote M. Neymarck, "always easy to purchase and to sell on the Bourse, have been the real cause of credit expansion. They were instrumental in accomplishing real marvels in France and abroad. As personal property has increased, endeavors have been made to render exchanges easy, and to make transfers as little expensive as possible; transferable securities, owing to their denomination, their form, their mode of maturity for the payment of interest, their conditions for redemption, and the ease with which they are negotiated, have been brought within the reach of all purses, and have thus developed the spirit of saving. The consolidation of capital, under the form of stock companies, issuing shares and bonds that everybody can obtain, encompasses on all sides the civilized nations of the world.

"We may say, with Paul Leroy-Beaulieu, that now, owing to capital being accumulated in the shape of negotiable instruments, it is the stock company which takes us on a journey; often it provides us with food and lodging, sells us coal and light, makes up our clothing, and even sells it to us; it procures news for us and inspires our newspapers. Further, it insures our lives and our dwellings; it feeds the unassuming Parisian in the 'Bouillons' (cheap cook-shops), and feasts the stylish Parisian in the fashionable wine taverns.

"The distribution of all these securities has materially contributed to the formation of small inheritances. It has influenced the development of savings institutions, mutual benefit societies, pension funds, and insurance; it has thus rendered invaluable service in the public rôle it has fulfilled. Thanks to it, these companies multiply and increase as the capitalization of their funds is made easier.

"It has also had another result. It has shown that there is no longer a plutocracy, but a veritable financial democracy; when these thousands of millions of certificates are minutely segregated, there are only found atoms of certificates of stocks and bonds, and atoms of income — so great is the number of capitalists and independent individuals who divide these securities and these incomes among themselves."*

* Remarks of M. Alfred Neymarck, at the International Congress of Securities, 1900, quoted by Vidal, pp. 166–7.

APPENDIX

THE REPORT OF THE HUGHES COMMISSION OF 1909

APPENDIX

REPORT

OF THE GOVERNOR'S COMMITTEE ON SPECULATION IN SECURITIES AND COMMODITIES

1909

New York, June 7, 1909

Hon. Charles E. Hughes,
Governor, Albany, N. Y.:

Dear Sir: The committee appointed by you on December 14, 1908, to endeavor to ascertain

"what changes, if any, are advisable in the laws of the State bearing upon speculation in securities and commodities, or relating to the protection of investors, or with regard to the instrumentalities and organizations used in dealings in securities and commodities which are the subject of speculation,"

beg leave to submit the following report:

We have invited statements from those engaged in speculation and qualified to discuss its phases; we have taken testimony offered from various sources as to its objectionable features; we have considered the experience of American States and of foreign countries in their efforts to regulate speculative operations. In our inquiry we have been aided by the officials of the various exchanges, who have expressed their views both orally and in writing, and have afforded us access to their records.

THE SUBJECT IN GENERAL

Markets have sprung into being wherever buying and selling have been conducted on a large scale. Taken in charge by regular organizations and controlled by rules, such markets become exchanges. In New York City there are two exchanges dealing in securities and seven in commodities. In addition there is a security market, without fixed membership or regular officers, known as the "Curb." The exchanges dealing in commodities are incorporated, while those dealing in securities are not.

Commodities are not held for permanent investment, but are bought and sold primarily for the purpose of commercial distribution; on the other hand, securities are primarily held for investment; but both are subject of speculation. Speculation consists in forecasting changes of value and buying or selling in order to take advantage of them; it may be wholly legitimate, pure gambling, or something partaking of the qualities of both. In some form it is a necessary incident of productive operations. When carried on in connection with either commodities or securities it tends to steady their prices. Where speculation is free, fluctuations in prices, otherwise violent and disastrous, ordinarily become gradual and comparatively harmless. Moreover, so far as commodities are concerned, in the absence of speculation, merchants and manufacturers would themselves be forced to carry the risks involved in changes of prices and to bear them in the intensified condition resulting from sudden and violent fluctuations in value. Risks of this kind which merchants and manufacturers still have to assume are reduced in amount, because of the speculation prevailing; and many of these milder risks they are enabled, by "hedging," to transfer to others. For the merchant or manufacturer the speculator performs a service which has the effect of insurance.

In law, speculation becomes gambling when the trading which it involves does not lead, and is not intended to lead, to the actual passing from hand to hand of the property that is dealt in. Thus, in the recent case of Hurd vs. Taylor (181 N. Y., 231), the Court of Appeals of New York said:

"The law of this State as to the purchase and sale of stocks is well settled. The purchase of stocks through a broker, though the party ordering such purchase does not intend to hold the stocks as an investment, but expects the broker to carry them for him with the design on the part of the purchaser to sell again the stocks when their market value has enhanced is, however, speculative, entirely legal. Equally so is a 'short sale,' where the seller has not the stock he assumes to sell, but borrows it and expects to replace it when the market value has declined. But to make such transactions legal, they must contemplate an actual purchase or an actual sale of stocks by the broker, or through him. If the intention is that the so-called broker shall pay his customer the difference between the market price at which the stocks were ordered purchased and that at which they were ordered sold, in case fluctuation is in favor of the costomer, or that in case it is against the customer, the customer shall pay the broker that difference, no purchases or sales being made, the transaction is a wager and therefore illegal. Such business is merely gambling, in which the so-called commission for purchases and sales that are never made is simply the percentage which in other gambling games is reserved in favor of the keeper of the establishment."

This is also the law respecting commodity transactions.

The rules of all the exchanges forbid gambling as defined by this opinion; but they make so easy a technical delivery of the property contracted for, that the practical effect of much speculation, in point of form legitimate, is not greatly different from that of gambling. Contracts to buy may be privately offset by contracts to sell. The offsetting may be done, in a systematic way, by clearing houses, or by "ring settlements." Where deliveries are actually made, property may be temporarily borrowed for the purpose. In these ways, speculation which has the legal traits of legitimate dealing may go on almost as freely as mere wagering, and may have most of the pecuniary and immoral effects of gambling on a large scale.

A real distinction exists between speculation which is carried on by persons of means and experience, and based on an intelligent forecast, and that which is carried on by persons without these qualifications. The former is closely connected with regular business. While not unaccompanied by waste and loss, this speculation accomplishes an amount of good which offsets much of its cost. The latter does but a small amount of good and an almost incalculable amount of evil. In its nature it is in the same class with gambling upon the race-track or at the roulette table, but is practised on a vastly larger scale. Its ramifications extend to all parts of the country. It involves a practical certainty of loss to those who engage in it. A continuous stream of wealth, taken from the actual capital of innumerable persons of relatively small means, swells the income of brokers and operators dependent on this class of business; and in so far as it is consumed like most income, it represents a waste of capital. The total amount of this waste is rudely indicated by the obvious cost of the vast mechanism of brokerage and by manipulators' gains, of both of which it is a large constituent element. But for a continuous influx of new customers, replacing those whose losses force them out of the "street," this costly mechanism of speculation could not be maintained on anything like its present scale.

THE PROBLEM TO BE SOLVED

The problem, wherever speculation is strongly rooted, is to eliminate that which is wasteful and morally destructive, while retaining and allowing free play to that which is beneficial. The difficulty in the solution of the problem lies in the practical impossibility of distinguishing what is virtually gambling from legitimate speculation. The most fruitful policy will be found in measures which will lessen speculation by persons not qualified to engage in it. In carrying out such a policy exchanges can accomplish more than legislatures. In connection with our reports on the different exchanges, as well as on the field of investment and speculation which lies outside of the exchanges, we shall make recommendations directed to the removal of various evils now existing and to the reduction of the volume of speculation of the gambling type.

THE NEW YORK STOCK EXCHANGE

The New York Stock Exchange is a voluntary association, limited to 1100 members, of whom about 700 are active, some of them residents of other cities. Memberships are sold for about $80,000. The Exchange as such does no business, merely providing facilities to members and regulating their conduct. The governing power is in an elected committee of forty members and is plenary in scope. The business transacted on the floor is the purchase and sale of stocks and bonds of corporations and governments. Practically all transactions must be completed by delivery and payment on the following day.

The mechanism of the Exchange provided by its constitution and rules, is the evolution of more than a century. An organization of stockbrokers existed here in 1792, acquiring more definite form in 1817. It seems certain that for a long period the members were brokers or agents only; at the present time many are principles as well as agents, trading for themselves as well as for their customers. A number of prominent capitalists hold memberships merely for the purpose of availing themselves of the reduced commission charge which the rules authorize between members.

The volume of transactions indicates that the Exchange is to-day probably the most important financial institution in the world. In the past decade the average annual sales of shares have been 196,500,000 at prices involving an annual average turnover of nearly $15,500,000,000; bond transactions averaged about $800,000,000. This enormous business affects the financial and credit interests of the country in so large a measure that its proper regulation is a matter of transcendent importance. While radical changes in the mechanism, which is now so nicely adjusted that the transactions are carried on with the minimum of friction, might prove disastrous to the whole country, nevertheless measures should be adopted to correct existing abuses.

PATRONS OF THE EXCHANGE

The patrons of the Exchange may be divided into the following groups:

(1.) Investors, who personally examine the facts relating to the value of securities or act on the advice of reputable and experienced financiers, and pay in full for what they buy.

(2.) Manipulators, whose connection with corporations issuing or controlling particular securities enables them under certain circumstances to move the prices up or down, and who are thus in some degree protected from dangers encountered by other speculators.

(3.) Floor traders, who keenly study the markets and the general conditions of business, and acquire early information concerning the changes which affect the values of securities. From their familiarity with the technique of dealings on the Exchange, and ability to act in concert with others, and thus manipulate values, they are supposed to have special advantages over other traders.

(4.) Outside operators having capital, experience, and knowledge of the general conditions of business. Testimony is clear as to the result which, in the long run, attends their operations; commissions and interest charges constitute a factor always working against them. Since good luck and bad luck alternate in time, the gains only stimulate these men to larger ventures, and they persist in them till a serious or ruinous loss forces them out of the "Street."

(5.) Inexperienced persons, who act on interested advice, "tips," advertisements in newspapers, or circulars sent by mail, or "take flyers" in absolute ignorance, and with blind confidence in their luck. Almost without exception they eventually lose.

CHARACTER OF TRANSACTIONS

It is unquestionable that only a small part of the transactions upon the Exchange is of an investment character; a substantial part may be characterized as virtually gambling. Yet we are unable to see how the State could distinguish by law between proper and improper transactions, since the forms and the mechanisms used are identical. Rigid statutes directed against the latter would seriously interfere with the former. The experience of Germany with similar legislation is illuminating. But the Exchange, with the plenary power over members and their operations, could provide correctives, as we shall show.

MARGIN TRADING

Purchasing securities on margin is as legitimate a transaction as a purchase of any other property in which part payment is deferred. We therefore see no reason whatsoever for recommending the radical change suggested, that margin trading be prohibited.

Two practices are prolific of losses — namely, buying active securities on small margins and buying unsound securities, paying for them in full. The losses in the former case are due to the quick turns in the market, to which active stocks are subject; these exhaust the margins and call for more money than the purchasers can supply. The losses in the latter case are largely due to misrepresentations of interested parties and unscrupulous manipulations.

To correct the evils of misrepresentation and manipulation, we shall offer in another part of this report certain recommendations. In so far as losses are due to insufficient margins, they would be materially reduced if the customary percentage of margins were increased. The amount of margin which a broker requires from a speculative buyer of stocks depends, in each case, on the credit of the buyer; and the amount of credit which one person may extend to another is a dangerous subject on which to legislate. Upon the other hand, a rule made by the Exchange could safely deal with the prevalent rate of margins required from customers. In preference, therefore, to recommending legislation, we urge upon all brokers to discourage speculation upon small margins and upon the Exchange to use its influence, and, if necessary, its power, to prevent members from soliciting and generally accepting business on a less margin than 20 per cent.

PYRAMIDING

"Pyramiding," which is the use of paper profits in stock transactions as a margin for further commitments, should be discouraged. The practice tends to produce more extreme fluctuations and more rapid wiping out of margins. If the stockbrokers and the banks would make it a rule to value securities for the purpose of margin or collateral, not at the current price of the moment, but at the average price of, say, the previous two or three months (provided that such average price were not higher than the price of the moment), the dangers of pyramiding would be largely prevented.

SHORT SELLING

We have been strongly urged to advise the prohibition or limitation of short sales, not only on the theory that it is wrong to agree to sell that what one does not possess, but that such sales reduce the market price of the securities involved. We do not think that it is wrong to agree to sell something that one does not now possess, but expects to obtain later. Contracts and agreements to sell, and deliver in the future, property which one does not possess at the time of the contract, are common in all kinds of business. The man who has "sold short" must some day buy in order to return the stock which he has borrowed to make the short sale. Short sellings endeavor to select times when prices seem high in order to sell, and times when prices seem low in order to buy, their action in both cases serving to lessen advances and diminish declines of price. In other words, short selling tends to produce steadiness in prices, which is an advantage to the community. No other means of restraining unwarranted marking up and down of prices has been suggested to us.

The legislation of the State of New York on the subject of short selling is significant. In 1812 the Legislature passed a law declaring all contracts for the sale of stocks and bonds void, unless the seller at the time was the actual owner or assignee thereof or authorized by such owner or assignee to sell the same. In 1858 this act was repealed by a statute now in force, which reads as follows:

"An agreement for the purchase, sale, transfer, or delivery of a certificate or other evidence of debt, issued by the United States or by any State, or municipal or other corporation, or any share or interest in the stock of any bank, corporation or joint-stock association, incorporated or organized under the laws of the United States or of any State, is not void, or voidable, because the vendor, at the time of making such contract, is not the owner or possessor of the certificate, or certificates, or other evidence of debt, share or interest."

It has been urged that this statute "specifically legalizes stock gambling." As a matter of fact, however, the law would be precisely the same if that statute were repealed, for it is the well-settled common law of this country, as established by the decisions of the Supreme Court of the United States and of the State courts, that all contracts, other than mere wagering contracts, for the future purchase or sale of securities or commodities are valid, whether the vendor is, or is not, at the time of making such contract, the owner or possessor of the securities or commodities involved, in the absence of a statute making such contracts illegal. So far as any of these transactions are mere wagering transactions, they are illegal, and not enforceable, as the law now stands.

It has been suggested to us that there should be a requirement either by law or by rule of the Stock Exchange, that no one should sell any security without identifying it by a number or otherwise. Such a rule would cause great practical difficulties in the case of securities not present in New York at the time when the owner desires to sell them, and would increase the labor and cost of doing business. But even if this were not the effect, the plan contemplates a restriction upon short sales, which, for the reasons set forth above, seems to us undesirable. It is true that this identification plan exists in England as to sales of bank shares (Leeman act of 1867); but it has proved a dead letter. It has also been used in times of apprehended panic upon the French Bourse, but opinions in regard to its effect there are conflicting. While some contend that it has been useful in preventing panics, others affirm that it has been used simply for the purpose of protecting bankers who are loaded down with certain securities which they were trying to distribute, and who, through political influence, procured the adoption of the rule for their special benefit.

MANIPULATION OF PRICES

A subject to which we have devoted much time and thought is that of the manipulation of prices by large interests. This falls into two general classes:

(1.) That which is resorted to for the purpose of making a market for issues of new securities.

(2.) That which is designed to serve merely speculative purposes in the endeavor to make a profit as the result of fluctuations which have been planned in advance.

The first kind of manipulation has certain advantages, and when not accompanied by "matched orders" is unobjectionable *per se*. It is essential to the organization and carrying through of important enterprises, such as large corporations, that the organizers should be able to raise the money necessary to complete them. This can be done only by the sale of securities. Large blocks of securities, such as are frequently issued by railroad and other companies, cannot be sold over the counter or directly to the ultimate investor, whose confidence in them can, as a rule, be only gradually established. They must therefore, if sold at all, be disposed of to some syndicate, who will in turn pass them on to middlemen or speculators, until, in the course of time, they find their way into the boxes of investors. But prudent investors are not likely to be induced to buy securities which are not regularly quoted on some exchange, and which they cannot sell, or on which they cannot borrow money at their pleasure. If the securities are really good and bids and offers bona fide, open to all sellers and buyers, the operation is harmless. It is merely a method of bringing new investments into public notice.

The second kind of manipulation mentioned is undoubtedly open to serious criticism. It has for its object either the creation of high prices for particular stocks, in order to draw in the public as buyers and to unload upon them the holdings of the operators, or to depress the prices and induce the public to sell. There have been instances of gross and unjustifiable manipulation of securities, as in the case of American Ice stock. While we have been unable to discover any complete remedy short of abolishing the Stock Exchange itself, we are convinced that the Exchange can prevent the worst forms of this evil by exercising its influence and authority over the members to prevent them. When continued manipulation exists it is patent to experienced observers.

"WASH SALES" AND "MATCHED ORDERS"

In the foregoing discussion we have confined ourselves to bona fide sales. So far as manipulation of either class is based upon fictitious so-called "wash sales," it is open to the severest condemnation, and should be prevented by all possible means. These fictitious sales are forbidden by the rules of all the regular exchanges, and are not enforceable at law. They are less frequent than many persons suppose. A transaction must take place upon the floor of the Exchange to be reported, and if not reported does not serve the purpose of those who engage in it. If it takes place on the floor of the Exchange, but is purely a pretence, the brokers involved run the risk of detection and expulsion, which is to them a sentence of financial death. There is, however, another class of transactions called "matched orders," which differ materially from those already mentioned, in that they are actual and enforceable contracts. We refer to that class of transactions, engineered by some manipulator, who sends a number of orders simultaneously to different brokers, some to buy and some to sell. These brokers, without knowing that other brokers have countervailing orders from the same principal, execute their orders upon the floor of the Exchange, and the transactions become binding contracts; they cause an appearance of activity in a certain security which is unreal. Since they are legal and binding, we find a difficulty in suggesting a legislative remedy. But where the activities of two or more brokers in certain securities become so extreme as to indicate manipulation rather than genuine transactions, the officers of the Exchange would be remiss unless they exercised their influence and authority upon such members in a way to cause them to desist from such suspicious and undesirable activity. As already stated, instances of continuous manipulation of particular securities are patent to every experienced observer, and could without difficulty be discouraged, if not prevented, by prompt action on the part of the Exchange authorities.

CORNERS

The subject of corners in the stock market has engaged our attention. The Stock Exchange might properly adopt a rule providing that the governors shall have power to decide when a corner exists and to fix a settlement price, so as to relieve innocent persons from the injury or ruin which may result therefrom. The mere existence of such a rule would tend to prevent corners.

FAILURES AND EXAMINATION OF BOOKS

We have taken testimony on the subject of recent failures of brokers, where it has been discovered that they were insolvent for a long period prior to their public declaration of failure, and where their activities after the insolvency not only caused great loss to their customers, but also, owing to their efforts to save themselves from bankruptcy, worked great injury to innocent outsiders. For cases of this character, there should be a law analogous to that forbidding banks to accept deposits after insolvency is known; and we recommend a statute making it a misdemeanor for a broker to receive any securities or cash from any customer (except in liquidating or fortifying an existing account), or to make any further purchases or sales for his own account, after he has become insolvent; with the provision that a broker shall be deemed insolvent when he has on his books an account or accounts which, if liquidated, would exhaust his assets, unless he can show that he had reasonable ground to believe that such accounts were good.

The advisability of requiring by State authority an examination of the books of all members of the Exchange, analogous to that required of banks, has been urged upon us. Doubtless some failures would be prevented by such a system rigidly enforced, although bank failures do occur in spite of the scrutiny of the examiners. Yet the relations between brokers and their customers are of so confidential a nature that we do not recommend an examination of their books by any public authority. The books and accounts of the members of the Exchange, should, however, be subjected to periodic examination and inspection pursuant to rules and regulations to be prescribed by the Exchange, and the result should be promptly reported to the governors thereof.

It is vain to say that a body possessing the powers of the board of governors of the Exchange, familiar with every detail of the mechanism, generally acquainted with the characteristics of members, cannot improve present conditions. It is a deplorable fact that with all their power and ability to be informed, it is generally only after a member or a firm is overtaken by disaster, involving scores or hundreds of innocent persons, and causing serious disturbances, that the Exchange authorities take action. No complaint can be registered against the severity of the punishment then meted out; but in most cases the wrongdoing thus atoned for, which has been going on for a considerable period, might have been discovered under a proper system of supervision, and the vastly preponderant value of prevention over cure demonstrated.

REHYPOTHECATION OF SECURITIES

We have also considered the subject of rehypothecating, loaning, and other use of securities by brokers who hold them for customers. So far as any broker applies to his own use any securities belonging to a customer, or hypothecates them for a greater amount than the unpaid balance of the purchase price, without the customer's consent, he is undoubtedly guilty of a conversion under the law as it exists to-day, and we call this fact to the attention of brokers and the public. When a broker sells the securities purchased for a customer who has paid therefor in whole or in part, except upon the customer's default, or disposes of them for his own benfit, he should be held guilty of larceny, and we recommend a statute to that effect.

DEALING FOR CLERKS

The Exchange now has a rule forbidding any member to deal or carry an account for a clerk or employee of any other member. This rule should be extended so as to prevent dealing for account of any clerk or subordinate employee of any bank, trust company, insurance company, or other moneyed corporation or banker.

LISTING REQUIREMENTS

Before securities can be bought and sold on the Exchange, they must be examined. The committee on Stock List is one of the most important parts of the organization, since public confidence depends upon the honesty, impartiality, and thoroughness of its work. While the Exchange does not guarantee the character of any securities, or affirm that the statements filed by the promoters are true, it certifies that due diligence and caution have been used by experienced men in examining them. Admission to the list, therefore, establishes a presumption in favor of the soundness of the security so admitted. Any securities authorized to be bought and sold on the Exchange, which have not been subjected to such scrutiny, are said to be in the unlisted department, and traders who deal in them do so at their own risk. We have given consideration to the subject of verifying the statements of fact contained in the papers filed with the applications for listing, but we do not recommend that either the State or the Exchange take such responsibility. Any attempt to do so would undoubtedly give the securities a standing in the eyes of the public which would not in all cases be justified. In our judgment, the Exchange, should, however, adopt methods to compel the filing of frequent statements of the financial condition of the companies whose securities are listed, including balance sheets, income and expense accounts, etc., and should notify the public that these are open to examination under proper rules and regulations. The Exchange should also require that there be filed with future applications for listing a statement of what the capital stock of the company has been issued for, showing how much has been issued for cash, how much for property, with a description of the property, etc., and also showing what commission, if any, has been paid to the promoters or vendors. Furthermore, means should be adopted for holding those making the statements responsible for the truth thereof. The unlisted department, except for temporary issues, should be abolished.

FICTITIOUS TRADES

Complaint is made that orders given by customers are sometimes not actually executed, although so reported by the broker. We recommend the passage of a statute providing that, in case it is pleaded in any suit by or against a broker that the purchase or sale was fictitious, or was not an actual bona fide purchase or sale by the broker as agent for the customer, the court or jury shall make a special finding upon that fact. In case it is found that the purchase or sale was not actual and bona fide the customer shall recover three times the amount of the loss which he sustained thereby; and copies of the finding shall be sent to the district attorney of the county and to the Exchange, if the broker be a member.

UNIT OF TRADING

The Exchange should insist that all trading be done on the basis of a reasonably small unit (say 100 shares of stock or $1000 of bonds), and should not permit the offers of such lots, or bids for such lots, to be ignored by traders offering or bidding for larger amounts. The practice now permitted of allowing bids and offers for large amounts, all or none, assists the manipulation of prices. Thus a customer may send an order to sell 100 shares of a particular stock at par, and a broker may offer to buy 1000 shares, all or none, at 101, and yet no transaction take place. The bidder in such a case should be required to take all the shares offered at the lower price before bidding for a larger lot at a higher price. This would tend to prevent matched orders.

STOCK CLEARING HOUSE

We have also considered the subject of the Stock Exchange Clearing House. While it is undoubtedly true that the clearing of stocks facilitates transactions which may be deemed purely manipulative, or virtually gambling transactions, nevertheless we are of the opinion that the Exchange could not do its necessary and legitimate business but for the existence of the clearing system, and, therefore, that it is not wise to abolish it.

The transactions in stocks which are cleared are transcribed each day on what are called "clearing sheets," and these sheets are passed into the Clearing House and there filed for one week only. In view of the value of these sheets as proving the transactions and the prices, they should be preserved by the Exchange for at least six years, and should be at the disposal of the courts, in case of any dispute.

SPECIALISTS

We have received complaints that specialists on the floor of the Exchange, dealing in inactive securities, sometimes buy or sell for their own account while acting as brokers. Such acts without the principal's consent are illegal. In every such case recourse may be had to the courts.

Notwithstanding that the system of dealing in specialties is subject to abuses, we are not convinced that the English method of distinguishing between brokers and jobbers serves any better purpose than our own practice, while its introduction here would complicate business. It should also be noted that the practice of specialists in buying and selling for their own account often serves to create a market where otherwise one would not exist.

BRANCH OFFICES

Complaint has been made of branch offices in the city of New York, often luxuriously furnished and sometimes equipped with lunch rooms, cards, and liquor. The tendency of many of them is to increase the lure of the ticker by the temptation of creature comforts, appealing thus to many who would not otherwise speculate. The governors of the Exchange inform us that they realize that some of these offices have brought discredit on the Exchange, and that on certain occasions they have used their powers to suppress objectionable features. It seems to us that legitimate investors and speculators might, without much hardship, be compelled to do business at the main offices, and that a hard-and-fast rule against all branch offices in the city of New York might well be adopted by the Exchange. In any event, we are convinced that a serious and effective regulation of these branch offices is desirable.

INCORPORATION OF EXCHANGE

We have been strongly urged to recommend that the Exchange be incorporated in order to bring it more completely under the authority and supervision of the State and the process of the courts. Under existing conditions, being a voluntary organization, it has almost unlimited power over the conduct of its members, and it can subject them to instant discipline for wrongdoing, which it could not exercise in a summary manner if it were an incorporated body. We think that such power residing in a properly chosen committee is distinctly advantageous. The submission of such questions to the courts would involve delays and technical obstacles which would impair discipline without securing any greater measure of substantial justice. While this committee is not entirely in accord on this point, no member is yet prepared to advocate the incorporation of the Exchange and a majority of us advise against it, upon the ground that the advantages to be gained by incorporation may be accomplished by rules of the Exchange and by statutes aimed directly at the evils which need correction.

The Stock Exchange in the past, although frequently punishing infractions of its rules with great severity, has, in our opinion, at times failed to take proper measures to prevent wrongdoing. This has been probably due not only to a conservative unwillingness to interfere in the business of others, but also to a spirit of comradeship which is very marked among brokers, and frequently leads them to overlook misconduct on the part of fellow-members, although at the same time it is a matter of cynical gossip and comment in the street. The public has a right to expect something more than this from the Exchange and its members. This committee, in refraining from advising the incorporation of the Exchange, does so in the expectation that the Exchange will in the future take full advantage of the powers conferred upon it by its voluntary organization, and will be active in preventing wrongdoing such as has occurred in the past. Then we believe that there will be no serious criticism of the fact that it is not incorporated. If, however, wrongdoing recurs, and it should appear to the public at large that the Exchange has been derelict in exerting its powers and authority to prevent it, we believe that the public will insist upon the incorporation of the Exchange and its subjection to State authority and supervision.

WALL STREET AS A FACTOR

There is a tendency on the part of the public to consider Wall Street and the New York Stock Exchange as one and the same thing. This is an error arising from their location. We have taken pains to ascertain what proportion of the business transacted on the Exchange is furnished by New York City. The only reliable sources of information are the books of the commission houses. An investigation was made of the transactions on the Exchange for a given day, when the sales were 1,500,000 shares. The returns showed that on that day 52 per cent. of the total transactions on the Exchange apparently originated in New York City, and 48 per cent. in other localities.

THE CONSOLIDATED STOCK EXCHANGE

The Consolidated Exchange was organized as a mining stock exchange in 1875, altering its name and business in 1886. Although of far less importance than the Stock Exchange, it is nevertheless a *secondary market* of no mean proportions; by far the greater part of the trading is in securities listed upon the main exchange, and the prices are based upon the quotations made there. The sales average about 45,000,000 shares per annum. The fact that its members make a specialty of "broken lots," i. e., transactions in shares less than the 100 unit, is used as a ground for the claim that it is a serviceable institution for investors of relatively small means. But it is obvious that its utility as a provider of capital for enterprises is exceedingly limited; and that it affords facilities for the most injurious form of speculation — that which attracts persons of small means.

It also permits dealing in shares not listed in the main exchange, and in certain mining shares, generally excluded from the other. In these cases it prescribed a form of listing requirements, but the original listing of securities is very rarely availed of. The rules also provide for dealing in grain, petroleum, and other products. Wheat is, however, at present the only commodity actively dealt in, and this is due solely to the permission to trade in smaller lots than the Produce Exchange unit of 5000 bushels.

There are 1225 members, about 450 active, and memberships have sold in recent years at from $650 to $2000. In general the methods of conducting business are similar to those of the larger exchange, and subject to the same abuses.

Very strained relations have existed between the two security exchanges since the lesser one undertook in 1886 to deal in stocks. The tension has been increased by the methods by which the Consolidated obtains the quotations of the other, through the use of the "tickers" conveying them. It is probable that without the use of these instruments the business of the Consolidated Exchange would be paralyzed; yet the right to use them rests solely upon a technical point in a judicial decision which enjoins their removal.

COGNATE SUBJECTS

HOLDING COMPANIES

Connected with operations on the Stock Exchange are a class of manipulations originating elsewhere. The values of railway securities, for example, depend upon the management of the companies issuing them, the directors of which may use their power to increase, diminish, or even extinguish them, while they make gains for themselves by operations on the Exchange. They may advance the price of a stock by an unexpected dividend, or depress it by passing an expected one. They may water a stock by issuing new shares, with no proportionate addition to the productive assets of the company, or load it with indebtedness, putting an unexpected lien on the shareholders' property. Such transactions affect not only the fortunes of the shareholders, who are designedly kept in ignorance of what is transpiring, but also the value of investments in other similar companies the securities of which are affected sympathetically. Railroad wrecking was more common in the last half-century than it is now, but we have some glaring examples of it in the débris of our street railways to-day.

The existence and misuse of such powers on the part of directors are a menace to corporate property and a temptation to officials who are inclined to speculate, leading them to manage the property so as to fill their own pockets by indirect and secret methods.

A holding company represents the greatest concentration of power in a body of directors and the extreme of helplessness on the part of shareholders. A corporation may be so organized that its bonds and preferred stock represent the greater part of its capital, while the common stock represents the actual control. Then, if a second company acquires a majority of the common stock, or a majority of the shares that are likely to be voted at elections, it may control the former company, and as many other companies as it can secure. The shareholders of the subsidiary companies may be thus practically deprived of power to protect themselves against injurious measures and even to obtain information of what the holding company is doing, or intends to do, with their property.

As a first step toward mitigating this evil we suggest that the shareholders of subsidiary companies, which are dominated by holding companies, or voting trusts, shall have the same right to examine the books, records, and accounts of such holding companies, or voting trusts, that they have in respect of the companies whose shares they hold, and that the shareholders of holding companies have the same right as regards the books, records, and accounts of the subsidiary companies. The accounts of companies not merged should be separately kept and separately stated to their individual stockholders, however few they may be.

We may point out the fact that the powers which holding companies now exercise were never contemplated, or imagined, when joint stock corporations were first legalized. If Parliament and Legislatures had foreseen their growth they would have erected barriers against it.

RECEIVERSHIPS

Our attention has been directed to the well-known abuses frequently accompanying receiverships of large corporations, and more especially public service corporations, and the issue of receivers' certificates. We feel that the numerous cases of long-drawn-out receiverships, in some instances lasting more than ten years, and of the issue of large amounts of receivers' certificates, which take precedence over even first mortgage bonds, are deserving of most serious consideration.

Legislation providing for a short-time limitation on receiverships or for a limitation of receivers' certificates to a small percentage of the mortgage liens on the property, could be rendered unnecessary, however, by the action of the courts themselves along these lines, so as to make impossible in the future the abuses which have been so common in the past.

EFFECT OF THE MONEY MARKET ON SPECULATION

It has been urged that your committee consider the influence of the money market upon security speculation.

As a result of conditions to which the defects of our monetary and banking systems chiefly contribute, there is frequently a congestion of funds in New York City, when the supply is in excess of business needs and the accumulated surplus from the entire country generally is thereby set free for use in the speculative market. Thus there almost annually occurs an inordinately low rate for "call loans," at times less than 1 per cent. During the prevalence of this abnormally low rate speculation is unduly incited, and speculative loans are very largely expanded.

On the other hand, occasional extraordinary industrial activity, coupled with the annually recurring demands for money during the crop-moving season, causes money stringency, and the calling of loans made to the stock market; an abnormally high interest rate results, attended by violent reaction in speculation and abrupt fall in prices. The pressure to retain funds in the speculative field at these excessively high interest rates tends to a curtailment of reasonable accommodation to commercial and manufacturing interests, frequently causing embarrassment and at times menacing a crisis.

The economic questions involved in these conditions are the subject of present consideration by the Federal authorities and the National Monetary Commission. They could not be adjusted or adequately controlled either through Exchange regulation or State legislation.

THE USURY LAW

The usury law of this State prohibits the taking of more than 6 per cent. interest for the loan of money, but by an amendment adopted in 1882 an exception is made in the case of loans of $5000, or more, payable on demand and secured by collateral. It is claimed by some that, since this exception enables stock speculators, in times of great stringency, to borrow money by paying excessively high rates of interest, to the exclusion of other borrowers, a repeal of this provision would check inordinate speculation. We direct attention, however, to the fact that the statute in question excepts such loans as are secured by warehouse receipts, bills of lading, bills of exchange, and other negotiable instruments. Hence its operation is not limited to Stock Exchange transactions, or to speculative loans in general. Moreover, the repeal of the statute would affect only the conditions when high rates of interest are exacted, and not those of abnormally low rates, which really promote excessive speculation. Finally, our examination indicates that prior to the enactment of the statute of 1882 such loans were negotiated at the maximum (6 per cent.), plus a commission, which made it equivalent to the higher rate; and a repeal of the statute would lead to the resumption of this practice. Therefore, as the repeal would not be beneficial, we cannot recommend any legislation bearing upon the interest laws of the State, unless it be the repeal of the usury law altogether, as we believe that money will inevitably seek the point of highest return for its use. In nine States of the Union there are at present no usury laws.

THE CURB MARKET

There is an unorganized stock market held in the open air during exchange hours. It occupies a section of Broad Street. An enclosure in the centre of the roadway is made by means of a rope, within which the traders are supposed to confine themselves, leaving space on either side for the passage of street traffic; but during days of active trading the crowd often extends from curb to curb.

There are about 200 subscribers, of whom probably 150 appear on the curb each day, and the machinery of the operations requires the presence of as many messenger boys and clerks. Such obstruction of a public thoroughfare is obviously illegal, but no attempt has been made by the city authorities to disperse the crowd that habitually assembles there.

This open-air market, we understand, is dependent for the great bulk of its business upon members of the Stock Exchange, approximately 85 per cent. of the orders executed on the curb coming from Stock Exchange houses. The Exchange itself keeps the curb market in the street, since it forbids its own members engaging in any transaction in any other security exchange in New York. If the curb were put under a roof and organized, this trading could not be maintained.

ITS UTILITY

The curb market has existed for upward of thirty years, but only since the great development of trading in securities began, about the year 1897, has it become really important. It affords a public market-place where all persons can buy and sell securities which are not listed on any organized exchange. Such rules and regulations as exist are agreed to by common consent, and the expenses of maintenance are paid by voluntary subscription. An agency has been established by common consent through which the rules and regulations are prescribed.

This agency consists solely of an individual who, through his long association with the curb, is tacitly accepted as arbiter. From this source we learn that sales recorded during the year 1908 were roughly as follows:

Bonds	$66,000,000
Stocks, industrials, shares	4,770,000
Stocks, mining, shares	41,825,000

Official quotations are issued daily by the agency and appear in the public press. Corporations desiring their securities to be thus quoted are required to afford the agency certain information, which is, however, superficial and incomplete. There is nothing on the curb which corresponds to the listing process of the Stock Exchange. The latter, while not guaranteeing the soundness of the securities, gives a *prima facie* character to those on the list, since the stock list committee takes some pains to learn the truth. The decision of the agent of the curb are based on insufficient data, and since much of the work relates to mining schemes in distant States and Territories, and foreign countries, the mere fact that a security is quoted on the curb should create no presumption in its favor; quotations frequently represent "wash sales," thus facilitating swindling enterprises.

EVILS OF UNORGANIZED STATUS

Bitter complaints have reached us of frauds perpetrated upon confiding persons, who have been induced to purchase mining shares because they are quoted on the curb; these are frequently advertised in newspapers and circulars sent through the mails as so quoted. Some of these swindles have been traced to their fountain heads by the Post Office Department, to which complaint has been made; but usually the swindler, when cornered, has settled privately with the individual complainant, and then the prosecution has failed for want of testimony. Meanwhile the same operations may continue in many other places, till the swindle becomes too notorious to be profitable.

Notwithstanding the lack of proper supervision and control over the admission of securities to the privilege of quotation, some of them are meritorious, and in this particular the curb performs a useful function. The existence of the cited abuses does not, in our judgment, demand the abolition of the curb market. Regulation is, however, imperative. To require an elaborate organization similar to that existing in the Exchanges would result in the formation of another curb free from such restraint.

As has been stated, about 85 per cent. of the business of the curb comes through the offices of members of the New York Stock Exchange, but a provision of the constitution of that Exchange prohibits its members from becoming members of, or dealing, on, any other *organized* Stock Exchange in New York, Accordingly, operators on the curb market have not attempted to form an organization. The attitude of the Stock Exchange is therefore largely responsible for the existence of such abuses as result from the want of organization of the curb market. The brokers dealing on the latter do not wish to lose their best customers, and hence they submit to these irregularities and inconveniences.

Some of the members of the Exchange dealing on the curb have apparently been satisfied with the prevailing conditions, and in their own selfish interests have maintained an attitude of indifference toward abuses. We are informed that some of the most flagrant cases of discreditable enterprises finding dealings on the curb were promoted by members of the New York Stock Exchange.

REFORMATON OF THE CURB

The present apparent attitude of the Exchange toward the curb seems to us clearly inconsistent with its moral obligations to the community at large. Its governors have frequently avowed before this committee a purpose to co-operate to the greatest extent for the remedy of any evils found to exist in stock speculation. The curb market as at present constituted affords ample opportunity for the exercise of such helpfulness.

The Stock Exchange should compel the formulation and enforcement of such rules as may seem proper for the regulation of business on the curb, the conduct of those dealing thereon, and, particularly, for the admission of securities to quotation.

If the curb brokers were notified that failure to comply with such requirements would be followed by an application of the rule of non-intercourse, there is little doubt that the orders of the Exchange would be obeyed. The existing connection of the Exchange gives it ample power to accomplish this, and we do not suggest anything implying a more intimate connection.

Under such regulation, the curb market might be decently housed to the relief of its members and the general public.

THE ABUSE OF ADVERTISING

A large part of the discredit in the public mind attaching to "Wall Street" is due to frauds perpetrated on the small investor throughout the country in the sale of worthless securities by means of alluring circulars and advertisements in the newspapers. To the success of such swindling enterprises a portion of the press contributes.

Papers which honestly try to distinguish between swindling advertisements and others may not in every instance succeed in doing so; but readiness to accept advertisements which are obviously traps for the unwary is evidence of a moral delinquency which should draw out the severest public condemnation.

So far as the press in the large cities is concerned the correction of the evil lies, in some measure, in the hands of the reputable bankers and brokers, who, by refusing their advertising patronage to newspapers notoriously guilty in this respect, could compel them to mend their ways, and at the same time prevent fraudulent schemes from deriving an appearance of merit by association with reputable names.

Another serious evil is committed by men who give standing to promotions by serving as directors without full knowledge of the affairs of the companies, and by allowing their names to appear in prospectuses without knowing the accuracy and good faith of the statements contained therein. Investors naturally and properly pay great regard to the element of personal character, both in the offering of securities and in the management of corporations, and can therefore be deceived by the names used in unsound promotions.

BRITISH SYSTEM CONSIDERED

We have given much attention to proposals for compelling registration, by a bureau of the State government, of all corporations whose securities are offered for public sale in this State, accompanied by information regarding their financial responsibility and prospects, and prohibiting the public advertisements or sale of such securities without a certificate from the bureau that the issuing company has been so registered. The object of such registration would be to identify the promoters, so that they might be readily prosecuted in case of fraud. Such a system exists in Great Britain. The British "Companies Act" provides for such registration, and the "Directors' Liability Act" regulates the other evil referred to above. Some members of your committee are of the opinion that these laws should be adopted in this country, so far as they will fit conditions here.

This would meet with some difficulties, due in part to our multiple system of State government. If the law were in force only in this State, the advertisement and sale of the securities in question would be unhindered in other markets, and companies would be incorporated in other States, in order that their directors and promoters should escape liability. The certificate of registration might be accepted by inexperienced persons as an approval by State authority of the enterprise in question. For these reasons the majority of your committee does not recommend the regulation of such advertising and sale by State registration.

In so far as the misuse of the post-office for the distribution of swindling circulars could be regulated by the Federal authorities the officials have been active in checking it. They inform us that vendors of worthless securities are aided materially by the opportunity to obtain fictitious price quotations for them on the New York Curb market.

LEGISLATION RECOMMENDED

For the regulation of the advertising evils, including the vicious "tipster's" cards, we recommend an amendment to the Penal Code to provide that any person who advertises, in the public press, or otherwise, or publishes, distributes or mails, any prospectus, circular, or other statement in regard to the value of any stock, bonds, or other securities, or in regard to the business affairs, property, or financial condition of any corporation, joint stock association, copartnership or individual issuing stock, bonds, or other similar securities, which contains any statement of fact which is known to such person to be false, or as to which such person has no reasonable grounds for believing it to be true, or any promises or predictions which he cannot reasonably justify, shall be guilty of a misdemeanor; and, further, that every newspaper or other publication printing or publishing such an advertisement, prospectus, circular, or other statement, shall, before printing or publishing the same, obtain from the person responsible for the same, and retain, a written and signed statement to the effect that such person accepts responsibility for the same, and for the statements of fact contained therein, which statement shall give the address, with street number, of such person; and that the publisher of any such newspaper or other publication which shall fail to obtain and retain such statement shall be guilty of a misdemeanor.

BUCKET-SHOPS

Bucket-shops are ostensibly brokerage offices, where, however, commodities and securities are neither bought nor sold in pursuance of customers' orders, the transactions being closed by the payment of gains or losses, as determined by price quotations. In other words, they are merely places for the registration of bets or wagers; their machinery is generally controlled by the keepers, who can delay or manipulate the quotations at will.

The law of this State, which took effect September 1, 1908, makes the keeping of a bucket-shop a felony, punishable by fine and imprisonment, and in the case of corporations, on second offences by dissolution or expulsion from the State. In the case of individuals the penalty for a second offence is the same as for the first. These penalties are imposed upon the theory that the practice is gambling; but in order to establish the fact of gambling it is necessary, under the New York law, to show that *both* parties to the trade intended that it should be settled by the payment of differences, and not by delivery of property. Under the law of Massachusetts it is necessary to show only that the bucket-shop keeper so intended. The Massachusetts law provides heavier penalties for the second offence than for the first, and makes it a second offence if a bucket-shop is kept open after the first conviction.

AMENDMENT OF LAW RECOMMENDED

We recommend that the foregoing features of the Massachusetts law be adopted in this State; also that section 355 of the act of 1908 be amended so as to require brokers to furnish to their customers *in all cases*, and not merely on demand, the names of brokers from whom shares were bought and to whom they were sold, and that the following section be added to the act:

Witness's privilege:
No person shall be excused from attending and testifying, or producing any books, papers, or other documents before any court or magistrate, upon any trial, investigation, or proceeding initiated by the district attorney for a violation of any of the provisions of this chapter, upon the ground or for the reason that the testimony or evidence, documentary or otherwise, required or him may tend to convict him of a crime or to subject him to a penalty or forfeiture; but no person shall be prosecuted or subjected to any penalty or forfeiture for or on account of any transaction, matter, or thing concerning which he may so testify or produce evidence, documentary or otherwise, and no testimony so given or produced shall be received against him upon any criminal investigation or proceeding.

There has been a sensible diminution in the number of bucket-shops in New York since the act of 1908 took effect, but there is still much room for improvement.

Continuous quotations of prices from an exchange are indispensable to a bucket-shop, and when such quotations are cut off this gambling ends; therefore every means should be employed to cut them off.

SALES OF QUOTATIONS

The quotations of exchanges have been judicially determined to be their own property, which may be sold under contracts limiting their use. In addition to supplying its own members in New York City with its quotations, the Stock Exchange sells them to the telegraph companies, under contracts restricting the delivery of the service in New York City to subscribers approved by a committee of the Exchange; the contracts are terminable at its option. This restriction would imply a purpose on the part of the Exchange to prevent the use of the quotations by bucket-shop keepers. But the contracts are manifestly insufficient, in that they fail to cover the use of the service in places other than New York City; if corroboration were needed it could be found in the fact that the quotations are the basis for bucket-shop transactions in other cities. In such effort as has been made to control these quotations the Exchange has been hampered to some extent by the claim that telegraph companies are common carriers, and that as such they must render equal service to all persons offering to pay the regular charge therefor. This claim has been made in other States as well as in New York, and the telegraph companies have in the past invoked it as an excuse for furnishing quotations to people who were under suspicion, although it was not possible to prove that they were operating bucket-shops. Recent decisions seem to hold that this claim is not well-founded. We advise that a law be passed providing that, so far as the transmission of continuous quotations is concerned, telegraph companies shall not be deemed common carriers, or be compelled against their volition to transmit such quotations to any person; also a law providing that if a telegraph company has reasonable ground for believing that it is supplying quotations to a bucket-shop, it be criminally liable equally with the keeper of the bucket-shop. Such laws would enable these companies to refuse to furnish quotations upon mere suspicion that parties are seeking them for an unlawful business, and would compel them to refuse such service wherever there was a reasonable ground for believing that a bucket-shop was being conducted.

LICENSING TICKERS

Tickers carrying the quotations should be licensed and bear a plate whereon should appear the name of the corporation, firm, or individual furnishing the service or installing the ticker, and a license number. Telegraph companies buying or transmitting quotations from the exchanges should be required to publish semi-annually the names of all subscribers to the service furnished, and the number and location of the tickers, in a newspaper of general circulation published in the city or town in which such tickers are installed. In case the service is furnished to a corporation, firm, or person, in turn supplying the quotations to others, like particulars should be published. A record, open to public inspection, should be kept by the installing company showing the numbers and location of the tickers. Doubtless local boards of trade, civic societies, and private individuals would, if such information were within their reach, lend their aid to the authorities in the enforcement of the law.

Measures should be taken also to control the direct wire service for the transmission of quotations, and for the prompt discontinuance of such service in case of improper use thereof. In short, every possible means should be employed to prevent bucket-shops from obtaining the continuous quotations, without which their depredations could not be carried on a single day.

THE COMMODITY EXCHANGES

Of the seven commodity exchanges in the city of New York, three dealing with Produce, Cotton, and Coffee, are classed as of major importance; two organized by dealers in Fruit and Hay, are classed as minor; and two others, the Mercantile (concerned with dairy and poultry products) and the Metal (concerned with mining products) are somewhat difficult of classification, as will appear hereafter.

THE MAJOR EXCHANGES

The business transacted on the three major exchanges is mainly speculative, consisting of purchases and sales for future delivery either by those who wish to eliminate risks or by those who seek to profit by fluctuations in the value of products. "Cash" or "spot" transactions are insignificant in volume.

The objects, as set forth in the charters, are to provide places for trading, establish equitable trade principles and usages, obtain and disseminate useful information, adjust controversies, and fix by-laws and rules for these purposes.

Trading in differences of price and "wash sales" are strictly prohibited under penalty of expulsion. All contracts of sale call for delivery, and unless balanced and canceled by equivalent contracts of purchase, must be finally settled by a delivery of the merchandise against cash payment of its value as specified in the terms of the contract; but the actual delivery may be waived by the consent of both parties. Possession is for the most part transferred from the seller to the purchaser by warehouse receipts entitling the holder to the ownership of the goods described.

DEALING IN "FUTURES"

The selling of agricultural products for future delivery has been the subject of much controversy in recent years. A measure to prohibit such selling, known as the Hatch Anti-Option bill, was debated at great length in Congress during the years 1892, 1893, and 1894. Although it passed both House and Senate in different forms, it was finally abandoned by common consent. As shown hereafter, similar legislation in Germany has proved injurious; and when attempted by our States it has either resulted detrimentally or been inoperative. The subject was exhaustively considered by the Industrial Commission of Congress which in 1901 made an elaborate report (Vol. VI), showing that selling for future delivery, based upon a forecast of future conditions of supply and demand, is an indispensable part of the world's commercial future delivery has been the subject of machinery, by which prices are, as far as possible, equalized throughout the year to the advantage of both producer and consumer. The subject is also treated with clearness and impartiality in the Cyclopedia of American Agriculture, in an article on "Speculation and Farm Prices"; where it is shown that since, the yearly supply of wheat, for example, matures within a comparatively short period of time somebody must handle and store the great bulk of it during the interval between production and consumption. Otherwise the price will be unduly depressed at the end of one harvest and correspondingly advanced before the beginning of another.

Buying for future delivery causes advances in prices; selling short tends to restrain inordinate advances. In each case there must be a buyer and a seller and the interaction of their trading steadies prices. Speculation thus brings into the market a distinct class of people possessing capital and special training who assume the risks of holding and distributing the proceeds of the crops from one season to another with the minimum of cost to producer and consumer.

HEDGING

A considerable part of the business done by these exchanges consists of "hedging." This term is applied to the act of a miller, for example, who is under contract to supply a given quantity of flour monthly throughout the year. In order to insure himself against loss he makes a contract with anybody whom he considers financially responsible, to supply him wheat at times and in the quantities needed. He "hedges" against a possible scarcity and consequent rise in the price of wheat. If the miller were restricted in his purchases to persons in the actual possession of wheat at the time of making the contract he would be exposed to monopoly prices. If the wheat producer were limited in his possibilities of sale to consumers only, he would be subjected to the depressing effects of a glut in the market in June and September, at times of harvest.

To the trader, manufacturer, or exporter, the act of transferring the risk of price fluctuations to other persons who are willing to assume it, has the effect of an insurance. It enables him to use all of his time and capital in the management of his own business instead of devoting some part of them to contingencies arising from unforeseen crop conditions.

ALTERNATIVE CONTRACTS

In order to eliminate the risk of a shortage of specific grades of the merchandise thus traded in, contracts generally permit the delivery of alternative grades, within certain limits, at differential prices; and if the grade to be delivered be not suitable for the ultimate needs of the purchaser, it can under ordinary circumstances be exchanged for the grade needed, by the payment of the differential. It is true that in this exchange of grades there is sometimes a loss or a profit, owing to some unexpected diminution or excess of supply of the particular grade wanted, due to the weather or other natural causes.

Deposits of cash margins may be required mutually by members at the time of making contracts, and subsequent additional ones if market fluctuations justify.

Dealings for outsiders are usually upon a 10 per cent. margin; obviously, if this margin were increased generally, say to 20 per cent., a considerable part of the criticism due to losses in speculation, particularly as to the Cotton Exchange, would be eliminated.

The major part of the transactions are adjusted by clearing systems, the method most prevalent being "ring settlements," by which groups of members having buying and selling contracts for identical quantities, offset them against each other, canceling them upon the payment of the differences in prices.

THE PRODUCE EXCHANGE

The New York Produce Exchange was chartered by the Legislature in 1862, under the style of the "New York Commercial Association." The charter has been amended several times; in 1907 dealing in securities, as well as in produce, was authorized. There are over 2000 members, but a larger number are inactive. Some members are also connected with the Stock and Cotton Exchanges. The business includes dealing in all grains, cottonseed oil, and a dozen or more other products; wheat is, however, the chief subject of trading, and part thereof consists of hedging by and for millers, exporters, and importers, both here and abroad. The quantity of wheat received in New York in the five years 1904–1908 averaged 21,000,000 bushels annually. No record of "cash" sales is kept. The reported sales of "futures" show in five years an annual average of 480,000,000 bushels, the year 1907 showing 610,000,000. Although some of these sales were virtually bets on price differences, all of them were contracts enforcible at law.

CLEARING SYSTEM

The greater part of the transactions are settled by a clearing system. The Clearing Association is a separate organization, duly incorporated, with a capital of $25,000. All members of the association must settle daily by the clearing system; other members of the Exchange may do so. The Clearing Association assumes responsibility for the trades of all its members, and accordingly controls the exaction of margins from members to each other, and may increase them at any time if the fluctuations require it. The records of the clearings show day by day the status of each member's trading — how much he may be "long" or "short" in the aggregate. Thus the members have a system of protection against each other; the welfare of all depends upon keeping the commitments of each within safe limits. The official margin system operates as a commendable restraint upon over-speculation.

From our examination of the trading in mining stocks recently introduced, we conclude that the lack of experience of this body in this class of business has resulted in a neglect of proper safeguards to the investor and an undue incitement to speculative transactions of a gambling nature, and should not be tolerated on the Produce Exchange.

THE COTTON EXCHANGE

The New York Cotton Exchange was incorporated by a special charter in 1871. Its membership is limited to 450. It is now the most important cotton market in the world, as it provides the means for financing about 80 per cent. of the crop of the United States, and is the intermediary for facilitating its distribution. In fact, it is the world's clearing house for the staple. Traders and manufacturers in Japan, India, Egypt, Great Britain, Germany, France, and Spain, as well as the United States, buy and sell here daily and the business is still increasing.

Cotton is the basis of the largest textile industry in the world. The business is conducted on a gigantic scale in many countries by means of vast capital, complicated machinery, and varied processes involving considerable periods of time between the raw material and the finished product. Selling for future delivery is necessary to the harmonious and uninterrupted movement of the staple from producer to consumer. Nearly all the trading, beginning with that of the planter, involves short selling. The planter sells to the dealer, the dealer to the spinner, the spinner to the weaver, the weaver to the cloth merchant, before the cotton of any crop year is picked. Dealers who take the risk of price fluctuations insure all the other members of this trading chain against losses arising therefrom and spare them the necessity of themselves being speculators in cotton. The risks connected with raising and marketing cotton must be borne by some one, and this is now done chiefly by a class who can give their undivided attention to it.

GRADING OF COTTON

The grading of cotton is the vital feature of the trade. When no grade is specified in the contract, it is construed to be middling. There are now eighteen grades, ranging from middling stained up to fair. This classification differs somewhat from that of other markets, and last January the Department of Agriculture at Washington took up the subject of standardizing the various grades for all American markets. The New York Cotton Exchange participated in this work; a standard was thus adopted, the types of which were supplied by its classification committee. It varies but little from the one previously in use here. The samples chosen to represent the several types are now sealed, in possession of the Department of Agriculture, awaiting the action of Congress.

The cotton plant is much exposed to vicissitudes of the weather. A single storm may change the grade of the crop in large sections of the country. It becomes necessary therefore to provide some protection for traders who have made contracts to deliver a particular grade which has become scarce by an accident which could not be foreseen. For this purpose alternative deliveries are allowed by the payment of corresponding price differentials, fixed by a committee of the Exchange twice annually, in the months of September and November.

Settlements of trades may be made individually, or by groups of members, or through a clearing system, the agency of which is a designated bank near the Exchange. No record is kept of the transactions, but it is probable that for a series of years the sales have averaged fully 50,000,000 bales annually.

INORDINATE SPECULATION

There have been in the past instances of excessive and unreasonable speculation upon the Cotton Exchange, notably the Sully speculation of 1904. We believe that there is also a great deal of speculation of the gambling type mentioned in the introduction to this report. In our opinion, the Cotton Exchange should take measures to restrain and so, far as possible, prevent these practices, by disciplining members who engage in them. The officers of the Exchange must in many cases be aware of these practices, and could, in our opinion, do much to discourage them.

THE COFFEE EXCHANGE

The Coffee Exchange was incorporated by special charter in 1885. It has 320 members, about 80 per cent. active.

It was established in order to supply a daily market where coffee could be bought and sold and to fix quotations therefor, in distinction from the former method of alternate glut and scarcity, with wide variations in price — in short, to create stability and certainty in trading in an important article of commerce. This it has accomplished; and it has made New York the most important primary coffee market in the United States. But there has been recently introduced a non-commercial factor known as "valorization," a governmental scheme of Brazil, by which the public treasury has assumed to purchase and hold a certain percentage of the coffee grown there, in order to prevent a decline of the price. This has created abnormal conditions in the coffee trade.

All transactions must be reported by the seller to the superintendent of the Exchange with an exact statement of the time and terms of delivery. The record shows that the average annual sales in the past five years have been in excess of 16,000,000 bags of 250 pounds each.

Contracts may be transferred or offset by voluntary clearings by groups of members. There is no general clearing system. There is a commendable rule providing that, in case of a "corner," the officials may fix a settlement price for contracts to avoid disastrous failures.

THE OTHER EXCHANGES

Of the exchanges which we have classed as minor, those dealing with Fruit and Hay, appear to be in nowise concerned with speculation. No sales whatever are conducted on them, all transactions being consummated either in the places of business of the members or at public auction to the highest bidder. No quotations are made or published.

In the case of the other two commodity exchanges, the Mercantile and the Metal, new problems arise. Although quotations of the products appertaining to these exchanges are printed daily in the public press, they are not a record of actual transactions amongst members, either for immediate or future delivery.

It is true that on the Mercantile Exchange there are some desultory operations in so-called future contracts in butter and eggs, the character of which is, however, revealed by the fact that neither delivery by the seller nor acceptance by the buyer is obligatory; the contract may be voided by either party by payment of a maximum penalty of 5 per cent. There are nominal "calls," but trading is confessedly rare. The published quotations are made by a committee, the membership of which is changed periodically. That committee is actually a close corporation of the buyers of butter and eggs, and the prices really represent their views as to the rates at which the trade generally should be ready to buy from the farmers and country dealers.

Similar, but equally deceptive, is the method of making quotations on the Metal Exchange. In spite of the apparent activity of dealings in this organization in published market reports, there are no actual sales on the floor of the Metal Exchange, and we are assured that there have been none for several years. Prices are, however, manipulated up and down by a quotation committee of three, chosen annually, who represent the great metal-selling agencies as their interest may appear, affording facilities for fixing prices on large contracts, mainly for the profit of a small clique, embracing, however, some of the largest interests in the metal trade.

These practices result in deceiving buyers and sellers. The making and publishing of quotations for commodities or securities by groups of men calling themselves an exchange, or by any other similar title, whether incorporated or not, should be prohibited by law, where such quotations do not fairly and truthfully represent any bona fide transactions on such exchanges. Under present conditions, we are of the opinion that the Mercantile and Metal Exchanges do actual harm to producers and consumers, and that their charters should be repealed.

THE EXPERIENCE OF GERMANY

In 1892 a commission was appointed by the German Government to investigate the methods of the Berlin Exchange. The regular business of this exchange embraced both securities and commodities; it was an open board where anybody by paying a small fee could trade either for his own account, or as a broker. The broker could make such charge as he pleased for his services, there being no fixed rate of commission. Settlements took place monthly. Margins were not always required. Under these circumstances many undesirable elements gained entrance to the Exchange and some glaring frauds resulted.

The commission was composed of government officials, merchants, bankers, manufacturers, professors of political economy, and journalists. It was in session one year and seven months. Its report was completed in November, 1893. Although there had been a widespread popular demand that all short selling should be prohibited, the commission became satisfied that such a policy would be harmful to German trade and industry, and they so reported. They were willing, however, to prohibit speculation in industrial stocks. In general the report was conservative in tone.

THE LAW OF 1896

The Reichstag, however, rejected the bill recommended by the commission and in 1896 enacted a law much more drastic. The landowners, constituting the powerful Agrarian party, contended that short selling lowered the price of agricultural products, and demanded that contracts on the Exchange for the future delivery of wheat and flour be prohibited. The Reichstag assented to this demand. It yielded also to demands for an abatement of stock speculation, and prohibited trading on the Exchange in industrial and mining shares for future delivery. It enacted also that every person desiring to carry on speculative transactions be required to enter his name in a public register, and that speculative trades by persons not so registered should be deemed gambling contracts and void. The object of the registry was to deter the small speculators from stock gambling and restrict speculation to men of capital and character.

The results were quite different from the intention of the legislators. Very few persons registered. Men of capital and character declined to advertise themselves as speculators. The small fry found no difficulty in evading the law. Foreign brokers seeing a new field of activity opened to them in Germany, flocked to Berlin and established agencies for the purchase and sale of stocks in London, Paris, Amsterdam, and New York. Seventy such offices were opened in Berlin within one year after the law was passed, and did a flourishing business. German capital was thus transferred to foreign markets. The Berlin Exchange became insignificant and the financial standing of Germany as a whole was impaired.

DETRIMENTAL CONSEQUENCES

This, however, was not the most serious consequence of the new law. While bankers and brokers, in order to do any business at all, were required to register, their customers were not compelled to do so. Consequently the latter could speculate through different brokers on both sides of the market, pocketing their profits and welching on their losses as gambling contracts. Numerous cases of this kind arose, and in some the plea of wagering was entered by men who had previously borne a good reputation. They had yielded to the temptation which the new law held out to them.

Another consequence was to turn over to the large banks much of the business previously done by independent houses. Persons who desired to make speculative investments in home securities applied directly to the banks, depositing with them satisfactory security for the purchases. As the German banks were largely promoters of new enterprises, they could sell the securities to their depositors and finance the enterprises with the deposits. This was a profitable and safe business in good times, but attended by dangers in periods of stringency, since the claims of depositors were payable on demand. Here again the law worked grotesquely, since customers whose names were not on the public register could, if the speculation turned out badly, reclaim the collateral or the cash that they had deposited as security.

MODIFICATION OF LAW IN 1908

The evil consequences of the law of 1896 brought about its partial repeal in 1908. By a law then passed the government may, in its discretion, authorize speculative transactions in industrial and mining securities of companies capitalized at not less than $5,000,000; the Stock Exchange Register was abolished; all persons whose names were in the "Handels-register" (commercial directory), and all persons whose business was that of dealing in securities, was declared legally bound by contracts made by them on the Exchange. It provided that other persons were not legally bound by such contracts, but if such persons made deposits of cash or collateral security for speculative contracts, they could not reclaim them on the plea that the contract was illegal.

In so far as the Reichstag in 1896 had aimed to prevent small speculators from wasting their substance on the Exchange, it not only failed, but, as we have seen, it added a darker hue to evils previously existing.

Germany is now seeking to recover the legitimate business thrown away twelve years ago. She still prohibits short selling of grain and flour, although the effects of the prohibition have been quite different from those which its supporters anticipated. As there are no open markets for those products, and no continuous quotations, both buyers and sellers are at a disadvantage; prices are more fluctuating than they were before the passage of the law against short selling.

THANKS TO THE CHAMBER OF COMMERCE

Our cordial thanks are due to the Chamber of Commerce of the State of New York for the free use of rooms in its building for our sessions, and of its library, and other facilities.

Respectfully submitted,

HORACE WHITE, Chairman,
CHARLES A. SCHIEREN,
DAVID LEVENTRITT,
CLARK WILLIAMS,
JOHN B. CLARK,
WILLARD V. KING,
SAMUEL H. ORDWAY,
EDWARD D. PAGE,
CHARLES SPRAGUE SMITH,

MAURICE L. MUHLEMAN, Secretary.

THE END

INDEX

Asterisks indicate foot-notes